GEORGIA

GEORGIA

A REBEL IN THE CAUCASUS

PETER NASMYTH

ILLUSTRATIONS BY TAMARA ALAVIDZE

CASSELL

TO MY PARENTS – FOR PUTTING UP
WITH A WORLD TRAVELLER
FOR SO LONG

A CASSELL BOOK

First published in the UK 1992
by **Cassell**
Villiers House, 41/47 Strand, London WC2N 5JE

Copyright © Peter Nasmyth 1992

Distributed in the United States
by Sterling Publishing Co., Inc.
387 Park Avenue South, New York, NY 10016–8810

Distributed in Australia
by Capricorn Link (Australia) Pty Ltd
P.O. Box 665, Lane Cove, NSW 2066

CIP data for this book is available upon request
from the British Library National Bibliographic Service.

ISBN 0-304-34078-2

Typeset by Chapterhouse, The Cloisters, Formby L37 3PX, England
Printed and bound in Great Britain
by Mackays of Chatham PLC

CONTENTS

ACKNOWLEDGEMENTS

This book has come about as the result of several visits made to Georgia between 1987 and the present. It opens with the trip I took in May 1989. Most of the events follow chronologically from this, with just a few exceptions inserted from earlier, briefer visits. Needless to say, I encountered many helping hands along the way. Some have been included, some with their names disguised. Since books about countries are largely books about people, I must warmly thank the many supportive, hospitable and generous souls without whom none of this would ever have happened: Marika Didibulidze for her attentive aid and constant good nature; Iraklie Topuria for the patience of a saint; Ilya and his family for making me so welcome at their house; Alex Kahn for translating the interview with Sasha Bashlachov; Rusico, Tamrico, Gia, Yuri (008), Soso, and all my other and excellent Georgian hosts; Warner Chappell Music Ltd for permission to quote from 'Of Course I'm Lying' (Blank/Meier) by the group Yello; Simon Broughton for his co-conspiracy on Svaneti; Maya Aves (and Jonathan) for looking over the facts; David Rowson for transporting Tamara's beautiful drawings from Georgia; Anthea Norman Taylor for her dedication to all matters Russian; Heather Wallis and Maggie O'Hanlon for correcting my bad English; Rosie Anderson for seeing it all through; Jonathan Grimwood for such friendly editorship; and most importantly of all Frances Howard Gordon of Gothic Image Tours for providing the initial idea for a book, as well as for her many admirable Soviet tours.

INTRODUCTION

WHY GEORGIA?

All voyages are searches in disguise, and this one to the Republic of Georgia has turned out as no exception. But any discovery of this small nation first requires the discovery of a larger nation. Georgia has nestled for the last 200 years at the base of the Russian (later Soviet) empire. Until very recently access was controlled by Soviet Russia alone.

Thus this story opens not in the Caucasus but on a crowded Aeroflot jet bound from Delhi to London in 1982. Beyond the aircraft nose loomed my first visit to the Soviet Union – a three-day stop-over in Moscow – and an enormous gap in my knowledge.

As the plane thundered down the runway at Delhi, I wondered what had induced me to visit this morose empire. I was returning to England after seven months travelling in India, a journey taking the idea of a search very literally – if unsuccessfully – having propelled me from temple shrine to holy city across the Indian subcontinent.

In my estimation, the Soviet Union represented a spiritually disabled culture. What could it possibly teach someone hungry for religious explanations ūnavailable in Europe?

As if to confirm my thoughts the plane's intercom crackled into life, 'We are now entering Soviet air space. Please remember it is no longer permitted to take photographs.' But something then happened. I found myself gazing down at the miles and miles of indescribably white, celestial and now illegal clouds stretching away to the horizon – clouds similar to those on a poster of a Tibetan god I had once gazed at in northern India. Suddenly I sensed an eerie connection between the two.

I felt that behind those words – ostensibly to do with a Soviet fear of spies – lingered a sense of ownership, a possessiveness stemming from political certainty. Did not the culture that issued that statement pursue a goal as supremely idealistic as my quest for spiritual enlightenment?

What if both I and the political masters of this land-mass suffered from the same excesses of zeal? Might we not have both made big

Kasveti Church, Tbilisi.

mistakes and did we not now need to own up?

Within that tiny insight a curiosity was born that several years later would send me scurrying from coast to coast across the Soviet world, as eager for psychological truth as I had been for a religious solution in Sri Lanka, Nepal and India.

The momentum would lead me to its gem-like southernmost corner – the Georgian Republic, the nation whose fields and mountains had given birth to the Soviet Union's fiercest guiding light – Joseph Stalin.

But on that plane this new curiosity received a further prod as the wheels bounced down on to the tarmac of Moscow's Sheremetyevo airport. No wrathful Asian deity ever produced the same sense of awe as I experienced looking at the hardware of our own nuclear annihilation: the strange red-tipped bombers, the revolving radar towers, the uniformed men on the tarmac.

During the next three days, walking around the capital city of 'my' enemy, the sensation deepened. I began to realize just how profoundly the dread of eternal Communist damnation had installed itself in the West and myself.

A walk down Gorky Street evolved into a powerful lesson. I remember staring at the walls devoid of advertisements, the shop shelves filled with items outdated ten years earlier in London, and at those earnest, grim faces, trying to buy. All the clichés seemed true.

Then came the moment when I stepped out of the tourist bubble and into another reality. Reaching a suitably lonely phone-booth, I dialled the number given to me by a friend in Katmandu, whose letter I now carried. I listened as the anxious voice at the other end of the line asked immediately: 'Are you phoning from the airport or a hotel?'

'No,' I replied.

'Good,' she said and instructions were given that led me to a tiny flat somewhere in the centre of Moscow – the home of two religious dissidents.

There was a sheer James Bondishness in handing over the letter, then listening to the daughter sing the songs she had written in English, learned from the BBC World Service. Watching as her trembling, deep voice sent tears rolling down her father's eyes, under walls plastered with Western magazine photographs and Russian icons, I seemed to have arrived in a tiny centre of great spirituality, equivalent to anything I'd found in Asia. The next day they took me to see the Kremlin.

'This is the world capital of atheism,' the girl had said with more than a touch of irony. 'But *look* at it.'

It was stuffed full of Russia's most magnificent cathedrals. This couple who walked boldly across Red Square wearing crosses, proudly suffered the punishment of unemployment for their principles. Suddenly I realized that this country, whose nineteenth century I distantly admired through its literature, still proved in every way worthy of Dostoyevsky and his characters. His Karamazovs and Grushenskas still lived; they walked the streets, filled the twentieth-century flats and living-rooms with those same contradictory demons and saints. The same electrifying hysteria he'd described over 100 years earlier had survived with great ease through the Stalinist era.

It was five years before I returned to Moscow. By then Mr Gorbachev and his *glasnost* had arrived and with it a quite different atmosphere. Standing on Gorky Street that second time, the passing faces showed more curiosity, even hope.

Russian friends no longer asked me to keep my voice down when speaking in public. My latest mission – to research an article on Russian rock music – introduced me to people I'd had no idea existed in 1982, although many did: heavy-metal rockers, experimental jazz musicians, hippies, poets, artists, writers, even punks. In what was then Leningrad I was taken to see the Soviet Hari Krishnas jingling down Nevsky Prospekt, to the graffiti-covered stairway and home of Boris Grebenschikov, the Soviet Bob Dylan, to meet new pop-promoters and managers, and *samizdat* publishers. One young writer told me then, 'The USSR is now experiencing the unleashing of its underground' and went on, 'The identity crisis amid your Western youth culture is because you've forgotten your own underground, and its energy.'

Indeed, the streets of Moscow and Leningrad sang out with a rebellion newly fashionable among its young. Leningrad's Saigon Café carried the atmosphere of a Portobello café in the 1960s. People were discovering 'self' and individuality. Only here it came with the chaotic emotional supercharge of the Russian character.

Yet to me the purity, the sheer otherness of that first 1982 visit had faded, become tainted by something familiar. It invoked the memory of our own discovery of 'freedom' in the 1960s and 1970s. Their major event, *glasnost*, seemed to my Western eye to offer the same delirium of political and spiritual confusion set in motion a century and a half earlier, amid the chaos of an industrial revolution, the dilemmas Gogol, Dostoyevsky and others had investigated so eloquently.

I had arrived expecting to find the confident new voice of Soviet youth but instead met the proud inferiority complex of a people forced to strain their eyes at a forbidden culture for too long; an underground where the demands on artists were quite different to those on ours (or even theirs at the turn of the century). For the last fifty years the instinctive call of youth had been for the same basic freedoms as existed in the West. Before the subtleties of language could blossom, there had to come permission to speak.

But my selfish disappointment was about to receive a healthy crack on the head.

Towards the end of my visit to Leningrad I bumped into an unusually well-informed man at a party who, as so often happens at parties, then disappeared into one of the eddies of faces, never to be seen again. But I vividly recall our conversation.

His words had come at me from behind a thick black moustache, in excellent, relaxed English – acquired from two years working in Pakistan. Placing his hand on my shoulder, he appeared not so much to speak as to confide in me. I found myself astonished at this difference in manner from the impetuous, secretive Russians. Discovering my interest in the new directions in Soviet culture he insisted, almost to the point of arrogance, on giving me his brutally honest appraisal. He dismissed *glasnost* with a wave of the hand.

'It is a gallant but poor imitation of you in the West,' he said.

I detected an uncanny ability to grasp the Western perspective; but where had he learned it?

As I launched busily into my own ideas on 'the new Soviet rebellion', he stopped me short with the answer.

'It may be new here,' he said. 'But where I'm from it's already 200 years old.'

'And where is that?' I asked, noticing his darker features for the first time.

'Georgia,' came his reply, with a hint of pride. 'The Russians colonized us at the beginning of the last century. And it's been more or less the same story since then.'

Then his expression grew more serious. 'If you want to know about rebellion, look at Georgia,' he said more quietly. 'In fact it's better you go there. When you do, you'll find Georgia is not "Soviet". It's only a part of the Soviet Union. You'll find that when the Russians say "Soviet", they really mean Russian. Georgia is not Russian. It's not even European. The Russians see themselves as Europeans, they think they're a modern people; they put the first dog into space, etc., etc. But to be this modern thing they're so proud of, they've had to push aside the rest of their history and culture, forget all the lessons of the past. And do you know why?' He looked at me with the same faintly amused, hooked eyebrows. 'Because history failed them.'

He pronounced his verdict in such a charming, affable style that I hardly noticed it as criticism at all. But I had to disagree with his point on Russian culture, and defended its modern literature as among the world's finest.

'Yes,' he replied, 'And you know why it's so fine? Because it describes the decline of the human spirit exceptionally well. It shows the way Western man is steadily losing his way, losing touch with his instinct. It shows a man so hungry for what he believes is modern, he learns to ignore those who lived before this age, who could still interpret their instinct.'

He paused, then looked at me intently. 'If you want to see a modern *Asian* culture that's aware of this, then go to Georgia. You'll find a people whose past is still the most valued part of themselves.'

Following this line of inquiry among young Russian friends brought a curious reaction. Nobody was greatly impressed by the rock music of Georgia, but many expressed a liking for the Georgians and a respect for their determination to hang on to their culture.

The more I inquired into this southernmost republic, the more intriguing it grew. First came the discovery that a surreptitious *glasnost* existed there long before Gorbachev; that it even possessed official social structures – disguised within its so-called mafia. I began to hear about a nation with noticeably less stuffing knocked out of them from the years of Stalinism. After all, their present colonization by the Soviets had been preceded by those of the Russians, the Turks, the Arabs, the Persians, the Byzantines, the Mongols, the Romans and the Greeks! These people regarded their current masters as just one more in a long succession of landlords. Furthermore, as all Russians admitted, they had learned to preserve their culture – and much of their economic wealth – with a cheeky good humour (although with the advance of *glasnost* their calls for independence lost much of this charm).

I also found the name of the republic recurring again and again for other reasons. Georgia was the old USSR's favourite holiday resort, with a landscape of quite exceptional beauty. No Western brochure has ever unveiled the extraordinary variety of countryside hidden within this small nation.

In Georgia, a country the size of Ireland, you can ski in the morning and swim a couple of hours later in a warm Black Sea; you can stand with your back to some of the world's most awesome mountains (the Caucasus has twelve peaks higher than Mont Blanc), yet be facing an arid, treeless terrain, where former inhabitants once carved their towns into hillsides as the only shelter. You can visit one of the world's most prolific and least-known wine districts, and discover tea and tobacco plantations thriving only 70 kilometres away from regions too cold even to grow tomatoes.

Every Russian I'd ever met praised the Georgian wines – the most popular in the old USSR – and longed to drink them at source, on Georgia's Black Sea coast, nicknamed the 'Russian riviera'.

The more I heard about this small nation of five and a half million people snuggling between mountain ranges just beyond the Turkish border, the more it emerged as the richest jewel in the Soviet crown. It seemed to possess the most dramatic mountains, the most exotic agriculture, the hottest blood, the strongest mafia, the most hospitable, wealthiest, religious citizens in the entire crumbling Soviet empire.

Talking to Soviet writers about nineteenth-century literature, I discovered that Georgia, while claiming almost no internationally-known writers of its own, served as a formative inspiration to many of Russia's greatest. Pushkin, Lermontov, Tolstoy and Gorky all visited the area and set major works there. Indeed, the famous nineteenth-century Russian critic Belinsky once had to admit, 'The Caucasus seem fated to have become the cradle of our poetic talent; the source and mentor of its muse, its poetic homeland.'

A particular favourite of mine, Lermontov, set his celebrated novel of the 1830s, *A Hero of Our Time*, in the foothills of the Caucasus. To me this is a novel strikingly more modern than many written today, and the clear forerunner to all the great 'psychological' Russian novels to follow. In it, Lermontov's young hero Pechorin – a Russian officer of the Caucasian Army – attacks the decaying Tsarist society all around him with the kind of predatory boredom that now so saturates modern European and American culture.

Yet Lermontov possessed a huge romantic passion for the desolate Caucasian passes, and their people. It is said his fascination with these chivalrous tribesmen gave him the strength to openly criticize his Tsar – for which he, ironically, found himself banished to the Caucasian Army. Thus this early hero of modern European literature sank his archetypal roots into a soil just beyond Europe.

Tolstoy's literary beginnings also uttered their birth-cry in the Caucasus. As a frustrated young aristocrat, he travelled to the area between the crucial years 1851 and 1854. Like his predecessors he was struck forcefully by the Caucasian cult of honour, chivalry and hospitality. Almost certainly, it was here he found the germ of his crusading sense of natural justice. Tolstoy's first significant stories, *The Raid* and *Childhood*, were written while living in Tiflis (the former Russian name for Tbilisi, the Georgian capital), and many of his Caucasian experiences returned to haunt his later work, particularly *The Cossacks* and *Hadji Murat*.

Not so long ago in this century, Boris Pasternak described Georgia as 'my second motherland', and there are those who argue that his passion for Stalin's motherland greatly assisted in his survival through the purges.

So why did so much mighty literary talent find itself drawn to this remote area? Possibly it was because the Caucasus has always represented a line of mutability between the Asian and European cultures. While Georgia was one of the earliest nations to convert to Christianity (in 337) – second only to Armenia – its people have always liked to leave a couple of fingers, if not a whole arm, in the wilder psychic regions of Asia. Ask a Georgian today whether he is a European or an Asian, and he will more often than not stop and think for a moment with his European mind, then give the answer with his Asian heart. 'Asian', tends to be the reply, especially if a European is doing the asking. Georgia is a blend of the two and, if the truth be known, probably Asian by nature while fervently Christian in belief. Men like Lermontov and Tolstoy drew in gulps of inspiration from what they saw as this healthy contradiction. The repeated invasion of Georgia from the south (it several times became a province of Persia) produced an interesting blend in the character, mixing cool mountain blood with the hotter Muslim Persians and Arab cultures from the plains below.

Thus Georgian culture contains many Muslim elements – such as its elegant, balconied architecture, a more traditional role for women and an extravagant sense of hospitality. In many ways the Georgian character has taken some steps towards resolving the seemingly insurmountable polarization between the Christian and Muslim religions. However, the Georgians themselves shy away from such analysis.

My frustrated quest into the old Soviet Union had found focus again in an Asian country, but one with European beginnings. Apart from sharing Saint George with England as its patron saint, Georgia also carried tantalizing archaeological and mythological links with our own European background: the so-called 'Caucasian' races and Caucasoid Man, from whom European Man reportedly evolved, emerged from this area, along with six entirely separate language groups (the Georgians have one all to themselves and the other fifty or so peoples living in the Caucasus region share the other five); surely this sudden wall of ice and rock shooting up out of the Nogay Steppe – for many centuries the official limits of Russia – concealed a zone both alien and yet integral to Europe.

Approached from its Black Sea side, Georgia was regarded by the Greeks and Romans as 'the ends of the earth'. Within it, Prometheus had been chained to the flanks of Mount Kazbek, 100 kilometres into the Caucasus from Tbilisi; Jason found his Golden Fleece beside the moutain rivers of Svaneti in the western Caucasus; and Medea, of the great Euripidean tragedy, lived with her father, King Medes, in her Colchis home (today the western Georgian area of Mingrelia). And most of these myths even today find astonishing hints of authentication. Perhaps the most striking is the ongoing evidence of panning for gold through staked-out sheeps' hides in the Lower Svaneti district – an ethnographic link with a 'golden fleece'.

Georgia seemed to contain more and more of the exotica I had once fallen for in the East. But this time the East had become resiliently Christian. Then, added to this, came the sounds of a new political awakening. Among the Soviet republics calling for independence, Georgia shouted with the loudest voice. Ever since *glasnost* restored a freedom of speech, these cries for full separation had stoked up a fire inside this small country. But unlike the Baltic republics, Georgia possessed a population still 70 per cent Georgian (some of the Baltics can barely manage 50 per cent their own). The blood of the country now seethed at another crucial juncture in its history. Rising to the surface in this ancient pot of cultures, came a bubbling cacophony of socialism, monarchism, hysterical nationalism and liberal democratic ideas, propelled with a do-or-die ambition to launch Georgia far into the future and the past, at one and the same time.

During my research, I had encountered many other Europeans equally captivated by Soviet culture. I began to ask myself why so many of us had fallen under the thrall of the comparatively dire Soviet experience. Was it simply the issue of befriending the enemy; taming the nuclear monster? Or did a matter of soul raise itself here? Did the Soviet world not represent that 'opposite' world to our own; a glimpse, but a glimpse only, into a place whose Communist experiment attempted to disprove much of what we believed as sacrosanct.

I met many Westerners expressing difficulty in accepting the Eastern bloc's fervent desire to pursue our own standard of materialism – feeling that the levels of discontent hidden within our wealth hardly merited such a demonic pursuit. It seemed that our quest for 'soul' balanced theirs for a new economy. But here, hovering uncertainly between both worlds, hung the enigma of Georgia, a culture gloriously intermixing both these impulses. There could be no avoiding it; as the man at the party had predicted, I would have to see for myself.

■Pyatigorsk

RUSSIAN FEDERATION

ABKHAZIA

■Pitsunda

MOUNT ELBRUZ

Novy Afon
■Sukhumi

SVANETI

■Mestia

MIN GRELIA

■Ushguli

Enguri river

Black

Sea

Rioni river

■Kutaisi

■Poti

I MERETIA

AJARIA

■Batumi

Vardzi

TURKEY

Mtkvari river

| 0 | | 50 | | 100 Miles |
| 0 | | 100 | | 200 Km |

16

CHAPTER ONE

BEFORE THE CAUCASUS

The southernmost steppe of the Russian Federation is one of the healthiest and greenest areas in what is now the former Soviet Union. It spreads before the Greater Caucasus mountains like a luscious doormat, sprinkled with spa towns and health resorts. This almost flat covering is occasionally ruffled by the odd green lump – like the five hills around the resort of Pyatigorsk.

It was up the last of these that the Intourist bus now climbed, and with it my expectations. After so many months of preparation, the mighty Caucasus lay just over this ridge. The bus's intercom crackled into life as our representative from Intourist, Victor, peppered us with facts about the town we approached.

'Pyatigorsk was formed in 1780 as a fort to protect the Russians against the Caucasian mountain rebels to the south. Its height is 530 to 630 metres above sea-level, its climate 15 to 25 degrees in the summer and the number of different minerals in the waters here is fifteen. Today it is a model resort town. Its population is 170,000 and this is the twelfth five-year plan . . .'

The bus-driver changed gear ready for the imminent descent and I knew the moment had arrived. I glued my eyes to the dirty window, glancing up at the huge grey sky above, imagining those literary Russians also anticipating these mountains, now just 70 kilometres to the south – the Tolstoys, Lermontovs, Pushkins, who'd been bowled over by what I was about to see. These European writers never quite grasped the Caucasus, and returned again and again trying to understand what they experienced here. I remembered in particular Tolstoy's account of their white ridges riding across the horizon in *The Cossacks* – a sight causing his character Father Olenin to shake himself vigorously, quite convinced they belonged to a dream.

A dream they had remained, if a dying one, to later travellers like the American journalist Negley Farson, who arrived here in 1929 and later wrote his poignant *Caucasian Journey* – the tale of his trek into the

Saint George slaying the infidel emperor Diocletian.

mountains several years before Stalin's purges in the Caucasus. This was an end-of-an-epoch journey up among the pre-Soviet cultures of these mountains, many of whom, as he rightly predicted, were to disappear for ever.

Then suddenly the downtown area of Pyatigorsk spread itself before us. I strained my eyes above the tree line, searching for the rude row of Asiatic teeth baring themselves across the horizon, the place where the Asian world crashed into the European and . . . saw nothing. I couldn't believe it – not a cleft or snowy peak anywhere, just drizzle. Furthermore it was that mean-minded, unrelenting, British variety of drizzle, cutting visibility down to a few dour kilometres. Victor addressed us again. In an inappropriately cheerful voice, he announced that according to the forecast, the weather 'will be cloudy for the rest of your stay'.

Through the water-streaked glass I stared disbelievingly at this, my opening into Belinsky's 'cradle of poetic talent'. The white-hot mountains of poetry had clammed themselves up tight. In fact, as the bus wound its way down the hill, past the lounging concrete slabs of the Soviet sanatoriums, the surprisingly neat roadside verges, clean signposts – very much the model Soviet town – an uncanny feeling of familiarity crept over me. Bar the few Cyrillic road signs and the number of Lada cars, this overcast panorama of smart tarmac and trees could easily be mistaken for a well-wooded corner of south-east England. No matter how far you push yourself across the globe, a part of you always seems to end up right back where you started. I remembered the deflating scorn Dr Johnson used to pour on all travel-romantics, declaring: 'The use of travel is to regulate imagination with reality.'

Victor (along with the brochures) had neglected to tell us of Pyatigorsk's British climate and high rainfall – hence its abundance of mineral waters. His optimistic socialist lists of facts were, like any political statement East or West, notable more for their omissions. He'd also stretched the truth on Pyatigorsk's original military garrison. It stood not so much to protect Russia from the wild Caucasian tribesmen, as to serve as a forward base for the Tsarist empire's progressive expansion southwards. Pyatigorsk, like the other fortress towns on the Caucasian borders, represented the gleam in eighteenth-century Russia's eye as it gazed on the territory it desired more than any other – the rich kingdom of Georgia.

Victor clicked his microphone back on. 'Not far from here used to be the land of Russia's most famous horsemen, the Cossacks. We now have many stud farms here.' Then his voice began to swell with mysterious pride. 'You know their horses are now turning into a more interesting product.' He paused for effect. 'Race-horses! You know in 1981 Armand Hammer bought one stallion for 1 million dollars and then from it he earned 35 million dollars!' One could almost hear his eyes light up.

I began to realize that in Victor stood that good, clean innocence of Soviet Man idealized since the 1930s, as portrayed in those Constructivist posters on sale in the bookshops along Moscow's Kalinin Prospekt – an innocence so pure it failed to notice the enormous ironies underlying it. I remembered the poster which I had bought for a few kopeks and pinned trophy-like on my wall; the sweeping image of young men and women lifting trowels, operating heavy machinery, eyes shining towards a pure and profitless future of five-year plans. And now race-tracks...

Yet I told myself Victor would almost certainly be my last view of this 'traditional' Soviet Man. Within a couple of days I would stand worlds away in the Asian 'beyond' of Georgia, where the Soviet ideal had never taken hold.

Later, at the hotel bar, I mulled over these first impressions of southern Russia: Pyatigorsk, the town I knew from Lermontov's 1830s novel, *A Hero of Our Time*; then the fashionable nexus for numerous peoples and cultures, all milling together in the same streets and bath-houses. Cossacks, Tartars and dagger-swinging Circassian warriors filled these streets, along with the conquistador Russian soldiers and their St Petersburg consorts, for whom Pyatigorsk was to serve as the fashionable launching-pad for Trans-Caucasia.

For Lermontov, the town was a symbol of the decaying Tsarist Russia. He describes it first as:

> A small town all prim and new with the babbling of medicinal springs and the sounds of a multi-languaged throng. Beyond it stands a massive amphitheatre of mountains... with Mount Kazbek at one end and the twin peaks of Elbruz at the other. What a delight to live in a place like this.... The air is pure and fresh as the kiss of a child, the sun is bright, the sky is blue – what more can one want?

But then, a few pages later: 'Our life here is pretty dull. Those who drink the waters in the morning are spiritless like all invalids, and those who drink wine in the evening are insufferable like all healthy people.'

He wrote these words at a time when Pyatigorsk came as close as Russia would ever come to having a 'wild west'. In those heady days, the cult of Byron struck deep into Russian high society, and Pyatigorsk functioned as a perfect literary foil, a blending of the delicate, St Petersburg society with war heroes from the southern front. Lermontov liked nothing better than to watch the mingling military caps and ladies' bonnets aim their telescopes at Mount Elbruz and declare to himself they 'didn't have a scrap of poetry in them', then sink his literary teeth into their daily social habits, via his brilliant and utterly believable anti-hero Pectorin.

How much had it changed? Judging from the town's exclusive spas and the many overweight Russian faces dotted round our hotel, the contingents from the capital still came. Before me, in my glass, was that other well-known ambassador from the south, the sweet, earthy-tasting Georgian wine. As for its people, from a nearby table came the sound of a loud, laughing group of Georgians. But where were the other tribes? They still existed, now intermixed and compressed together over three generations by the homogenizing Soviet model. One made guesses at the blood lines lingering in the passing figures. Perhaps a Terek Cossack in the adroit, swarthy manner of the bartender; a Circassian in the waiter?

At the second glass of wine, my thoughts returned to that moment of disappointment in the bus, and Victor's odd statement about the weather. I sensed in myself a European confusion, not so much a genuine 'disappointment' as the pains of adjustment to this upside-down world. Here people lived to be pleasantly surprised when something worked as planned, instead of unpleasantly surprised when it didn't. For Victor, drizzle came as the standard kit of life. I had to remind myself I now sat at a bar in the far corner of a land whose national characters rose from foundations of appalling loss: loss of life in the Second World War, followed by the further loss of 20 million during the Stalinist purges and relocations, and then a loss of initiative – withered down to an unforgiving, disciplinarian stick in the years to follow. This was a society that had decided that human instinct could not be trusted, whose inevitable frustrated intelligence had turned back on itself.

The noise from the Georgians at the next table increased in volume. Snatches of a ragged, deep-voiced, southern tongue hit me. A minute later they all suddenly stood up and raised their glasses solemnly for a long toast ending with the word '*Sakartvelo!*' – the ancient (and now the modern) word for Georgia.

They sat down again and the loud voices, the laughing, the back-slapping resumed. These noisy, dark-haired men, with thick necks, grandiloquent hand-gestures and standing toasts indulged themselves regardless of any political climate. A fact observed over a hundred and fifty years ago by Lemontov's 'Moscow dandies'.

As a thicket of empty wine and cognac bottles gradually stacked up between these tragi-comic rebels, I found myself wondering how it could be possible that but one month earlier the nation of Georgia had suffered its most wounding event of the last 30 years.

23

Twenty Georgian protesters had been butchered by Soviet soldiers on the steps of their State Government Building in Tbilisi. This act of Soviet savagery had sent chills down the spines, not only of all Georgians but of every rebellious republic in the Union. Suddenly the ugly black hand of Soviet repression had been raised again. Everybody (and not just the Georgians) now asked whether the once all-powerful Soviet state would resort to its old means of dealing with dissent: the Stalinist tactic – rule by terror.

Gradually the evening geared itself up, and soon the room spread before me a delectable sample of the many peoples jostling for position in this new post-colonial struggle. At the front tables were groups of Russians of the Party, the 'official' strata, in Pyatigorsk on their All-Union 'cures'. Then came various East European holidaymakers, a few odd Caucasian faces, then a good number of those mysteriously rich Georgians who crop up in expensive restaurants all across the old USSR. Before them, on the white tablecloths, the coveted rich pickings appeared: fresh melon, strawberries, apricots and aubergines – items which usually commanded black-market prices far too high for ordinary Intourist catering up north but here were close to their source, the warm, well-irrigated valleys of Georgia just over those drizzling mountains.

When Victor joined us later at the table, he responded to our curiosity towards this fine spread with that bright-eyed candour which so often directly contradicted his sentences.

'Here in Pyatigorsk I've eaten two bananas, and once I saw a pine-apple!'

Then all further conversation ceased. In its place came that dreaded Russian dining custom, 'the floor show'. The lights dimmed ominously, a Yamaha drum-machine and keyboard sprang to life with a joyous, folky vibrato, and so began a most extraordinary exhibition of Soviet evening entertainment.

Parading out before the diners came a procession of almost naked girls, but not in the standard 'costume'. For in brazen defiance of the Las Vegas 'look-alike' styles now the rage in Moscow, in came a group of dancing hammers and sickles. Perfectly proportioned girls in bright-red skimpy leotards and hats emblazoned with Communist insignia began to gyrate and spin before the delighted diners. Donning coy imitations of militia caps, they strutted and saluted with military precision, or shivered seductively before the front row of tables, flinging back their heads in abandon – a startlingly honest display of eroticism, and utterly faithful to the licentiousness saturating every strata of Soviet society. (What first-time visitor wasn't taken aback by the number of hard-currency prostitutes haunting the hotel bars?)

The music propelling the dancers seemed to blend traditional Russian folk-ballad and Western pop. The Yamaha belted out the hits; 'Misha Misha' gave way to 'You're in the Army Now', a Status Quo hit from the early 1980s, as the girls paraded half-mockingly, half-reverently before the rows of holidaying Party officials, who gazed back with glassy smiles.

Was this a glorious parody of Soviet socialist style or a stylish glorification that ended up as parody? I couldn't tell. Yet as I watched it steadily ceased to matter; the event took on a ghostly quality all of its own. The macabre death-dance of the Soviet ideal was being performed out in the open, thinly disguised as its opposite. Male soldiers' faces were replaced by women's, their limbs responding not to the clean-living Soviet Russian melody but to the decadent siren call of Western rock music; the new revolution was starting to eclipse that of October 1917.

Whoever selected this entertainment for Pyatigorsk must have been an impresario of genius. The act was an instant hit across the restaurant. The Georgian and East European men saw these nymphetic symbols of collapsing Communist power as an absurd and delicious challenge to their prowess at seduction after the show. The good, solid Soviet patriots watching from their All-Union tables had their egos stroked by this female reincarnation of the May Day parade with its iconography of power. And the delighted Western Europeans . . . we just couldn't believe our eyes.

But one thing was certain; there could be no better finale to this short stay in the Soviet Union. The following evening we would dine in Georgia.

The Massacre: 9 April 1989

Before we left Pyatigorsk, our group was joined by a Georgian woman called Marika. She arrived from Tbilisi to act as cultural guide for our small group during the journey over the Caucasus. All eyes turned to greet a striking olive-skinned woman. What a dramatic physical change from those Slav onlookers all around the restaurant: the intensely black eyes, the round, eagle-like nose of Persian or Arab cultures. This was a face accustomed to sun and hot southern climate rather than the snow-bound north, yet the skin also showed a tone just slightly paler than that of all those many generations living among the mountains.

Her arrival brought a chorus of questions, all on the same subject. What had really happened a month ago in Tbilisi, on 9 April? Western press reports spoke of demonstrations calling for independence, unleashed by the arrival of *glasnost*; a gradual escalation of marches, strikes and non-cooperation with the Soviet system had culminated on 9 April when sixteen Georgian women and four men on hunger-strike on the steps of the Government Building were butchered by an angry Soviet Army militia.

The strike had apparently focused on the recent Abkhazian call to secede from Georgia (the Abkhazians are one of the many nationalities living within Georgia's boundaries, in their case within what was a small autonomous republic on the Black Sea coast). While the Georgians were wanting to secede from the Soviet Union, the Abkhazians were calling for secession from Georgia – in favour of Soviet rule. The Georgians believed the Abkhazians had been put up to this by Moscow. When the Soviet Army's 'Special Forces' arrived on the Tbilisi streets to restrain the protest, this itself became yet another cause for protest.

Marika decided to try and answer our questions all in one go, by giving us an authentic Georgian account of the terrible event. Her words came at us in one continuous river of emotion. Nobody dared interrupt.

'On 9 April Soviet Special Forces troops were sent into our city, and all of us had the horror of seeing Soviet tanks and soldiers on our streets like an occupying army.'

Immediately I was struck by the completely different tone to her voice. The sharp, strident accent of Russia had been replaced by a far softer, more mellifluous sound. Marika chose her words slowly, carefully matching sound with meaning, as if both carried equal importance.

Her hands entered the discussion, moving like a conductor's baton. Sometimes, as they came up against unknown English expressions, they almost attempted to mould words before us. Hers was such a different personality from that of the Russians, with their swift, nervous gestures, their sudden dark silences.

'Our people demonstrated, threw themselves in front of the tanks until eventually the tanks withdrew. There followed a strange calm. The city came to a standstill and many people celebrated the disappearance of the Army on Rustaveli Avenue. Yet at the same time everyone sensed something awful was being planned.'

She paused, and in the silence that followed we could sense the rising emotion. 'Then our General Secretary came on TV telling us we were on the edge of a great catastrophe. We thought he was saying this just to frighten us, but suddenly the tanks appeared again, this time heading up Rustaveli Avenue towards the Government Building. This time nobody attacked them or resisted. Everyone just said, 'Let them go', stepped out of the way and began to sing Georgian songs. But the Special Forces troops were right behind, carrying shields and batons.

The Soviets advanced through the crowd and surrounded the hunger-strikers on the Government Building steps. Then, all of a sudden, they threw gas in the air, and began to attack the protesters – most of whom were young women – beating them with spades.

Then the troops took out aerosols and sprayed these in their faces, broke ampoules full of poison under their noses. Many died right there and then in violent spasms, but without showing any visible wounds. When the protesters tried to run away, they found they were trapped inside the cordon and the soldiers chased them. The male protesters and the Georgian police tried to stop this and break the cordon, but without weapons. Our police had been disarmed two days before. They were attacked too, and many of our Georgian police ended up in hospital. The Special Force soldiers behaved like savages, almost as if they were mad. One seventeen-year-old girl was chased half a kilometre and cut down with a spade outside the Iveria Hotel.'

As the feeling rose, Marika's hands cupped the air before her, as if holding out the weight of the atrocity for us to see. 'Afterwards our government came on the TV and said it was very sorry for what had happened. They said that sixteen people had 'unfortunately' died accidentally within the crush of the rioting, that they weren't murdered and it was an unfortunate accident. But can you believe it!' She looked at us beseechingly. 'It was so absurd. Half of Tbilisi was there that night and saw it all with their own eyes. Nobody believed them.'

She sighed deeply and one sensed the long-standing anger and hurt of this small nation, its ages of helplessness before mighty neighbours. What could they have done before the omnipotent Red Army? To me the event smacked of a carefully planned military operation, as if the old-guard Army leaders still believed they could rewrite history, as if *glasnost* never existed. By not killing with bullets, they thought they could get away with a statement that the rioters were killed in the struggle to escape. I remembered those grinning Party officials at the front row of the 'floor-show' half an hour earlier, and realized one should never underestimate such a mentality in the Soviet hierarchy, as the August 1991 coup attempt was to bear out all too vividly.

'After this' Marika continued, 'the commander of the Caucasian Army appeared on TV to announce martial law. For several days our streets were full of soldiers stopping everyone, at times threatening to kill us – and everybody believed they would kill.'

Her strained expression lightened slightly. 'But just when we all felt the most helpless about twenty cars, with our boys and girls leaning out of their windows, began driving at great speed through the streets of Tbilisi, their horns blaring, our old Georgian and pre-Soviet flags hanging out of the window.

When they found the soldiers, they drove up and down in front of them as a challenge. They said, "You're cruel but we're not afraid of you. You can kill Georgians, but that's all. You cannot break us." You know, when I saw this I suddenly had a feeling of joy. I suddenly sensed the spirit of our nation, a spirit that would stand up to even them.'

Looking round her small audience of rapt faces, I realized we'd all just taken several solid steps closer to that precious feeling all Georgians hold for their country. The moment she stopped talking, there was a chorus of questions. She then explained that shortly afterwards Eduard Shevardnadze, Mr Gorbachev's right-hand man and also a Georgian, had arrived in Tbilisi to take control of the army. After that the turbulence gradually subsided.

Someone asked what had been her most memorable moment during the whole of the event. She thought for a moment. 'I don't really know, but I remember how at the darkest time, when there seemed to be nobody willing to support us, when everyone seemed to have given up, a group of Georgian soldiers who had fought in the Soviet army in Afghanistan suddenly came to the TV station and said on air that next time they would put themselves between the protesters and the Special Forces. They said they would be prepared to die first. They gave out a telephone number that people could ring if there was trouble. And you know, they *really* defended us.'

She emphasized the word 'really', as if to imply that nobody could ever properly describe the event. She continued: 'They drove about the city at any time, during the day or night, and without weapons they fought the Special Forces, heroically pushing them away from people. You know, when I saw this happening, and all these young people standing up and prepared to die, for the first time during the whole event I cried.'

CHAPTER TWO

THE MOUNTAINS OF POETRY

On that final morning at Pyatigorsk my alarm rang at 7.00 a.m. I'd decided on one last reckless bid for the 'silver-capped Caucasus' of Pushkin. The hotel lift took me to the seventeenth floor, then I strode down the corridor towards the south-facing balcony door like a bleary-eyed modern Lermontov, with cameras, tripod and lenses clanking under my arm.

By half-way along the threadbare carpet, I noticed myself squinting at the light pouring in through the far door. It seemed as if a brilliant neon strip had been lit at the point where the earth and sky collided. With every step it grew brighter and fiercer until, finally, pushing the door – and unleashing a blast of freezing mountain air – I understood why. There they stood! Set into a dazzling blue sky were the stunning white ridges of Asia striding across the horizon, disappearing over the curve of the earth 400 kilometres in either direction. The silver, glittering peaks of the Greater Caucasus, exactly as Pushkin and Tolstoy saw them 150 years ago.

I leaned against the balcony railing and stared, quite oblivious to the bitter wind. The sun had already crept up over the Dagestan Caucasus to the east, converting the far western mountaintops into pink-tipped fingers as dawn spread across the Black Sea. Such deceitful flirtations of light that overcome the first-time viewer every time. Standing slightly thunderstruck by such painterly beauty, I remembered once before another snowy first glimpse, this time of the Himalayas in Nepal, how almost hypnotically they had drawn me into their glaciers, only to turn all ideas of beauty upside down by leading me straight into the arms of disaster. I found myself having to help two Sherpas carry the tombstone of their friend, an English climber, up to the base of Anapurna One. I'll never forget cementing it into place at the foot of that deadly lily-white mountain, in a ceremony filled with more loneliness than I care to experience ever again.

But now all tragedies were blithely ignored, for lording over the entire range stood the twin volcanic peaks of Mount Elbruz. At a full 5,642 metres they pressed into the icy air like two 'white breasts' (as 'Elbruz' translates). Through my 300-mm lens I could even see their nipples – small dark areas of rock around the summit.

With fingers now shrinking in the cold I fumbled to change the camera settings, reflecting on how these mountains had taunted poets, politicians and armies alike, over and over again. When the Nazis first saw Mount Elbruz during their 1941 invasion of the north Caucasus, they'd apparently vowed to climb and ritually reconsecrate it as the mother of their Aryan ancestry. (They believed the ancient tribe of Caucasian Alans played a crucial role in fathering the Teutonic master race.)

Such a provocative domination of the skyline had led to numerous switches of ownership, and today Elbruz belongs not to Georgia but to the Kabardino–Balkaria Autonomous Republic – the part of the Russian Federation containing most of the highest Caucasian peaks. But the mountain was not without its own human catastrophies. In 1941, the mountain's nearby inhabitants, the highland Balkars, chose to side with the Germans in the hope that Hitler might free them from Soviet domination. As a punishment Stalin relocated the entire tribe to Khazakstan.

The other major bump in the panorama, Mount Kazbek, belonged to Georgia and represented our journey's next destination.

With hands almost too cold to move, I just managed to press the shutter. Elbruz was now mine too.

The Ends of All the Earth

The main road into this formidable rockscape is the Georgian Military Highway, a Russian road built to supply the colonizing army during its steady push southwards in the nineteenth century. It begins outside Georgia, in North Ossetia and ends, effectively, beyond it (although technically Tbilisi marks the finale). Our bus quickly picked up the road's scent in the Pyatigorsk suburbs with a cantering, swerving motion. The driving style prompted a sharp glance towards the driver – yes, we were now in the hands of a Georgian. Like most Georgians, he was a hugely friendly, spirited man, with a tree-trunk of a neck and many grins for his guests, as well as those he attempted to drive off the road. And our first stop?

'Tbilisi,' he shouted back.

I rephrased the question. Not the ultimate destination, our first one.

'Tbilisi!', came the reply again.

According to our schedule, we were not due to arrive for four more days. A joke surely?

To begin with nobody commented on his desire to drive a forty-four-seater bus like a Ferrari coupé. This gusto was the Georgian way, and we'd elected to be willing guests. But eventually our anxiety transmitted itself to Marika, who passed it on, and he slowed just enough for us to relax our grip on the seats ahead and begin a hesitant observation of the scenery.

The opening miles took us along the rippling southern steppe towards the town of Vladikavkaz, at the time still called Ordzhonikidze – in honour of Stalin's hatchet-man, Sergo Ordzhonikidze. He was another zealous Soviet monster who, in the 1920s, inflicted such a vicious campaign against 'counter-revolutionaries' in his native Georgia that the cruelty horrified even Dzerzhinsky, the head of the Cheka (the Soviet secret police). Lenin too had been appalled, and Ordzhonikidze's brand of Bolshevism played an important role in his break with Stalin in 1923. Unfortunately, due to his illness, Lenin's pronouncement never saw the light of day until 1956 – one of those great mistimings of history. By then the Communists had promoted Ordzhonikidze across the Soviet Union as a People's Hero and most of Georgia's major towns collected their own Ordzhonikidze Streets, Plazas or statues.

Needless to say, his name suffered its own purge: the statues were being felled – the one in Tbilisi had been paint-bombed until it had to be removed as an eyesore – the 'Ordzhonikidze Streets' renamed, and praise-giving records rewritten. The town Ordzhonikidze itself teetered on the brink of returning to the name of the former Russian fortress, Vladikavkaz, which translates as 'rule the Caucasus'. But today, with this now safely achieved, the local Ingush tribe are standing up and calling for yet another change, back to its pre-Russian name.

Outside the window the land grew steadily greener and wetter, the white caps of the Greater Caucasus darting in and out of the roadside trees – poplar, ash, chestnut and sycamore. Every so often an open field of deep-brown earth put a space between them, and occasionally small, green burial mounds would sprout from the furrows, topped by primitive crosses or heaps of stones. Clearly we'd entered the territory of a proudly ancient people, a population whose history refused to be ploughed under or rewritten by the universal imposition of the collective farm. This earth carried the names of tribes whose ancestors still haunt the pedigrees of many modern Europeans. The bones of the Scythians, Parthians, Alans, Huns and Khazars all nourished this soil, as do those of their tribal offspring of today – the first of whom we were

31

about to meet.

Marika had clicked on the intercom. 'We're now entering the territory of Ossetes, or North Ossetia,' she said. 'The Ossetians are both Christian and Muslim, with many pagan elements to their religion. Their language is the only one in the Caucasus of Indo-Iranian origins. We don't know why.'

At the time, the dispute between the Ossetians and Georgians had yet to flare up into the virtual war of 1991. Marika spoke of this Caucasian people with a trace of pride. Their roots sank deep into this area and earned them a noble lineage. She continued: 'The Ossetians are said to come from the tribe of ancient Alans, who came here around the sixth century before Christ. Later this tribe migrated to North Africa, France and Spain, and lost its originality. But the Ossetes here still have a very pure blood.'

Purity of blood – I would hear this phrase again and again in Georgia. It referred to strong cultural resilience and determination, qualities much admired by the intermixed Georgians. Yet this determination also now led the Ossetians to dispute the ownership of their recently colonized area of Georgian territory, known as South Ossetia. As just one more element of the raging nationalistic whirlwind ripping across the Soviet Union, they wished to be joined to North Ossetia, thus re-creating their own pure-blooded nation of Ossetia. In spite of this, Marika's voice couldn't conceal its enthusiasm for this ancient race.

'The Ossetian mythology is very interesting and has influenced many Caucasian tribes, especially the Ingush and Chechens. The Ossetians believe they are descended from the Narts, a legendary tribe, half-giant and half-human. We think Nart comes from the Indo-Iranian word *nar*, which means "strong man". Today Ossetians will even show you ruins of Nart villages.'

I wondered about these former 'strong men', now steaming ahead with visions of independence just like the Georgians. 'Autonomous Socialist Republic' no longer sufficed for the Ossetians, just as 'Socialist Republic' no longer suited the Georgians' new image of themselves. During the years of brutal central planning these small nationalities had lost not only much of their self-esteem but also that crucial everyday initiative to direct their own trades and professions. They'd watched stunned as Gosplan (the Soviet Central Planning Committee) blundered through their local industries and agriculture again and again. Now those years of frustration finally found voice in a single, all-encompassing cry of 'independence'. After seventy years of silence, it cut through the mountain air with a hysteria that saw little beyond its own volume. As a result, the Ossetians and Abkhazians now glared at the Georgians with hatred and lust for independence just as the Georgians glared at the Russians (and the Ossetians and Abkhazians).

When Marika switched off the microphone, I asked her about these Ossetian grumblings.

'It's so silly,' she said. 'We get *glasnost* and suddenly everybody, down to the smallest tribe, wants independence.'

I wondered what gave the Georgian claim for independence more authority than anyone else's, but decided to keep an open mind. Meanwhile, the bus thundered on its way towards the tribal melting-pot that never melted, these mountains of peoples that even Stalin's almighty stick couldn't mix together. The road deteriorated, and the number of potholes dramatically increased, due to a winter thaw that plainly found little to forgive here, under the foothills. We passed several boulder-strewn, shaly rivers, their unconvincing bridges showing all the evidence of violent flash-floods. My confidence wavered at the sight of one brand-new metal-girder bridge washed away, obviously just a few weeks earlier. But our driver shot fearlessly across its wooden replacement, still driving his Ferrari.

With these scenes of destruction, the road offered up reminders of just how thoroughly its surrounding population had followed its example. First came a tall minaret (the Minaret of Tartartub), marking the place where in 1395 Tamerlane the Great won a great battle over Tokhtamysh, leader of the Mongol White Horde; then a monument proudly proclaiming the limits of the German advance in 1942 during the Great Patriotic War. These markers could just as easily have stood for the numerous battles fought along the famous Cossack Terek Line, which until the nineteenth century represented the high-water mark of the Russian empire. In these fields the Russians had repeatedly fought Persians, Turks and the various Muslim warrior tribes, such as the Circassians from the northern Caucasus. Today the Circassians still survive to the west, just as the remnants of Cossack tribes still mingle among the local foothill populations. Tolstoy had visited the Cossack villages in his youth and observed the deep codes of honour, the strength of character forming the backbone of their communities. If the northern Caucasus had ever been a melting-pot, these fields and washed-out floodplains on either side of the bus had to be the crucible.

Then briefly came and went the town of Vladikavkaz – a row of spiritless tower-blocks encircling the former Russian fortress, the goal and haven for those like Lermontov, who travelled from Tbilisi through these mountains in the nineteenth century. For me the town remained memorable for one giant spotted pig, indolently strolling along the street. But more importantly, here began the Georgian Military Highway, a route unchanged since Pushkin's day, when it served as the Russian Army's lifeline to the front. And here we picked up a faithful companion and chaperon for the high Caucasus to come, the much-praised, richly poeticized River Terek.

This 'laughing', 'smokey', 'agonized' torrent had drawn the adjectives of all nineteenth- and twentieth-century poets passing through the Caucasus. Its origins, high up in the rugged Caucasian glaciers, were much gazed upon by Pushkin, Lermontov, Tolstoy, Mayakovsky and so many others, before they too poured forth their devoted lines. The Terek would remain our companion along the Military Highway all the way to the Krestovy Pass, the highest point on the road.

However, then came a sudden shout from the back of the bus. 'Turn right!' This emanated from one of our group, someone who had carried out some earnest research before leaving England.

'Turning right somewhere round here will lead us to the Fiagdon valley and the Ossetian City of the Dead,' he announced confidently.

Did the driver know anything about these places, or indeed the turn-off?

'*Ho*,' came the cheerful reply (Georgian for 'yes').

But would he, or our representative from Intourist, permit such a major deviation from the Moscow-approved route? To my complete surprise a few minutes later the driver simply swung the wheel to the right, away from the Georgian Military Highway, and we were careering up a narrow, car-free mountain road, heading straight into the Greater Caucasus.

Densely wooded foothills quickly closed in on either side. Then came high cliffs, a narrow gorge and dense vegetation, as the road converted into a violently winding band of tarmac, pitching left and right as it followed the course of the gushing Fiagdon River. Watching a shaggy, Chinese-like hillock passing by, I suddenly experienced the distinct feeling of entering Asia. To greet it, the engine roared, the gears crashed and the bus leaned horribly round corners, until suddenly another shout came from the back of the bus and we skidded to a halt. Someone had spotted a mural high up on the cliff-face beside the road.

Following the direction of the pointing fingers I saw the image of a man's face painted in a seemingly inaccessible position high on the rock, at least 10 metres from any solid ground. The cleanness of the colours indicated a recent creation, yet its position directly above the raging torrent gave it the air more of an act of inspired bravery than a work of art. Clearly the face carried a deep significance for those who lived up here in the middle of nowhere. But who could it be? An Ossetian saint? Our driver answered the question monosyllabically.

'Stalin.'

He then lurched us forward again up into this, the Kurdish Gorge, and towards the City of the Dead. I was still mulling over his casual tone of voice when the bus shot round a corner and out into a vast and treeless valley. With it came the signs of former human habitation: ruined houses, hamlets and the remains of the famous Caucasian lookout towers – gaunt stone pillars of great antiquity, standing along

Stalin Monument to WWII.

with their decaying homesteads, in various states of collapse. Here in the Fiagdon valley came the first clues of the dramatic shifts in the Caucasian populations, begun after the Revolution and the relocations and continuing to this day, as these remote valleys continue to depopulate. At the end of the last century 50 per cent of the entire Caucasian population lived in mountain valleys like this. Today the figure barely touches 10 per cent.

As if to confirm the statistic there was yet another shout and more pointing of fingers, levelled this time at a dramatic ruined village clinging to a mountainside high up above the valley. With ghostly walls and crumbling towers it was silhouetted against an awesome backdrop of snow-streaked summits and steaming black cliffs. It looked more like an abandoned earth-base for aliens than any human settlement, and for the first time I felt that creeping sense of otherness that was to return again and again in the Caucasus – as if we'd just glided up a valley on a whim and discovered a lost civilization.

'Is this the City of the Dead?' someone asked.

Marika consulted the driver. 'No,' she then answered. 'The city is further on and is too far for us to visit today. This term refers to the Ossetian burial towers. From the Middle Ages they buried people in towers. But I can't tell you any more than that.'

The driver revealed the name of the hilltop town as Tsimitar, and explained that the so-called City of the Dead was a large Ossetian cemetary comprising many large burial towers.

Tsimitar's ragged outline, with its fan of drastic snowy peaks beyond, made it obvious why all those nineteenth-century poets found themselves compelled to return to the Caucasus. Then the villages were thriving communities, before the five-year plans and intense Soviet industrialization in the plains below, with its demand for workers.

At that point, as if to remind everyone that the process still continued, a 2-metre high display board appeared at the roadside. It stood out in the empty landscape like a forlorn iron stump, its flaking surface portraying a young Soviet woman holding her fist in the air in a gesture of defiant workers' solidarity. Yet its rusting paintwork stood more as an appropriate symbol of the decaying system that designed it. Socialism had come and now gone from this faraway region; it had left a few relics in the hillsides, but these soon would be forgotten.

The driver wanted to know how much further to go. 'We go to Stalin?' he asked.

Marika translated his words, then looked at me inquiringly. I just nodded. About a kilometre further on the bus slowed to a halt beside a small statue on a hillock and yes, contrary to all my reading on the

Caucasus, there, right in the centre of this enormous barren valley, stood a bust of Stalin, the eyes of his mustachioed face gazing solemnly up into the snowfields.

What on earth did he see up here? What kind of inspiration did he give to these local villagers – illegally? Officially only one statue of Stalin had been permitted to remain in the Soviet Union and that is at his birthplace in Gori, a couple of hundred kilometres to the south. But even the wisdom of having this statue had been hotly disputed, while up here, just below the snowline, the personality cult flourished gloriously untouched. At the base of the statue a number of fresh-cut flowers had lovingly been placed, an ongoing and spontaneous tribute to the tyrant. I'd yet to see any Lenin in the USSR so well cared for. It seemed that this great monster continued to blossom long after Khrushchev's famous reversal of the cult in 1956. Stalin, the greatest Caucasian of all time – responsible for the deaths of between 7,000 and 10,000 Georgians during the Georgian uprising of 1924; for sending a further 20,000 to Siberia; for wiping out the Georgian intelligentsia and many of his supporters in the insane purges of 1937 then deporting whole tribes from their homelands, including the nearby Chechens, Balkars and Ingush after the war – was still treated as a god.

I turned to Marika for help.

'The people in valleys like this are quite simple,' she said hesitantly. 'They feel their world to be small, and Joseph Stalin was very big. He won the Second World War and saved the world. He was internationally famous. He was also half-Ossetian, on his father's side. It sounds silly, but they're probably proud of him.'

'Is it not also a little sinister perhaps?' I suggested.

'No, not at all,' her voice broke into an affectionate laugh, as if she were talking about children. 'These are just country people. They don't support his ideas, they just like him. The big man.'

But one could tell, to this educated, liberal woman from the capital, the ongoing presence of the Stalin cult caused some embarrassment.

'What about the purges and the local deportations?' I asked.

'They think, well, he made a few mistakes, but so does everybody.' Her voice sounded conciliatory, as if playing them down as but minor blemishes on what was at heart a liberal nation.

On our way back down the valley, still not entirely convinced, I found myself concocting an exotic explanation of my own, connecting the Ossetian myths of the 'strong men' Narts to the big man Stalin. Had this early race been given human form, after religious worship had been suppressed by the atheist Soviets? Did the modern personality cult in any way resurrect the ghosts of the Zoroastrian gods of light and darkness, the truth and the lie, which dominated these mountains before Christianity?

My thoughts were drowned out by more shouts from the back of the bus.

'Stop!'

'City of the Dead!'

'Nart houses!'

Everybody looked towards a fortified Ossetian farm under a cliffside, with strange, stupa-like outbuildings. We piled out of the bus – hungry for anything which approached the sepulchrous city now denied us. For clearly here were a few of the Ossetian burial houses.

They stood behind the farm, looking more like tiny stone barns than towers, the blocks of their roofs stepped into each other in jagged, oriental shapes. These were obviously smaller versions of the 'City of the Dead' towers up the valley, but hardly less macabre. I wondered about the innocent foreign visitor to this 'City', wandering around believing it was just another Ossetian village. (From photographs I saw later, their towers did appear similar to buildings in nearby villages.) What about the moment he peered inside one of the buildings, only to discover the village peopled not by living families but thousands of corpses, layered one on top of the other in various stages of decomposition?

I approached the nearest burial house with caution, but I found my way barred by a viciously barking dog, leaping at me from the end of a thin rope. I retreated smartly, but as I did so I felt the Asian world take several steps towards me. These towers bore strong resemblances to the twelfth- and thirteenth-century *turbes*, or tomb towers, of Iran and Anatolia. Furthermore, the jagged stupa-like shape of the roofs offered a clear architectural connection with those I'd seen in Ladakh and Nepal.

I remembered reading about Georgia's key position on the old Silk Road: how its mountains once served as crucial repositories for religious texts and ideas as they flowed from East to West; how Caucasian monasteries preserved several critical religious and philosophical texts at a time when the Europeans persecuted them out of existence. One of the first accounts of the Buddha to arrive in the West came via Georgia in the tenth century – translated into Greek by Saint Euthymius at the Georgian monastery at Mount Athos. The story survives today as a folk-tale of Balavari. Among the writings otherwise lost to history were *On Nature* by Zeno, the founder of the Stoic school, and the neo-Platonic writings of Porphyry (saved by Armenian and Georgian scholars, then transmitted to the West). The people who today tend these strange single-windowed chambers certainly know nothing of this, yet the designs hinted at a time when their ancestors did.

Back at the bottom of the valley, lying on the rich green grass, engaging in that fine Caucasian tradition of the picnic, I began to feel the centuries-old fingers of legend slowly wrapping themselves around our journey. The ghosts of these ancient Caucasian cultures still haunted the hillsides, moving between the trees. In the grass around us, daisies, wild garlic and any number of different herbs and flowers sprouted from the same soil. Above, I noticed a white-winged eagle circling lazily among the crags. I felt we'd just glided up into a majestic, disappearing world of a former mankind, then back again to the modern Soviet world. It had all taken place in an instant and now seemed too much like a dream. I wondered how much I indulged in the popular condition of modern nostalgia, that self-manufactured state of yearning towards delight and terror – the same sort of feeling that motivated the European Romantic Movement and all nineteenth-century poets who visited the Caucasus; the phenomenon Marxists had described as 'drowning in honey' and 'rural idiocy'. But the Marxists were now being drummed brazenly from the Caucasus. The space they left behind would be filled by new winds rushing into the vacuum. Might not one of these be our modern European nostalgia industry? Would this unquenchable cultural thirst inflict any less damage on these valleys than Leninism? Only the silent barometer of eagles and wild herbs would ever let us know.

The Daryal Gorge

The entrance into the true Greater Caucasus begins when the Georgian Military Highway delves into its first gorge in the company of the rushing Terek. From here the assualt on Georgia begins in earnest with the endless climb to Kazbegi (Qazbegi in Georgian), the first major town after Vladikavkaz. I had been told the Georgian Military Highway ranked among the world's most dramatic when not cloaked in mist, rain or snow, but that it had a habit of dropping down all three on its most eager visitors. However, for us the vapours held back at the entrance to the cavernous Terek valley, allowing the sun to dab down patches of burning golden light on to the valley-floor stones.

But as the haggard mountainsides closed in, so the promise of drama fulfilled itself. Our tiny red speck of an Intourist bus crept slowly upwards among the rock ramparts and cliffs, a landscape far more suited to Narts than to mechanical conveyance. As the first glimpse from Pyatigorsk suggested, these mountains shoot up with great determination at the end of the former Russian empire. At every gear-change and battered road sign, I sensed this angry Asian curtain stiffen at our advance. These formidable ridges quietly loathed all intrusions, but as always the Terek obliged us Europeans with its persistent and rapidly narrowing slice up into the massif.

We now followed the route that for many centuries served as the main artery into the kingdom of Georgia. Until the arrival of the Russians, the river provided the most reliable guide south, in the form of a bridle-path. By the end of the eighteenth century, this had evolved into a rough-shod, frequently avalanched, often subsiding carriage-path. In the Soviet era, the military road was built up, widened and given today's decaying, pot-bellied tarmac surface, while a separate rail link had been established via Baku. Yet for all its modernity, this road amounted to no better than a narrow two-lane thoroughfare, one that most Americans would declare a single. This fact seemed only to spur on our driver, who recommended his imaginary death-race, wrenching the bus up the winding, clinging highway as if views never existed.

Leaning back in my seat, trying to enjoy the calamitous drops and fleeting panoramas, I took a philosophical stance. His return to the death-track simply replaced the former bandit threat of this road with a modern equivalent. Our senses now attuned themselves not to sword-waving Chechen warriors but to the next sixteen-wheeled, Soviet-built truck careering round a corner, under the control of a driver just like ours – an easy match for any disaster inflicted by the nineteenth-century Muslim rebels.

But the miraculous absence of traffic preserved us and we rocked and swerved our way ever upward towards a descending snowline. The gorge below us sunk deeper, the mountains stretched ever higher as the road increased its supply of heart-stopping blind corners – with only the occasional tyre-marked bollard between us and the smokey Terek. Marika then added to everyone's paranoia by announcing a purely historical fact.

'They say in the 1830s a great avalanche brought down a boulder of 2,000 tons, dropped it across the highway and closed the road for two years.'

Neither the road nor the driving perturbed her in the least. But from my own front seat I missed nothing and, after one last-minute wrench at the wheel, only just saving us from an instantaneous visit to the Terek hundreds of metres below, I couldn't restrain a comment. Marika just smiled.

'This is nothing. If you ever go to Svaneti, then you'll find out about

Georgian driving!'

I vowed never in my life to visit Svaneti. (I was proved wrong, of course.)

Meanwhile, she switched on the microphone again. 'We are now approaching the Iberian gates, the point at which the Roman general Pompey ceased his advance into Asia. Classic historians have described this place as "the ends of all the earth", but we Georgians call it the Daryal Gorge or Dary Alan, which translates as "the Gates of Alan". It was traditionally the doorway to Ossetia, the land of the Alans. For you, it's the doorway into Georgia. It is one of the narrowest parts of the Military Highway and was much attacked.'

As the 12-kilometre-long gorge clamped itself around us, one could easily see why. Its cliffs rose up a good kilometre on either side of the road, and at times plunged down to the same depth below. When Pushkin travelled through this deep crevasse of rock he described the sky as 'a narrow blue ribbon far above. Today the mountains disappeared into swirling mists and cloud, never able to decide whether to drop rain, fog or burning sunshine. How easy for bandits to drop something else – which they frequently did. In 1804 the local tribes almost brought the Russian Army to its knees by severing its supply line in this gorge.

As if still afraid of attack, the bus never slowed until the moment we flew round a corner and found ourselves face to face with a Crusader-type castle, perched on a bank beside the Terek.

'This is the Daryali Fortress,' announced Marika. 'It dates from medieval times and is one of the last in the ancient string of fortress-castles and watch-towers running across the Caucasus from early Christian times. They would light fires on the flat roofs when an army approached in order to warn the kings of Georgia on the other side of the mountains.'

Her words conjured up images of the numerous dark watch-towers of the kind found in the Fiagdon valley, igniting one after the other across the Greater Caucasus, creating a long orange necklace of light all the way to Tbilisi.

This particular fortress, restored and then used by the Russians in the eighteenth-century, had now been left to rot. Yet its turrets held up sturdily in spite of years of neglect, leaning crisply over the left bank of the Terek in readiness for the next supply train from Vladikavkaz. Above it rose the shadowy gorge 'of depths obscure and dismal', into which Lermontov landed the tormented demon in his narrative poem of the same name.

I found myself remembering the young poet again and his self-portrait at the beginning of *A Hero of Our Time*: perched on his bullock cart, his face battered by the wind, his 'portmanteau half-filled with travel notes on Georgia', a young man possessed by what he described as a 'mania for romantic places' and that terrible new malaise afflicting the officer classes of Tsarist Russia – boredom. In an unnervingly modern and almost certainly autobiographical passage from the book, he describes the feelings of a twenty-five-year-old in the 1830s:

> As a young man, as soon as I gained my freedom I threw myself wildly into all the pleasures that money can buy, and needless to say, soon tired of them. Then I went in for society high-life and before long tired of that too. . . . I took to reading and study but even wearied of that. I began to realize I had no need of learning to win fame or happiness, for the happiest of people are the stupid, and fame is a matter of luck and you only need a little cleverness to achieve it.

Then, later in the same monologue, he admits: 'My soul's been corrupted by my society. My imagination is eternally restless, my heart insatiable. . . . All that's left for me is to travel.'

In this passage can be found the first germs of that universal despair which eventually lead to the popularization of nihilism by Turgenev and other nineteenth-century writers. It also laid down the opening moves for the idealistic cult of the 'Young Man', a phenomenon much more 'of our time' than Lermontov's.

Lermontov had travelled to Georgia, searching for an experience of 'otherness' to lift him above the deadening sophistications of his own society – the motive that took me to India in the early 1980s. In these mountains he clearly found something, although not enough to make him forgo his passion for duelling, which ended his life (like Pushkin before him) at the age of twenty-six.

A century later the Russian Constructivist and poet Vladimir Mayakovsky, travelled through these mountains believing he carried the torch his predecessors lacked – Bolshevik socialism. He passed through this very gorge in 1924, composing his own irreverent sequel to Lermontov's *The Demon*. As in previous poems, such as 'Ode to Revolution', Mayakovsky proselytized on behalf of the new Communist regime with unruly zeal, fusing his Bolshevik fury with Nature mysticism. Again this zeal propelled him to an untimely end: he committed suicide in 1930, a bitterly disappointed man, having turned on the system he had once so wholeheartedly promoted.

With my head lolling against the velvety headrest, I looked up at the twisting rock formations, the fog funnelling between cracks in the cliffs. These mountains seemed to hold their breaths, anxiously awaiting the next set of idealists and poets, the newest, furiously improved system of human government.

Minutes later our bus shot out of the gorge and into the luxurious, wide open valley around Kazbegi. Finally, we'd arrived in the generous heartland of Georgia.

CHAPTER THREE
KAZBEGI

To enter the spacious Kazbegi valley straight out of the Daryal Gorge is to transfer from one absolute of landscape into another. From the shadowy, claustrophobic cliffs of the canyon we sped out into a brilliant white arena of peaks and luscious alpine meadows. Before us a transparent green grass rolled out welcomingly across the valley floor, climbing up the steep hillsides towards the white snow-line and finally ebbing away into the frosty blue firmament.

Through the bus windscreen I saw the next watch-tower in the line leading straight into the heart of Georgia's old kingdom, Mtskheta, beyond the Greater Caucasus. But unlike those in the Ossetian Fiagdon valley, it stood in perfect repair. Beside the road the Terek had also changed, from a violent, steaming attack on rocks hundreds of metres below to an obedient river burbling quietly beside the road. To celebrate the change in mood the highway gaily crossed and recrossed the water, making up for all those embittered kilometres clinging desperately to the western valley wall.

'From here the river's name is Tergki,' said Marika. 'Its Georgian name.'

Then buildings appeared beside the road and, without warning, the bus suddenly swung off the highway, climbed the valleyside, passed a few blocks of well-spaced tin-roofed houses and pulled up before a long, balconied building.

'The Kazbegi Intourist Hotel,' announced Marika.

With my back to our new home I looked down on my first Georgian town: a community of perhaps 4,000 people whose houses nosed down to the Terek (or Tergki), then on up the other side as an untidy scattering of silver and brown roofs, smallholdings and miniature market gardens. The only real landmark was a rusty pylon rising up in the centre of the village on the opposite side (Gergeti) like a fleshless totem-pole. Plainly, it was the centre station of a cable car, but where was the cable? The base station in Kazbegi also seemed dysfunctional or broken. I was about to ask Marika what had happened, when a casual glance up into what I thought was the sky stopped me dead. For there in place of empty space stood one utterly vast mountain. It rose up into the air like a menacing white hammerhead, poised to strike down on a submissive community below. Directly before it, as if in supplication to stay the execution, a picturesque twin-peaked church (the Gergeti Trinity Church) knelt on a small mountaintop.

So this was it, Mount Kazbek, the great pivot, the horn of rock and ice around which the ancient Caucasus revolved, the father of our own Prometheus legend. It lifted up another 3,250 metres above the tin roofs of the town, most of it in a single gigantic thrust of granite to scrape the heavens at 5,047 metres. Seeing it in the crystal-clear air, so cleanly defined, generated a rush of exhilaration, followed by a slight twinge of anxiety. This monster stood a shade too close for comfort. Experience had by now taught me to beware of all breath-taking beauties, mountains in particular. For in spite of all the grandeur, something afflicted this town. It had to do with that abandoned cable car and the numerous fluttering strips of black cloth hanging off buildings and road-signs.

Marika offered the first clue: 'These flags are flying all over Georgia at the moment,' she said gravely. 'They are marking the forty-day period of mourning for the protesters killed on 9 April. Many are choosing to dress in black, to go to churches, light candles and place these flags in public places as a mark of respect and also as a protest.'

This would explain why none had been seen before, as North Ossetia stood within the Russian Federation, not Georgia. Yet here, just across the border, the atmosphere changed dramatically. I walked down to the town square and discovered small knots of loitering men, their burnt Asian faces glancing at me from under flat cloth caps. They seemed disgruntled, apathetic, or both. The streets oozed the same sense of unease and decay. Mountain cattle (like the local Khevsuretian cow) and chickens strolled untended along the main avenues, as the men idly watched on. Beyond the town I noticed a bulldozer left to rust in the middle of a field, as if once broken down it immediately became useless, irreparable – like the Soviet system that supplied it. I watched a cow push open the gate of the Intourist hotel and amble in towards the lusher tourist grass beyond, and in the main square a pig sniffed her way around the black granite platform bearing up the serious statue of the town hero, the nineteenth-century poet, A. Kazbegi. Nobody cared.

Walking up the hill I encountered a large vandalized building. On its walls the words 'Kazbegi Cultural Centre' were written in Russian.

Next to it, sitting under a statue of Lenin (since removed), three local teenage girls chatted among themselves, all wearing knee-length dresses. Could I take a quick photo?

'*Ya, danke schön*,' came a casual reply, imagining me an East German tourist.

I tried a few words of Russian.

'Why is the Cultural Centre broken?'

'We don't use it,' came the off-hand reply.

'But why break it?'

My question received a shrug in reply. They'd already lost interest in me, by now just another part of this lackadaisical Georgian mountain village. Yet back in England, the processed film revealed three utterly charming and alert smiles, all overhung by the thickest, darkest female eyebrows I've yet seen.

Back at the hotel the atmosphere of lethargy and staggering beauty only deepened. We stood in the lime-disinfected reception area (the hallmark of all Intourist hotels) for half an hour before finding anybody able to supply us with room keys. Eventually a Russian woman provided the solution. She pulled open a drawer in the small table beside the front door, then simply spread out all the room keys.

'Take,' she said, trying to show willing.

When one of our group asked if the hotel had room service, the question prompted a confused look.

'Er . . . yes. Where would you like to visit?' she replied.

This in turn confused the asker. The manageress had mistaken the question for 'Do you have a Service Bureau?' – a kind of internal travel agency/information service, common to most large Moscow hotels. Since this hotel had neither, I couldn't understand why she'd answered 'Yes', so I asked where it might be.

'Here,' she replied, pointing at the humble table with its three now empty drawers.

I realized that this wooden table stood as the solution to all tourist dilemmas, whether manned or unmanned. As long as a 'Service Bureau' existed, Moscow would be satisfied. The staff to operate it amounted to a mere incidental.

Then another of our group descended from her second-floor room to complain of unmade beds, no sheets, toilet paper or towels.

'Where is our floor lady?' she asked hopefully.

'Here.' The Russian manager pointed to herself and smiled feebly.

'Well perhaps you could just get the maid to bring it by later,' our group member suggested, trying to be tactful.

The manageress just smiled again, quickly stepped through a nearby doorway and reappeared a minute later, clutching sheets and a toilet roll.

'Isn't there anybody here to do the rooms?' someone asked.

'Yes, but not now . . . or so often,' came the awkward reply.

These words turned out to be prophetic, and for the next three days we appeared to live in a medium-sized hotel run by one person. She explained later that Intourist had great difficulty recruiting staff from the local Kazbegi population. When asked why, she just shrugged a little too casually.

'Not money from Moscow,' she replied.

Again and again in Georgia I experienced hotels just as inefficient as those up north. Much of the reason, as Marika later explained, was to do with the fact that hotel jobs, especially the menial ones, tended to be carried out by non-Georgians. And the reason for this? Marika smiled a little sheepishly.

'Well, you know Georgians don't like to be servants. And although many Georgian women would be willing, our men don't allow us. Once it was even a shame to be a merchant here, but then the Armenians came in and started taking over everything, so we Georgians had to learn.'

And then came dinner. Informing the kitchen of my vegetarian needs (a practice not recommended to travellers in the former Soviet Union), I awaited my meal with anxiety while the others first received a slice of bread, then a bowl of greasy soup, followed by a lump of boiled mutton. Then, when all around me were scraping their chairs to leave, my food finally arrived – a single boiled potato in the middle of a chipped white plate.

I stared at this piece of fluffy conceptual art with disbelief. Kazbegi knew no shortage of food or produce. We'd passed plenty of prosperous vegetable gardens and farms on the way in, some only yards away from the hotel. No, my steaming potato had been placed before me as a message. It spelled out the words 'Go away' as vividly as if they'd been emblazoned across the hotel front door. Tourists were not wanted in Kazbegi, even foreign (hard-currency-bearing) tourists. As for those with eccentric, unreasonable eating habits, what kind of a nerve was this!

Sitting in that deserted restaurant I ate my potato in silence, chewing over its brief significance. Since they didn't know me personally, the kitchen obviously hated what I represented. I, who arrived in Kazbegi not at their invitation but on behalf of the Moscow regime, as one more unit of Intourist's currency-earning machinery. And what did Moscow do with this currency? It simply furthered its own ends, or furtively invested it in more hard-currency projects, like cable-car schemes, designed to transform peaceful Caucasian villages into booming holiday resorts. In return the Intourist head office on Prospekt Marxa, would pay these minor, rebellious outposts a few worthless roubles.

These villagers detested what they saw as the Moscow dictatorship, long before the arrival of the Soviets. Georgia had entered the Russian empire willingly in 1801, only then to watch the Russians renege on their treaty of 1783 by banishing the Georgian royal family and attempting to disestablish their Orthodox Church. Resistance had passed on from generation to generation. Georgians had no desire to please their masters in any way. If guests at this hotel carried away terrible reports, so much the better. Intourist might simply drop Kazbegi from its schedule altogether.

The Mountain

The following evening I sat alone on the first-floor balcony watching the sun slide away to the west beneath Mount Kazbek. The town before me seemed ravaged by beauty and decay at one and the same time. Furthermore, up here in the high Caucasus there existed a quality of light I'd never seen before: a translucent, airy emerald in the grass that seemed to penetrate everything – the rock, the sky, the people, one's thoughts. In the presence of so much snowy splendour, so much infinity right up before one's face, what did the smaller things in life (like work) matter?

As the sun settled down over the valley, I watched it spread a delicious deep glow behind the mountain, gradually erecting its enormous golden dome over our heads, pricked with stars. Night now approached from the east, and out along the Military Highway the lights of traffic blinked on, hurrying their journeys south towards Tbilisi. Above us all, and still kneeling before the colossus of Mount Kazbek, the mountain-top Gergeti Trinity Church (Tsminda Sameba) now pushed itself to centre-stage, its twin towers crisply silhouetted against the radiant sky.

According to Marika the church had stood in that position since the sixteenth century and the bell-tower beside it since the fifteenth century. But under this flood of other-worldly light, what did the facts of history matter? Its sentinel shape, set prominently beside the holy mountain, conveyed everything that needed to be known about the importance of religion in Georgia.

Then as I gazed at it, to my complete surprise the church suddenly ignited in a brilliant bath of yellow light. I could hardly believe my eyes.

The villagers must have run up a cable and floodlights from the town a good 500 metres below. I stared at the now luminous twin towers floating up against the glowing darkness like a squat celestial lord. What an extraordinary place: human indolence below and fierce religious enterprise burning above; plainly representing the only political force they trusted.

Georgia's Orthodox Church, founded in the fourth century, had been the single rock to which this smal nation had clung throughout its terrible history of subjugation. After the Muslim Persians and Turks had done their utmost to destroy it, their allies, the Christian Russians, attempted the same by abolishing its autocephaly in 1811 (viciously reneging on the 1783 treaty) and replacing it with their own Russian Orthodoxy. Instead of razing the churches to the ground (like former invaders), they simply abolished its hierarchy and painted over the fine Georgian frescoes. Yet the many previous centuries of similar atrocities had only hardened Georgian will to maintain its Church. By the time the Communists arrived with their own crusade – to eradicate religion altogether (establishing an extraordinary organization called the Georgian League of the Militant Godless), the Georgians were well equipped to outride this one too. In the end, Stalin himself restored the autocephaly in 1943, as an attempt to woo fuller Georgian support during the Great Patriotic War (the Second World War).

But to the locals at Kazbegi, their religion sank down roots beyond even the Christian arrival in Georgia. While they still call Mount Kazbek the Mountain of Christ, they also believe the tent of Abraham is pitched on the summit (in some versions of the myth it becomes an inaccessible citadel) and that inside an infant sleeps in a cradle held up by unseen hands. Some also say a sacred tree grows on the top with treasure spread around its base, a treasure with the ability to let some see it and others not. It is said that most human beings are now too impure to see these wonders – including the London Alpine Club, who first climbed the mountain in 1868, in defiance of predictions that they would be driven back from the summit by furious storms and invisible forces. In 1913 this mountain revealed more of its religious secrets when climbers discovered the ruins of a church bearing a cross at an astonishing 3,962 metres.

Next to the Gergeti Trinity Church, the Kazbegi skyline carried another man-made silhouette – an ugly concrete cube about 10 metres high, set 30 metres to the side of the church. This Soviet-built structure announced, more effectively than any plaque or statue, the attempt to force modern leisure values into this valley. Set prominently on the skyline (I suspect deliberately, for the building could easily have been

Kazbegi.

dropped 6 metres or so to preserve the panorama) it stood like the trademark of materialism stamped on the mountainside. As the cable-car terminus it was intended to serve a thriving tourist industry – much resented by the locals – by sparing visitors the two-hour switchback trek up to the 'tourist attraction', Gergeti Church. But where had the cable gone?

Marika could tell us nothing. Eventually our local bus-driver solved the mystery, with the help of Marika's translation.

'The cable car was finished in October 1988,' he replied flatly to my question.

'But what about the cable?'

'It's there,' he replied, then adding quietly, 'on the ground. Go to the base station. Look for yourself.'

He seemed very keen for us to go – which we did later, and found a brand-new concrete structure recently (and deliberately) destroyed. The giant pulley-wheels lay on the grass among twisted iron girders and lumps of concrete rubble. Spread between this debris lay sections of the cable, cut into pieces and left to rust.

After some determined questioning, the curious history emerged. Apparently the Soviet-designed cable car had taken no less than ten years to build. The protesting locals had eventually been persuaded to assist in its construction, earning lethargic roubles, joking and jeering at the thing they erected.

'It cost them $1\frac{1}{2}$ million roubles,' said our driver emphatically. 'It was being built for Russian workers in the All-Union holiday camp above your hotel.' His tone of voice clearly lumped our hotel in with the camp. 'We wrote to our First Secretary, asking him not to put the head station too close to our monument [the Gergeti Church], but he didn't listen.' He paused, before continuing in a matter-of-fact voice, 'So in December 1988 we knocked down the lower station,' then picking up enthusiasm he added. 'And we're going to do the upper one soon.'

Responding to my surprised remark, he said sternly. 'Nobody wanted that thing. Even the tourists didn't want it.' He turned round and glanced at me, not for confirmation but to let me know. Yet with this look the listlessness underneath the town began at last to make sense. Here was a community instructed by Moscow to participate in its grandest enterprise since building the Gergeti Church, and yet the only real achievement to these villagers would be to pull it down again.

Looking up at this huge mountain, now just a glowing shadow, I thought of the futility and despair experienced by the legendary Promethius and the Promethean ordeal suffered by these villagers at the hands of a covetous Moscow central planning committee.

The Greek Prometheus' crime had been to form mankind out of clay and give him fire. Yet his story bears a curious similarity to the local Caucasian legend of Amirani, another god-like man chained to this mountain. Amirani's sin had been to challenge the almighty (and here wise) Zeus or great spirit to a test of strength, but unlike Prometheus, Amirani's lack of psychological insight had been the cause of his imprisonment.

Looking at the now almost faded mountain, I found it easy to imagine a giant, tormented man strapped within the enormous silhouette. A few months later, driving along the Inner Kartli valley of central Georgia, I had the man in the mountain pointed out to me from the south. The knobbled shape of the old hero, hunched over as if by some burden, appeared clearly.

'You know why he looks so miserable and bent under the weight?'

asked my Georgian host at the time. 'Because he created the Russians!'

Later that night at 12.30 a.m. I lay in the room, waiting for my room-mate to return and turn off the light. From upstairs came the sound of a party hosted by a Georgian film crew from Tbilisi's Gruzia film studios. The sound of twin pipes and delighted off-key riffs floated through the hotel hall, past all the silent doors, a sound far more Oriental than European. I couldn't imagine such a wilful disturbance in any other Russian hotel at this hour; the *babushka*s and neighbours would have dealt with it swiftly. But in Georgia the rules of hospitality carried new meaning. Nobody complained. If you couldn't stand the noise, you joined in.

The volume of laughing, clapping and stamping steadily increased as the Georgian revellers gathered more guests, who began to join in the dance. Soon the floorboards were creaking directly above my bed, occasionally shuddering alarmingly as dancers stamped out the rhythm. Then suddenly the music stopped and in its place came one solitary male voice singing a single note; then another voice joined in with a different note, then another. Soon our two rooms quivered under the force of an entirely new vibration – the full-blooded dissonant harmony of a male choir, the sound for which Georgia has been famous for thousands of years.

I imagined the European and Russian tourists tossing in their sheets, trying to close their ears to these proud male chords peeling off one after the other. Yet for myself, I found the sound enlivening rather than annoying. These polyphonic chords – a Caucasian phenomenon unique to Georgia – date way back into prehistory. In 400 BC the Greek historian Xenophon described Georgian soldiers charging into battle while singing the chorus. To me in the twentieth century, they resonated with a refreshing, new brand of 'soul', quite unlike the relentless dull throb of 'soul music' emanating from speakers at European hotel parties.

But where was my room-mate? Then suddenly I was putting on my trousers and jacket, and hurrying off down the hall. There could only be one answer! Following the choir back to its source I knocked loudly on a door which immediately swung open. A grinning dark face invited me in, not even remotely curious about who I might be. And there sat my room-mate, a glass of red wine in hand, an embarrassed smile on his face, watching these Georgians gather steam. A glass was thrust into my hand, a slap deposited on my back and suddenly we'd been friends for life. A minute or two later the singing stopped and a dark mustachioed face stood up and proposed a toast.

'I give a toast to our faith, our Georgian faith. To Saint Nino, who brought it to us, to the glory of her work in Georgia, may it continue, may the Georgian Church flourish, may all who visit it grow bold . . . '

The glasses were all raised and, to my surprise, downed in one gulp, then immediately refilled. I glanced around the room full of Georgians and a couple of our group; a small silver pipe lay on the bed. But the ritual had not yet finished.

'To our guests from England,' shouted the *tamada*, or Georgian toastmaster. 'To their noble country.' Then he lowered his voice to an earnest whisper, 'May the Russians give up their empire as graciously as the British gave up theirs!'

A cheer erupted from the Georgians, most of whom understood English. All glasses were then raised again, and, in a sudden silence, downed to the dregs.

During that hushed, religious moment as the liquor flowed down the throat, I reflected on this Georgian style of hospitality. It gave the process of getting drunk a pleasant, ceremonial quality. Later, when I explained that in England anything declared with a glass in the hand, toast or not, is usually taken with a pinch of salt, the Georgians laughed heartily.

'To us Georgians, this means it is to be trusted!' they replied.

Not entirely convinced, I asked one of the toasting crew what they were up to in Kazbegi.

'We're making a film,' he said vaguely.

'What's the film?' I persisted.

'I think in English you'd call it *The Sons of Sin*. It's about the conflict between Christians and Muslims up here in the mountains. About a Christian who kills a Muslim and realizes he was a noble man, and so he prays for his enemy. It's a story of honour, because honour is really the only possession the people have up here. It's the same for both religions. Have another vodka. Now we will toast the Queen of England. May she live long. May she vanquish her enemies. God save her!'

Another profound silence gripped the room as we all solemnly raised our glasses and knocked back what in an English pub would amount to about five shots of neat vodka.

I asked him why he toasted our Queen. Didn't he realize she no longer wielded any power or vanquished enemies?

'Yes, I realize,' he said, adding emphatically, 'But she's your *Queen*. In Georgia, we still like kings and queens. We once had our own Queen . . . ' He took a deep draught of his vodka. 'Queen Tamar!' I could see him winding up for another toast and interceded quickly.

'In England our government takes the role of king now.'

'Yes, I know,' he interrupted. Then he grinned. 'Margaret Thatcher, Queen Tamar!'

I tried to ask more about the film, about the war between Muslims and Christians in these mountains that seemed to flare only when provoked by the surrounding Muslim and Christian great powers, two religions that otherwise contented themselves with the occasional token raid – as Tolstoy had noted in *The Cossacks*. Still, it was not to be.

'Now you, you make a toast!' he said boisterously. 'I saw you sitting on the balcony, alone, looking up at the church, writing. I thought then, "He's one of us!" A poet. So propose a toast!'

I faltered. Noticing my embarrassment, he stepped in to help with a question: 'What do you think of Stalin?'

Reaching for my glass in desperation, I remembered Marika's words a few days back on the bus, while responding to a similar question in reference to the Ossetian villagers. In a voice louder than I intended I replied. 'He was a big man.'

'Yes, a big man, yes!' he agreed heartily, then raised his glass. 'To Stalin!'

CHAPTER FOUR
KAZBEGI TO TBILISI

We left Kazbegi chewing on this blend of contradictory impressions. Georgia, regaled as one of the world's most hospitable nations, had supplied one of its most unaccommodating hotels. Georgia, the seething single voice of nationalistic rebellion against the Russians, seemed split within itself. Its Ossetian and Abkhazian populations sought separation, not from the USSR but from their old Georgian alliance.

Others in our group had encountered their own paradoxical experiences of Kazbegi. The novelist Fay Weldon – accompanying us with her husband and her mother – told the story of attending a Kazbegi wedding party. Joyfully accosted on the street, they accepted this first invitation of genuine 'Georgian hospitality', only to find themselves quickly elevated to the guests of honour at the dinner as 'the foreigners'. They then watched in stupefaction as the *tamada* proposed toasts not only to Stalin but to Hitler as well.

Almost certainly not Georgian fascists, these unsophisticated mountain people simply loved Stalin as 'the big man' – and Hitler as well, one supposed, as the attempted liberator of the area from the cruel Soviet regime. Somehow the deeds of Stalin had become completely separated from the man.

As the bus steered a southern course along the Khevi gorge, and across the wide floodplains of the Terek, I wondered about these 'gaps' in memory. Some purpose far more compelling than history had opened the gulf. The 'bigness' of the man remained too important to these remote villages.

Then I remembered Marika's description of the pre-Christian legend of Amirani. She insisted it stood as the 'central and formative myth underlying Georgian culture'. Could a pre-Bronze-Age myth of a stubborn superhuman still provide links with modern character? I doubted it. But the story was interesting, especially if one took the legendary Amirani to represent the emergence of the Georgian people.

Under this interpretive tack, many intriguing clues seem to reveal themselves about the mysterious beginnings of this nationality – so obsessed with all the links to its past.

Amirani was born in the midst of a dark forest to Dali, the Georgian goddess of the hunt. He grew up displaying prodigious strength with the capacity to outdrink and outeat three ordinary men. During his first quest for treasure he encountered a three-headed monster who, just before Amirani slayed him, begged the hero not to kill the three worms that would come from its mouth at death. Amirani agreed. After he'd dispatched the monster, the worms grew and transformed into three dragons, one white, one red and one black. Amirani killed the first two but was swallowed by the black dragon, leaving his brothers to cut him out from its stomach.

Amirani then began his quest for a beautiful maiden called Kamari, 'covered in silk as gold as sunbeams' and 'so beautiful even the sun daren't look at her'. He found her in a magnificent celestial castle suspended from the sky by a chain. Cutting the chain, he entered to find Kamari in the middle of her domestic chores. He begged her to run away with him and she agreed, but only once the dishes had been cleaned. Amirani began to help her but quickly lost his temper with a dish that refused to stand upright, and smashed it with his heel. At this, all the other dishes cried out in alarm and rushed up into the sky to alert Kamari's father.

A terrible pursuit and battle ensued. At one point, hearing about the deaths of his two brothers, Amirani committed suicide, only to be brought back to life by Kamari, with a magic herb she discovered by listening to the advice of a mouse.

After Amirani had rid the world of nearly all its dragons, monsters and wild animals, he threw down the gauntlet to God himself. God warned Amirani of the futility of this, but Amirani, in all his vanity, stuck doggedly to this quest for omnipotence. Answering Amirani's challenge, God plunged a stick into the ground and asked Amirani if he were man enough to pull it out. Amirani wrenched and wrenched but the stick had secretly sunk roots deep into the world and refused to budge. For punishment, Amirani was chained to a pole sunk into the side of Mount Kazbek. Each day, as he struggled to free himself, God sent a raven with a piece of bread and a glass of wine. But in his fury Amirani would hurl a stone at the raven, miss and knock in his pole ever more firmly.

From this I began to speculate on the emerging nation of Georgia, a train of thought that lasted a good many kilometres up the valley. With Amirani representing the Georgian race, I saw their dark beginnings as a Neolithic tribe hunting in the prehistoric forests, followed by their mysterious link or mating with the supernatural world (the goddess of the hunt, Dali). The birth of the child Amirani symbolized the attaining of a powerful semi-divine vision (or consciousness). This infant, born with enormous strength to follow quests, slay dragons, seek out unearthly and beautiful women, symbolized the new vision of the people. As the tribe (Amirani) pursued their new mission, they gradually progressed towards civilization.

After his various battles and successes – indicating the strength of human consciousness over the unconscious animal world – Amirani began to run out of heroic physical challenges. During his many quests, numerous tiny reminders kept hinting that he should stop focusing so intensely on the world of physical prowess and notice instead the smaller details of heroic life: tiny worms that grow into dragons, taking care of dishes, mice. Such incidents were pointing always towards the more subtle side of greatness. Yet amid all his successes he never noticed it was the smaller things in the end that led to his downfall. In his misguided belief in superiority, he finally attempted the impossible (like all great dictators). Thus he is crushed by his own lack of insight. Yet even God, when he threw the stick into the earth, tried again to remind Amirani that in order to mature, the warrior hero must stop looking at the top of the stick and recognize instead that all his victories, his quests for dragons, treasure and beautiful women, are but superficial triumphs and as nothing to the deep roots below the surface of consciousness. Now that he'd outgrown the tribe's early successes, he needed to add a level of philosophical introspection. This, in his dogged tugging at the head of the stick, he refused to do and thus found himself chained to the rock of futile conquest, power and rage for all eternity.

As we sped past the village of Kobi, its long plastic greenhouse tunnels of tomatoes and cucumbers, and on towards the highest point on the Military Highway, the 2,395-metre Krestovi Pass, I began to ponder Prometheus' role in all this. Could he be the reformed successor of this Caucasian hero – transformed into the god who moulded mankind out of clay and then, at great personal sacrifice, invested him with the fire of intelligence? Marika told us in some versions of the Amirani legend, Amirani had also given fire to mankind and suffered at the hands of opposing heavenly forces. But perhaps more significant, what about the lessons of Amirani when applied to Georgia's modern deity of masculine power, Stalin? As we passed more black flags, this message from the Bronze Age seemed to apply with equal urgency today. Amirani had not departed from Georgia, even with the death of his latest incarnation as almighty Communist leader. (The fact hit home with some force at the end of 1991 when Georgia's mini civil war erupted right in the heart of their newly independent capital. The foolish hero seemed to have returned again, this time in the shape of their new, non-Communist President Zviadi Gamsakhurdia. He too would receive his lesson against omnipotence and infallibility, at the hands of his former supporters in the National Guard, as they too turned into gun-slinging warrior heroes in their own right.)

The unusual sensation of the bus slowing brought me back to reality, and with it the sound of hundreds of tiny tinkling bells. Looking from the window, I found the bus suddenly afloat on what appeared as a rippling, choppy sea of wool. An enormous flock of sheep swarmed and bleated across the road, blocking out all sight of the ground for 100 metres on either side of our bus. Some distance away on the mountainside, a single shepherd leaned on a long crook, looking away, completely unconcerned. Our driver opened his window and shouted something unpleasant. The shepherd did nothing and then, a few seconds later, turned and shouted back something equally rude. But instead of thrusting the bus into gear and charging down the sheep, our driver suddenly leaned back in his seat and laughed heartily to himself, then nodded at the shepherd. A good joke in the Caucasus obviously carried much of the distance to forgiveness. The shepherd's humour saved his sheep from our despotic driver, and eventually we pulled forward respectfully.

On our final assault on the pass, we flashed past snowdrifts and abandoned avalanche-tunnels as the bus rapidly decelerated. The sheet of tarmac deteriorated drastically, often doubling as a river. At times the road surface disappeared altogether under stones, mud and bubbling water. As we climbed the light grew brighter on either side and the mountainsides shrank down.

I remembered reading about travellers in the last century who frequently climbed down from their carriages at this point, preferring to walk over the summit due to the road's treachery. One foreign diplomat apparently even had himself blindfolded and led through by hand.

As the light swelled all around us, the revving bus slowed to walking pace. On either side the mountains stretched down long fingers of snow that immediately converted to floods of wild Terek-like water the moment they touched the tarmac. The torrent then raced along the road, before diving over the far side and into the slim river beside us – the Terek's high-altitude beginnings. Every so often, vivid red gashes of mineral deposits coloured the riverbank, like flowing wounds. These open veins of the earth belonged to the bubbling Narzan spring water, common in many areas of the Caucasus, a tonic water popular for its high iron content – hence the colour.

About a couple of kilometres below the top of the pass a large growth of rusty, amber rock bulged out from the mountainside and beside it was a spring. We stopped to stock up with Narzan water. It tasted tingly and metallic, and a few hundred metres further up the hill we discovered why. Several loud pops from the back of the bus announced that corks on winebottles were blowing out, pouring Narzan water all over the seats.

'The water is also naturally carbonated,' remarked Marika rather too late.

Afterwards I was told of a nearby lake of this same gaseous water where, due to the water's carbonation, the surface appeared permanently on the boil.

At the crest of the Krestovi, Marika clicked on the microphone. 'This is what we in Georgia call the Djvari Pass. Djvari means "cross". If you look, on the left you should see a cross. It marks the top of the pass where the Terek's watershed ends and the Aragvi River begins. It's a very important cross for Georgians and is called Queen Tamar's cross. It's said to have been put there by King David the Builder during Georgia's golden era, between the twelfth and thirteenth centuries.' Then her voice picked up enthusiasm. 'Queen Tamar was the most famous and inspirational of all Georgia's monarchs. During her reign, 1184–1213, Georgia extended its empire through much of Armenia and into present-day Turkey. It also underwent a major cultural and spiritual renaissance. During her reign much of the great Georgian movements in religion, art and epic poetry were begun.' Then she added, 'She is also called Tamara.'

Still mopping up Narzan water, I missed it. But I also wondered why there was such a fuss over a simple cross. For the second time I'd heard the name of this queen spoken with reverence, almost as if she still lived. At 800 years old she obviously still played a pivotal role in the complicated self-image of modern Georgians, a guide perhaps for their uncertain reaction to the contradictory pulls and pushes of modernity.

As Marika was to say on a later occasion: 'We Georgians have a strong feeling for our past centuries; much stronger than Europeans. We feel very close to our twelfth century. For some of us, it's almost as if it were yesterday.'

At the time I thought it a strange statement, but the longer I spent in Georgia the truer it seemed.

The nose of the bus then dipped downwards for the first time in several days, beginning the long descent to Tbilisi, the capital of these enigmatic twelfth and twentieth centuries.

To our right the giant zebra-striped summit of Gud Gora slipped past and next to it the Gudaur Abyss, a 600-metre drop offering spectacular views of the southern mountains. But to the Soviet propagandists, not content with a majestic view of barren mountainscape and moraine boulders – known locally as the 'Stone Chaos' – this was not enough. They had added a stone chaos of their own. Disguised as a viewing platform, a giant semicircular piece of 'People's Art' had been constructed right on the edge of the abyss. An enormous, 70-metre-long mosaic replaced the view with a joyful Soviet proclamation of the fruits of the Russo-Georgian Treaty of 1783, a pact marking the formal beginnings of fraternity between the two nations (a treaty totally disregarded by the Russians a few years later when they abolished the Georgian monarchy and, later again, the Georgian Church). These facts were well known to every Georgian yet, in blithe obedience to that old slogan 'Tell a lie enough times and loudly enough and it becomes a truth', this mural portrayed in candy colours a history of the inseparable 'friendship' between the Russian and Georgian peoples (the Communists even renamed the Georgian Military Highway 'The Road of Friendship').

In the illustrative style of a child's colouring book, the mosaic depicted a carnival of Georgian mythological figures; Russian and Georgian churches side by side (both persecuted by the Communists); an enormous flowing red young man to signify the Revolution; a group of cheerful, obedient women workers; then a laughing soldier holding up a Kalashnikov and a bunch of flowers to represent the Great Patriotic War. At the end of this sugar-coated vision of the past came an image of the future. It apparently belonged to a teenaged boy and girl portrayed in rainbow colours, running beneath a firmament filled, not with angels but with flying cosmonauts, their arms outstretched towards empty space.

This enormous tableau of lies presented ever more gainfully not the truth but the images which the Soviet authorities intended other people (and themselves) to perceive as truth. It was as if they too sensed the imminent ideological collapse and hoped the tons of concrete poured into these enormous public monuments would somehow shore it up.

As a result of this monstrosity, none of the passing Georgian cars stopped here any more, preferring (quite naturally) an uninterrupted view of nature's achievements further up. The huge monument sat forlornly on the cliff edge like a pimple in open competition with everything unSoviet – in this case space itself.

I thought of those blandly smiling faces at the Pyatigorsk floor-show again. Did they ever genuinely consider the messages of their art? Did they not detect the blatant futility of these statements? Already nature had begun her first moves towards renovation by attacking the outer layers of concrete. Cracks shot along large sections of the platform, and parts had already crumbled back to the reinforcing bars.

Marika also expressed a healthy dislike of such monuments. 'I don't know who they think likes these things,' she remarked. 'They never ask us.'

In the meantime the ancient village of Gudauri passed by, a village that a few years ago nearly became the modern Austrian skiing village of Gudauri (and could still do so). A solo Austrian entrepreneur took it on himself to construct a thoroughly Western mini-resort close by, knitting parts of the Stone Chaos with chair- and ski-lifts, connecting roads and chalets. Unfortunately for his entrepreneurial zeal, he then had to rely on the centralized Soviet air transport (Moscow or Leningrad first) for his public's arrival. As a result, almost no currency-bearers came.

Yet as we slid past this strangely desolate skiing paradise, knowing that direct flights from Europe awaited just around the corner (they in fact did commence in 1991), I couldn't help but see this new addition to the landscape as an example of the future investment now lying ahead for Georgia.

Several kilometres later, along the edge of the Aragvi precipice, we arrived at the head of the infamous Mleti descent, a terrifying series of eighteen hairpin bends winding back on themselves, as the road slides down a 600-metre cliff to the river below. For our edification, the driver stopped so we could survey this death-trap from above, telling us he'd lost several friends here.

Glancing behind me, I suddenly noticed a huge metal figure of a man standing in an empty field unremarked on by Marika: more People's Art, this time of the Russian poet Mayakovsky. Marika's silence may have been explained by the fact that although born in Georgia (of Russian parents) Mayakovsky never endeared himself to his childhood compatriots; his point of view making itself all too obvious in poems like his 'Vladikavkaz to Tiflis', written in 1924, just two and a half years after the Bolshevik Red Army had brought the Georgian government to its knees (completely ignoring their 1920 Soviet–Georgian agreement) and then instigated a horrific purge.

I'm from the Georgians,
but not the old nation.
I'm an equal comrade in one federation,
the Soviet world which we forge.

And later in the same poem, exhorting the Georgians towards a bright bold Bolshevik future:

> Build with gusto, for all you're worth,
> from no demolition desist!
> If Kazbek's in the way
> raze the hill to the earth.

This terrible materialist zeal of the new Communists would be pursued, true to Mayakovsky's word, for decades to come, and almost to the letter (sparing Mount Kazbek). Looking down on the lush new panorama below, the fine silver thread of the Aragvi River snaking its way hundreds of metres below, I suddenly experienced a surge of relief. Below me spread a nation never falling for this manic, political ardour (and the chauvinism lurking beneath it). In the aftermath of the Revolution, the Georgians had rejected Bolshevism in favour of the opposing Menshevik socialist system. The Mensheviks, a non-Leninist wing of the Social Democratic Worker's Party, disagreed with the Bolshevik insistence on a highly centralized, dictatorial party, even declaring themselves willing to create a liberal capitalist regime as the precursor to full socialism. They were to achieve three halcyon years of office, from 1918 to 1921, the period now lovingly referred to by Georgians as 'Independent Georgia' and 'the world's first example of genuine democratic socialism'. Ramsay MacDonald, British prime minister to be, visited this socialist government in operation and hailed it as 'a great and bloodless social revolution'. But it didn't last. In 1921 this brand of socialism was snuffed out by the Russian Bolsheviks.

Standing on that cliff edge, I also looked down on a climate and geography equally separate, a landscape responsible not only for the fruit- and vegetable-laden central valleys of Georgia but for Marika's olive skin. With this change, the colour green bombarded us again, this time warming a few degrees, keeping pace with our steady progress southwards towards the arid Anatolian plateau, Turkey and Iraq.

The bus gradually zigzagged its way down to meet this luxurious new land. Softly wooded hillsides, wild fruit trees, ivy-clad cliffs, villages of silver- and rust-coloured roofs were dotted across the valley floor. At the bottom we accelerated down the Aragvi gorge, the river to our left steadily fattening as numerous streams and rivers cascaded down from the high Caucasus. The hillsides surrounded us, covered in an even green tree-fur, with watch-towers poking curiously above the leaves at every prominent crook in the valley.

Some 17 kilometres beyond the Mleti cliff we arrived at the village of Pasanauri, where the White Aragvi met with its twin sister the Black

Aragvi, bounding down from another quite distinct area of Georgia, the Khevsureti region. As if to acknowledge this, the waters refused to merge immediately, the light- and dark-coloured currents running side by side, like the independent tribes at their source.

I'd read about these tribes, like the remarkable Khevsurs and Pshavs, thought at one time to be descendants of the Crusaders. In the 1930s, travellers to Tbilisi told of Khevsur families walking round the capital wearing chain-mail shirts and large red-on-white crosses front and back – another example of time standing still in Georgia. Even today, these people ride their stocky mountain horses at festivals carrying shields and broadswords.

As we raced on towards the modern capital of Tbilisi, now less than 50 kilometres to the south, I felt myself suspended somewhere between the Middle Ages and the 1960s, unable to unhook my thoughts from misty images of Saint George, dragons and the almost Tolkienesque pictures and prancings that seemed inseparably tethered to this landscape.

Yet amid all this came the technological contradiction of the Soviet Space Age, within which tribes like the Khevsurs still existed (but only just). I began to wonder just how the Georgians handled the twentieth century in their humming capital now just down the road, a nation adoring its past with an almost disease-like passion. Did they need to glorify a former heroic image of Georgia simply to provide the only base they could trust in the face of an increasingly uncertain future?

Then, as if conjured up by my thoughts, an immaculately preserved church-fortress suddenly presented itself at the roadside. Situated, according to the Intourist guidebook, exactly 140 kilometres along the Highway, the heroic Middle Ages again pressed themselves right up to our faces – this time as the beautiful seventeenth-century Ananuri Church surrounded by a high walled keep. The bus stopped in the car park.

Stepping out I found the atmosphere completely changed. The temperature had risen and the air was filled with new scents and sounds – olive-groves, vineyards and buzzing insects. The church also seemed to have shifted hemispheres. We found its outer walls adorned by many deliciously enigmatic carvings. Cleanly set into the soft yellow stone were geometric designs, not quite Christian, not quite Oriental and not quite Celtic. They climbed the west facing wall of the transept then spread around the windows, flanked by a giant cross rising on the backs of two tiny dragons. Beside this hung two lions, two very strange angels with moustaches and wearing dresses, and two trees with grapes and domestic animals in their branches – pagan symbols which also hinted strongly at Persian influence. Marika spent quite some time discussing these symbols and their historical significance, without once mentioning the large lake close to the fortress base, now silting up as a result of the ill-placed Zhinvali hydro-electic station.

As we continued the tour around these fine old walls I found myself wondering about the widespread Georgian sense of 'the nation' or 'homeland' now tenaciously attaching itself to all icons of the past. These walls merely provided further confirmation of that elemental link between place, history and human identity. Nationalism grew from such foundations, and the need to elevate 'homeland' or 'nation' into something larger than oneself. These old churches gave Georgians the security to feel part of a long, noble, on-going process. The immortal 'national self' worthy of dying for, which all too frequently they did. (Goergia's tragic mini-civil war at the end of 1991 would bear out all too vividly.)

Climbing back on the bus I knew we were about to enter the now seething flash-point where this age-old requirement of identity encountered the stubborn 'internationalism' of the Soviet ideal. Tbilisi waited just sixty minutes away.

CHAPTER FIVE
TBILISI

Tbilisi has been the capital of Georgia for the last 1,400 years and, thanks to its unique position between the Greater and Lesser Caucasus, is also the unofficial sovereign of these 'mountains of languages'. Unofficial is a good word for this city. Ever since the fifth century, when it took control of the kingdom of Kartli (East Georgia), Tbilisi has had to disguise its economic activities within whatever system the current invading army decided to inflict. Its amiable riverside streets, numerous parks and tree-lined avenues have bustled with every brand of hot-blooded mountain man, trader, traveller and soldier, presenting at all times a veneer of respectability – the better to conceal the vigorous free-for-all of human instinct.

Today, the same tradition continues. Visitors are welcomed with wide-open, hospitable arms, then sweetly charmed towards the thriving black-market. As if to acknowledge this, the Soviets had built a giant twenty-storey Tower of Babel right in the centre of the metropolis and filled it with the bearers of the most desired commodity of all – *valuta* (foreign currency). The Iveria Hotel is where most foreign tourists usually find themselves. Named after the ancient Greek word for western Georgia, 'Iberia', Tbilisi's premier Intourist hotel perches precariously above a cliff-face at the head of the city's main street, the fast and furious Rustaveli Avenue. The building dominates the city like a beacon, visible from just about everywhere. In return it offers the privileged a stupendous panorama.

With fingers gripping the railing on the fourteenth floor, I looked out over this city of $1\frac{1}{4}$ million people, a city razed to the ground, its identity plundered so often that its existence at all is a miracle. (Bar rebuilt churches and the old town fortress and wall, almost no building prior to 1795 still stands in Tbilisi due to the ferocity of the final Persian invasion.) Yet there it lay, spreading leafily away across its many hillsides, expanding faster than ever before. Over to the north and east, the skyline sprouted thickets of tall, white tower-blocks, the proud

65

Tbilisi old town.

spires of socialism. Running through the centre of it all, like a boiling brown lifeline, flowed the powerful Mtkvari River (or Kura in Russian).

Along its banks, houses and roads swept north and south in diversifying waves of architecture. Like all Soviet municipalities, the city's layout had suffered at the hands of centralized planning, but less than most. In spite of its tower-block fever, and unlike many other Russian cities of the republics, Tbilisi has a substantial amount of nineteenth-century Russian architecture of the Moscow/St Petersburg ilk. These graceful pastel-painted buildings and avenues date back to 1801, when Georgia officially joined the Russian empire, having invited in the Tsarist army after the 1795 Persian demolition job. A good section of Tbilisi's 'Old Town' has also magically survived Soviet reconstruction: its maze of higgledy-piggledy homes, wooden back-alleys and charming Persian balconies crashing into each other beneath a dignified fourth-century clifftop fortification, the Narikala Fortress.

Then up to that balcony came another all-important impression of the modern city – its smell. In contrast to Moscow's odour of cheap sickly gasoline freezing against your cheek, Tbilisi gave off a faintly sweet, nutty fragrance. With a hint of the mountain air and a sniff of expensive black-market perfume and tobacco from the floors below, there came a feeling that life had suddenly returned to something closer to normal after all those unsettling hours and days in the cities of the north.

I'll never forget one visit to Tbilisi when, standing on an Iveria balcony, I was transfixed for a good half-hour as a thunderstorm swept its way across the city, to leave a trail of freshly washed cobbled streets, Oriental wooden balconies, colonial Russian avenues and a glistening forest of green, healthy trees rising between the roofs.

Yet this time I couldn't help but feel a slight sense of disappointment. Looking down at the squat, hell-for-leather Ladas, fast-moving figures earnestly squeezing between them, the cable-car slowly climbing Tbilisi mountain, it seemed too like any other fully modern, fully industrialized city. How could those anonymous scurrying figures represent a Christian belief blending with the enormous emotions of Islam, or a twelfth-century psychology living in the twentieth century? Had the forces of modernity, evidenced by these manic Ladas, now wiped clean all hopes of regaining this idealized Georgian character of the past?

My first steps into Tbilisi took me across the Iveria's gusty plaza straight into a shower of water flung from its large fountain of short, evenly jetted water – nicknamed 'Shevardnadze's hair', after Georgia's former First Secretary and later the Soviet Foreign Minister.

Beyond this, in perfect counterpoint to the fountain was a series of enormous triumphal arches rising above a small podium – Georgia's answer to Red Square's parade platform. The Georgians have nicknamed these arches 'Andropov's ears' – very aptly because the loops of concrete fit one inside the other like ears within ears and Andropov was once head of the KGB before becoming State President.

Impeccably situated directly opposite stands Tbilisi's telecommunications centre. Inside, a large marble floor serves as an eternal waiting-room for scores of Georgians passing hours, if not days, waiting to call distant relatives. The calls are connected somewhere within the five neon-lit floors above, and occasionally listened to. Most large international Soviet switchboards set aside a room for telephone surveillance. I once met an American girl who claimed intimate knowledge of the surveillance officer of the Moscow Hotel in St Petersburg, in the days it was still Leningrad. For the price of a drink, she'd sell information on his 'off-duty' periods. Such buildings always reminded me of a message I once found on an information sheet at the Intourist hotel in Novgorod.

'When leaving your room, please be sure to turn off your TV set, air conditioning, lights and the mike.'

No doubt it was a printing error for 'the like' but the ironies continued here in Tbilisi, for this telephone exchange/surveillance centre also doubled as a gathering-point for the city's street mafia.

'Hello!'

It didn't take long to announce itself.

'You're an American. Change money? You have something to sell? You talk English?'

'No, I don't. Not today. Sorry,' I replied to the standard one-liners.

Yet to my surprise, instead of being fired up at my refusal, nine out of ten Georgians simply nodded politely and walked away. For these assailants of every set of passing Western clothing, courteous manners seemed almost as important as becoming 'your friend', a status that could last for several blocks, or occasionally the entire length of Rustaveli Avenue.

I hurried on away from this bustling corner and down the Avenue, past a gaunt Lenin Museum (since deconsecrated), then the ebullient Zacharia Paliashvili Opera House and on down towards the old town. The local faces flowed past in a steady dark stream of olive-skinned southerners, their eyes glancing at me, registering 'foreigner' and glancing away. In Georgia, blond hair lit you up like a beacon. Unlike in Moscow, where I enjoyed certain levels of covert operation, here I stood out a block away.

The manner and the clothes of the locals also set them apart from the northeners. Here men walked with far more self-importance, confronting the world from under their dark eyebrows and moustaches, with almost regal composure. Later I discovered that until the abolition of the Georgian monarchy, one in every five Georgian men claimed noble blood.

The women, for their part, appeared correspondingly more demure than northerners, wearing knee-length dresses, late 1960s hairstyles, deep layers of make-up and not a single set of Levis among them. For a main drag, Rustaveli Avenue was remarkably free of European youth

The Opera House.

culture – those fully jeaned, ghetto-blasting teenagers associated with Nevsky Prospekt or Moscow's Arbat. Beneath the elegant nineteenth-century facades the street exuded a presence of refined watchfulness. Women appeared more interested in the 'art' shop beside the grand Rustaveli Theatre than the dismal cosmetics display in the nearby gift shop (where I counted the massive total of two lipsticks).

An impulse made me turn up a side street – beside, as it happened, the Communist Party Headquarters. I'd proceeded but 200 metres up the hill when a Lada suddenly screeched to a halt right next to me. The window was wound down frantically and a huge hairy arm presented itself, leading back to a bristly Georgian face.

69

'Hello, my friend!' said the man.

'Sorry, I have nothing to sell,' I replied automatically.

But his grin only widened enormously, and I noticed the back seat of the car full of his family, also beaming.

'No, no, no!' said the bristles. 'What's the time?'

Relieved, I pulled back my sleeve to look at my watch. 'It's . . .'

'Forty roubles,' he interrupted. 'No, fifty!' and the whole car erupted into raucous laughter.

As I recovered from my confusion, he gave me a bone-crushing handshake.

'No, my friend, don't worry. Enjoy Georgia, happy holiday, goodbye!' He engaged gears and the car roared off out of sight, ostentatiously disobeying every road-sign. How different from those secretive, suspicious approaches of Moscow!

Back on the Avenue, approaching the pre-Revolutionary Hotel Tbilisi, I spotted an unusual couple walking towards me: a dark-skinned boy and a blonde girl, both no more than twenty. The boy wore a flashy sports jacket of the thick, grey-flecked type then currently the rage at London's Camden Market, with a single 'identity' badge pinned to its lapel. The girl also wore snappy Western clothing – all of it remarkably high quality so far from the fashionable black-markets of Moscow and Leningrad.

As they drew up level I managed to read the words on the boy's badge. 'Fuck off and die' it announced flatly. I slowed down, gazing at this brazen exhibition of fashion rebellion, more flagrant than any I'd seen up north. Our eyes met.

'Hello. Do you speak English?' the boy asked, sensing my comprehension.

This time I nodded. I had to know why this boy adopted a punk slogan, so far away from anything to do with punk.

'Do you?' I asked.

'No, I don't,' he replied grinning, then added, 'Not well.'

'What part of America are you from?' the girl then asked in a heavy Russian accent.

I explained my British origins and we continued down the Avenue like old friends, with no mention of buying or selling. First they wanted to know if I'd arrived for business or holiday. Then how long would I stay, and what hotel was I staying at. Next came the important question . . .

'What is the name of Phil Collins's newest album? How much does a blank 180-minute video cassette cost in London? What was the concert at the Hammersmith Odeon when you left?'

These questions were fired at me with the urgency of life-saving requests. In my turn I wanted to know how they found that badge.

'From a foreigner.'

The Georgian looked surprised at the question, for where else would he get it? I asked if he knew why punks wore such slogans in England. He shrugged.

'It's not punk here. We don't have punks. It's just what we feel about those who are ordering us.' He glanced towards the Communist Party Headquarters.

I realized that our tribalized English youth culture, with its various uniforms of rebellion, no longer applied down here. The enemy of all Georgians, young or old, stood out far too clearly – the Russian system, its politics as abhorrent to the Russian girl as to her Georgian boyfriend. As we talked so the topics opened out and the boy suddenly developed an interest in my trainers.

'Where did you buy them?' he began, which soon led to, 'How much do you want for them.'

I told him they weren't for sale, but fearing the end of our meeting, suggested we change some money.

'You have a few minutes?' the girl asked, adding, 'We'll go somewhere. Don't worry, it's all right.'

But I already knew this. Those resisting the Soviet economic system usually came ready-stamped with the benefit of the doubt. Furthermore, street-level conversations normally unearthed swifter, sharper and more propaganda-free opinions on the country than those from any well-versed intellectual. Theirs was the instinctive response to laws that disobeyed human nature. In Georgia, they and their older cousins had illegally operated what for some time had been the only free market – estimated at up to 50 per cent of the entire economy. These streetwise black-marketeers simply lived the double lives of ordinary citizens, only more openly.

The boy introduced himself as Shota. We shook hands. I asked how he could be so open in his dealings, wondering how much of this boldness came from a sense of having little left to lose.

'We are not hiding so much now,' he said with the help of his girlfriend's English. 'They're all hypocrites,' he said, referring to those who tried to prevent him. 'They buy and sell the same as we do.'

'They're jealous,' added the girl, flagging down a passing Lada.

He asked her what 'jealous' meant, then, when she explained, added to himself, 'Dzarlian!', the Georgian word for 'very'.

The three of us climbed into the car and set off for somewhere in Tbilisi.

'Do you meet many foreigners?' I asked as the car swerved alarmingly through the traffic.

'No, not so many, but we like it,' she said.

I could sense her looking at me, trying to work out what kind of person they had landed from London, city of unlimited rock stars and black-market goods.

'What do you think of Madonna?' she asked suddenly, clearly curious about the new messages of female sexuality emanating from the West. 'Do you think she's too . . .' She paused, looking for the right word to describe Madonna's wanton sensuality, 'Loud?'

'I don't like her,' interrupted Shota. 'She's like a . . .' He made a circular motion with his hand.

'Balloon,' said the girl.

'Yes, balloon. All empty on the inside,' he said.

The Russian girl looked at him doubtfully. 'I thought you liked her,' she said cautiously. It was no secret that Georgian men liked Russian and foreign girls for their more liberal attitudes to sex.

'No,' he replied flatly. I guessed Madonna flaunted what he wanted just a bit too openly, even for him.

At this point the car-driver – a complete stranger – chipped in, also in English (which, I found, was widely spoken in Tbilisi).

'Madonna is like an American Russian girl.'

I glanced at our own Russian girl. She looked furious but said nothing.

'And the Pink Floyd?' I changed the subject.

'Yes, I like it,' said the girl, and her boyfriend swiftly agreed, adding: 'I've got the disc "Dark Side of the Moon".' He looked at me meaningfully. 'Disc not tape.'

Something to be proud of. Original Western records in the USSR were like gold-dust. The only way young Soviets could possess their favourite music was as duplicated tape-to-tape copies distributed underground, from one side of the Union to the other. Melodiya, the state record company, very rarely issued Western groups. (Even now, with the liberalized chaos of cooperatives and joint ventures, this great, searching hunger of youth is rarely met – save by foreigners, and then only inadequately.)

To discussions on The Rolling Stones, The Doors and Band Aid, the streets of Tbilisi flicked by at terrible speed. Peering through the front windscreen I witnessed a type of driving quite alien to Moscow or Europe. Traffic lights blinked from red to green almost without meaning. Rogue cars careered up the wrong side of the street, daring the oncoming traffic. Occasionally drivers would stop in the middle of the road, swing open their doors and gesticulate angrily about someone else's driving, swing their doors shut and continue on just as terribly themselves.

'Do you like Mr Gorbachev and what he's trying to do?' I asked, hoping to distract myself.

'No,' the driver said emphatically.

'But isn't he trying to reform the Soviet Union?' I asked.

'You foreigners are all fooled by him,' he said. 'Georgians aren't. We understand the Russians. They're colonists. Why can't I travel? Why do I have to be a Party member to travel? Look! I have money.' He fumbled in his pocket and held up a bundle of mauve twenty-five rouble notes. 'They're no use. There's nothing of worth from Russia. Their stereos last three months, their TVs a year. I like good quality and that has nothing to do with Russia.'

The other two sat in quiet agreement.

We drove on, eventually stopping before a tall, concrete tower-block. Stepping out of a creaking lift on to the ninth floor, we knocked on an apartment door. It opened and a boy introduced as 'the Armenian' led us into a spacious, undecorated flat. Inside we met another Georgian boy and a quite beautiful, white-skinned Russian girl. After a few words with Shota, a bottle of Georgian brandy and an enormous portable cassette-player were produced.

The Armenian reached into the wall – no sockets or switches had yet been installed – pulled out two live electrical cables and twisted them with his fingers into the cassette-player's lead. It immediately came to life.

'Pink Floyd,' he said casually.

'Is this your place?' I asked.

'Not really,' he said, and I guessed they just inhabited it in the evenings after the workmen left. Then the door opened and more people tumbled in – a couple of young Georgians followed by a nervous-looking, fifty-year-old East German. They also handed him a glass of brandy, then took him into a back room. There followed some terse private discussions, raised voices and then the German was shown smartly to the door.

The Armenian returned to the living room and said distastefully, 'They met him in a foreign-currency bar. He is homosexual, he wants a boy but we don't have any.' He spoke unemotionally, like a shopkeeper explaining that an item was out of stock.

I realized I'd just arrived at a local small-time mafia headquarters, and that I, like the German, represented just more business.

'How much do you want for your trainers?' Shota asked again. I tried to explain these were my only shoes – which they were – and not for sale. But he only interpreted this as a ploy to raise the price.

'OK, seventy roubles,' he said, quite unable to understand my refusal. Meanwhile, one of his Georgian friends started talking to me in an odd English accent.

'You talk the wrong English,' he said challengingly. 'You should talk American English.'

'Why?' I asked.

He put on a strong Chicago/Georgian accent, 'Because then you can talk like Al Capone.'

Everybody laughed. Confused, I wondered if this boy genuinely saw himself as a gangster (an impression that by 1992, with the steady arming of the population, had taken several ugly steps towards reality).

I asked him if he could pick up the BBC World Service.

'Oh yes, we pick it up.' He gave me a sideways glance. 'But I listen to Voice of America, to modern English. The World Service is for people living in the last century.'

Shota turned to me and said casually, 'Merab supports the IRA.' Meanwhile, Merab had tuned the cassette/radio into the World Service and, as chance would have it, slap bang into an *English by Radio* broadcast.

'Margaret is a teenager,' the clipped, schoolmistress voice was saying. 'She likes to go out and have a good time. On Tuesday nights she visits the town with her friend John ...' Merab shut it off, giving me a 'told you so' look.

When I suggested that the propaganda on the Voice of America might be similar in style to Soviet propaganda, he gave me another sideways look.

'You don't have to tell us about propaganda,' he said sourly.

The longer I stayed in Tbilisi, the more I realized that his attitude towards English – a language becoming almost as important as Russian – was by no means the norm. It was only those living a life dedicated to the electronic, the expensive and the illegal who preferred American. The American way of life appealed more to the Georgian materialists. The aesthetes, of whom I would meet many, preferred Euopean culture and languages.

As the others talked among themselves I turned to the white-skinned Russian girl and tried some English on her, asking if she preferred life here in Georgia to that up north in Russia.

'I don't know.' She shrugged. 'We do what we can.' She showed little interest in my questions, but her eyes continued to bore into mine.

I guessed she might be one of the hard-currency prostitutes. They usually work out of the tourist hotels, but in her case, her breathtaking beauty seemed to make that unnecessary. I knew that the bleak lack of opportunities in the USSR and restrictions on travel could draw remarkably well-educated and beautiful girls into the profession. (One 1990 survey of teenagers in a provincial Russian city unearthed a startling 50 per cent of the boys wanting to join the mafia and 50 per cent of the girls wishing to become hard-currency prostitutes.)

The Russians who came to Georgia, attracted by the climate, the fertility of the land and even the rebellious nature of the locals, often shared their disenchantment with the central authorities. Yet while Georgia politely tolerated the small population of Russians living in Tbilisi (unlike some of their Baltic counterparts), they never went out of their way to make them feel at home, and Russian women constantly report harassment fom Georgian men.

'Have you got what you wanted yet?' said the Russian girl suddenly. Her eyes looked at me enquiringly. I glanced round the room at this curious, dissatisfied, disobeying, spirited group of teenagers, people possessed by an energy I'd never experienced in the same circles in Moscow. Here, at the apex of the blissful black-market, it manifested itself in a gusto for adventure and rebellion, sanctioned (as I was to find out later) by the ideals of nationalism. Unlike the northerners, these youngsters, and their parents too, had never abandoned that crucial, life-sustaining sense of hope.

Standing there in that mini-den of iniquity, I tried to reconcile the sense of optimism I picked up here. On one side of me sat a prostitute, on the other a boy offering nearly half the average month's wages just for my battered shoes, yet that self-destructive cynical atmosphere of the north had vanished. These nefarious Georgians still saw an inherent goodness somewhere in the future, their days were still strung together by this faith. The Soviet system had been imposed on them from outside, and they'd known all along it would fail.

I made my excuses to leave, but my original companions insisted on accompanying me back to the hotel. Shota had still not achieved his aim – my shoes – although the price had now reached 100 roubles. He seemed to take perverse delight in going for the unattainable.

In the taxi home I pulled out my Walkman and slipped on the headphones. Pressing 'play' I found it half-way through 'Of Course I'm Lying' by the Swiss group Yello. As the tall, concrete, Brezhnev-era tower-blocks floated by outside the car, so the lyrics of a sophisticated but cynical Western future, the one lying in store for these young Georgians, filled my head:

I love your lies,
I love your games.
Look in my eyes.
I love your lies.
Just hold me tight.
I've got no one to blame.
You're lying,
I'm buying,
I'm buying every word . . .

This ironic song had always struck as an anthem for the eerie *savoir-faire* taking root among European youth.

'Have you heard this?' I asked the girl and handed her the headphones. A minute later she handed them back.

'It's OK,' she said without enthusiasm. Her boyfriend listened for a few seconds then handed them back without real comment. The words never engaged them. I slipped the headphones back on and listened again to those silky female whispers as the twenty-storey high stacks of Soviet living-rooms slid by. Surely nothing could be more appropriate than these aching sounds of a new European sophistication set against the architecture of the old Soviet alternative. These buildings, their architecture, their everyday appliances were all spawned within a system whose little political lies had steadily grown up into a massive fungus-like social institution. A bureaucratic system so cumbersome that in the end only terror itself could hold it together. Now the fungus had finally collapsed in on itself. Everyone here looked forward eagerly to the sparklingly clean, remote-control hi-fi of the West. Yet what slick messages lay at the heart of this brave new alternative?

The song's chorus sang out its warning again and again: 'You're lying, I love it . . .'

The following lunchtime I sat in the Iveria's foreign-currency bar, when to my surprise Shota suddenly appeared at the door, clutching a pair of brand-new Russian shoes. How he'd penetrated this well-guarded and exclusive domain of the tourist I'd no idea. Yet somehow he'd deceived the Iveria's severe front-door mafia and all the entrance-hall's official loiterers.

He noticed me and I hailed him cheerfully. He took a couple of steps towards me, then stopped, glancing at the two men behind the bar. They both glowered back. This bar was strictly out of bounds for Georgians, unless clearly escorted by a currency-bearing foreign guest.

'It's all right. He's with me.' I said. They nodded. He walked over to my table uncertainly. I asked what he wanted.

'Double whisky,' he replied. I passed the order on to the barman, who poured it reluctantly.

'These are for you,' Shota said quickly, putting the shoes on the floor. 'Try them.'

I asked for any news back at base. But he seemed stangely distracted, unwilling to talk. Finally he put his head close to mine. 'It's hard here. KGB here.' He glanced anxiously towards the men at the bar again, and as he did so, one of them raised a finger, beckoned him outside. Shota stood up immediately, and followed him. I found myself remembering his words about jealousy between official and unofficial mafias. During the couple of painful minutes he was gone, I tried on the shoes. They didn't fit.

When he returned, he gulped down his double whisky, took not one but five of my offered Marlboro, then, without even asking about them, grabbed the shoes and hurried for the door.

'I've got to go,' he said.

The next day, just outside the main door of the Iveria, I was approached by his friend, the one who arrived at the apartment with the East German.

'Have you seen Shota?' He looked at me anxiously. 'He came here yesterday and nobody's seen him since.'

I told him about the drink and the KGB. A frown suddenly spread across his face.

'Oh,' he said quickly, then hurried away without another word.

The Steps of Independence

While in Moscow I'd been given the Tbilisi phone number of a Georgian poet called Georgi. I was told he wrote Georgian and English songs, and kept his ear close to the ground as Georgian literature sank its feet into the soil of *perestroika*. We'd spoken briefly on the phone, and he had sounded a little surprised at the label 'poet'.

'I used to write a few songs . . .', he'd said. 'But anyway, let's meet at a "poetic" place.'

His directions left me standing outside the elegant Kashveti Church on Rustaveli Avenue, right across the road fom the State Government Building. With my back to this pre-Revolutionary centre of Georgian power – the Orthodox Church – I looked across at its replacement, the gargantuan arched façade of the Communist State Headquarters.

Georgi had been right about poetics – the atmosphere was charged. A continuous flow of people streamed in and out of the candle-lit church, their faces uncomfortably intense. A month earlier the twenty Georgian hunger-strikers had been butchered only a few metres away on the Government Building steps. A long blue fence now sealed off the entrance from the public. Shortly afterwards, many had reported symptoms of gas-poisoning due, they believed, to traces of chemicals still embedded in the slabs. No amount of scrubbing the concrete could rid them of this deadly residue, just as no manipulation of the media or rewriting of history would remove the event's imprint on Georgian consciousness. To reinforce this, the fence had been adorned with numerous strips of black cloth and, below it, wreaths lay on the pavement.

With no sign of anyone resembling Georgi's description, I gazed out at the traffic. There was the usual vortex of whirling Ladas, Volgas and the occasional black Zil trying to assert a forlorn claim on the centre lane. Every so often a high-speed Lada, horn blaring, lights blazing, roared hysterically down the Avenue. Out of its windows, teenagers thrust streaming nationalist flags, sometimes even themselves – perched up on the window-ledge – to add a death-defying quality to their proclamation. In their ecstatic faces, I saw Marika's description of the young car-drivers flaunting themselves before the Special Forces during the curfew a month ealier – the single act of heroism that restored the Georgian spirit of resistance. As a backdrop to these dramatic entrances and exits, the severe arches of Government Building looked sternly down, the red flag of Communism waving from its top, like a rag to a bull.

For all Georgians, this imposing structure, completed in the very year that Stalin died (1953), represented the accumulation of many years of paranoid, paper-pushing, mafia-enabling bureaucracies. Yet now, for the first time since Stalin took control of the Soviet state, another flag flew on many of the buildings of Rustaveli Avenue – the black, magenta and white tricolour of independent Georgia – an event unthought of even six months earlier. But time had now restarted again for this small nation. I wondered how long it would be before the dream of the Georgians came true and their flag flew on this building too. (In fact it would take only one and a half years.)

My reverie was broken by an unexpected change in the atmosphere – silence. The traffic on Rustaveli Avenue began mysteriously to dry up. The normally furious six lanes – impossible to cross on foot – slowly emptied themselves of cars. A quick glance up the Avenue revealed why Georgi had chosen this time and place to meet. For suddenly the street was filled again, this time not by cars but by thousands upon thousands of Georgian faces. Approaching us from the north, they poured forward in a slow, inexorable rising tide, filling from the side streets and stretching away out of sight beyond the Iveria Hotel. Then I remembered the date. Today the period of mourning for the 9 April disaster ended. To mark the occasion, a sea of olive-skinned humanity had risen up from all corners of Georgia to converge on Tbilisi and this wide Soviet building right before me – built on the site of a former Georgian church. As had happened so often before in Georgian history, the emotions of the massacre turned people to the candle-lit sanctuaries of their Orthodox Church. The prayers, the mysteries and communion with Georgia's martyrs and saints began to heal the affront to self-dignity, and now the emotions returned to the streets, stronger than ever.

As this army of the new Georgia closed in, I noticed the front marchers carried large black-and-white photographs of next of kin, murdered by the Special Forces. But most remarkable of all, the first half-kilometre of this great coiling snake of humanity made almost no sound at all. It piled ominously forward, its thousands of eyes training themselves on the Government Building, propelled by the weight of perhaps quarter of a million bodies behind. It was an almost supernatural sight, as if the dead rather than the living controlled this enormous stealthy force.

As the crowd drew level with the blue fence, handkerchiefs appeared and individuals broke away, hurried over and pinned red carnations or independence flags on to the wooden slats. Within minutes the surface of the fence had completely changed, brimming and weeping its own festoons of many red-petalled tears. Then suddenly the march stopped dead, and I felt a tap on my shoulder.

'Are you Peter?' said a voice.

Swinging round, I found myself looking at a tall Georgian in his mid-twenties, his nose large and hooked, and above it deep-set, sad eyes. Beside him stood a woman with jet-black hair, pale skin and the tell-tale Georgian female moustache. Georgi had arrived, along with his friend Tamoona. It hardly seemed the moment for elaborate introductions. After a few words we turned back to observe the spectacle. Right ahead of me on the Avenue, now chock-a-block with solemn southern faces, the marchers had arrived at the first of their goals, the Government Building. What on earth would they do?

Then without any instruction or orchestration, the front several thousand demonstrators suddenly sank down on to their heels and raised their fists defiantly in the air towards the building, a gesture carried out in almost complete silence. It must have sent shudders down the spines of the Soviet officials watching. Not only had most of the population risen up against it; it had also displayed the other much-feared quality of rebellion – discipline.

I noticed several rows of blue-uniformed police had now appeared on the top of the Government Building steps, their arms folded, facing the crowd. Above them the enormous five-storey façade rose up like raised eagle wings. I watched Georgi lift his fist too, not looking at the police but at the flag. He turned to me.

'I don't criticize our police. Some of them were wounded trying to defend the women on 9 April. It's the ones who aren't here . . .'

I asked him if he'd been at the steps on 9 April.

'Yes, I was here,' he said quietly, 'and it was the worst day of my life.' He lowered his fist and turned to me. 'I'll never forget when I walked up to that Special Forces soldier and asked him what he was doing, why they attacked peaceful demonstrators. He just shoved his Kalashnıkov into my ribs, hard, and told me to go away. You know, I looked at his face and . . .' He paused, glancing up at the blue fence, now ablaze with carnations. 'You know, I experienced a terrible feeling. Not of his gun, but of that blank, empty look in his eyes. This was not a man, this was a dead machine sent to exterminate Georgia. I saw the end of our nation in that face. I'll never forget it.'

As he spoke, I detected a tear creeping into the corner of his eye. Then suddenly he added in a new, harder voice. 'At 3.30 today our Communist government has announced a ten-minute silence all over the city. I think they want to join in.' His eyes held mine for a second to see if I caught the irony.

Then suddenly the spooky silence ended. A single defiant voice rose up out of the rows of crouching faces, shouting the word '*Gau-mar-jos*!' towards the Goverment Building. Everybody joined in, shouting the word back, and the sounds of protest, the centuries-old rebellion against Russia, recommenced. The crowd stood up and moved on. We stepped in among the bodies, and in the momentum somehow became separated. Surrounded by this swelling tide of dark strangers, their hands gripping banners, their lungs shouting the slogans of 'Free Georgia', I searched in vain for Georgi or Tamoona. Instead I found myself pressed forward with the thousands, caught up myself in this movement towards independence.

Right up next to me, rough male faces and women's voices shouted out resolutely. This was a people disowned of their own country for several centuries, a people not afraid to demonstrate if sufficiently moved. In 1956, at the height of the Stalinist deep-freeze, thousands had taken to the streets to protest against, of all things, the denunciation of Stalin by Khrushchev. It led to a horrific reaction from the Soviet authorities – over 100 shot dead, with many more wounded or exiled to labour camps in Siberia. But this didn't prevent demonstrations again in 1978, when the Communist government tried to lower the status of the Georgian language in a new draft constitution. On that occasion Eduard Shevardnadze, then the First Secretary of the Georgian Communist Party, had immediately given in to the demonstrators' demands.

As the chants filled my ears, I realized that these people emptied their lungs with that crucial declaration of separation from a culture they dispised. They shouted to restore their self-respect. Within these cries there also stirred the determination to believe in what they euphemistically called a 'free' future (free from Russia) and the rekindling of the enormous anger held down for so many years. Such demonstrations amounted to a kind of medicine against the last seventy years, and took place all over the USSR as an exercise in self-independence and self-assertion. (But this rediscovery of individuality and anger has also brought with it dramatically increased crime statistics in the 1990s.)

As one Georgian friend said later of that time, 'Even if we didn't quite know the meaning of the word "free", we were calling for the freedom to make our own mistakes, not theirs.'

Then, to my great relief, I spotted Marika standing by the road and hurried over to my only ally in this ocean of grievance. She greeted me and we stood together at the roadside, watching the faces surge past, each block of several thousand strong, stopping silently before the Government Building and raising their fists (a gesture ironically similar to the Red Front Fascist salute).

A huge cheer then rose up as a group of men and women in overalls joined the demonstration.

'Those are factory workers,' explained Marika. 'They've joined mid-shift.'

I asked her to translate the curling Georgian script on some of the passing banners, and she pointed to a dense thicket of posters approaching the Government Building.

'These say they're from Kutaisi. It's a large town in Imeretia, in East Georgia. I heard they had walked all the way here – it's about 250 kilometres.'

As they dropped on their heels for the salute, so they exposed a remarkable group of demonstrators standing right behind. Men and women in a splendid, multicoloured tribal dress, their leader standing

81

before them carrying a 2-metre silver mace like a chief. Beside him stood a score of similarly dressed companions. The men wore knee-length, richly patterned tunics with half-metre silver daggers strapped to their waists. The women wore dresses covered in beautiful embroidered stars and crosses. Across their foreheads they wore strange headpieces or mantles, also bearing the same crosses.

'These people are from Khevsureti,' explained Marika, 'one of the remote mountain tribes of Georgia.' Then she looked wistful. 'It's a great shame, because their culture is disappearing. Not many now can make these traditional clothes.'

Looking at their marvellous costumes, it did seem a great pity that they and their way of life would soon vanish for ever. I asked if these weren't the people European writers had described wearing chain-mail and Crusader crosses earlier this century.

'Yes, but they don't wear them any more,' Marika replied, adding, 'although many still have these costumes in their families, and the older women still know how to make chain-mail.'

I stepped out into the street to take a photograph. Several of the faces turned anxiously towards me. To these remote valley eyes I, with my blond, Russian-looking hair, represented police or KGB. I found myself remembering the faces of Jewish refusniks at a 1987 rally in Leningrad, an occasion drawing more KGB than demonstrators. Each agent, true to the 'Boy's Own' guide to the KGB, wore his trench-coat collar turned up and trained a long lens on everyone coming within 100 metres.

I took my snap, and then we stepped into the crowd, following perhaps a half a kilometre from the front. For me the rally had turned from a demonstration into a pageant of all the peoples of modern Georgia: a river of dark and occasionally pale mountain faces, shouting their way forward towards Tbilisi's rebuilt fifth-century Sioni Cathedral and the shrine constructed to commemorate the events of 9 April, like a totem to this people's long history of massacre. These faces encompassed all stages of civilization, from those Khevsur tribesmen to the spy-satellite operators in the Government Building. I found myself wanting to pin down some point or pivot in history from where they emerged. As usual, I turned to Marika. She smiled at my question, but answered politely.

'Nobody knows exactly where the Georgians come from. They emerged out of several Neolithic and Bronze-Age cultures in this area, growing up beside the world's great early civilizations: the Sumerians, Hittites, Babylonians, and the peoples of Urartu . . . .'

But her voice became increasingly difficult to hear between the shouts and the music now booming from the public-address system.

I tried to question her about the early Caucasian tribes, how they may have influenced or served as a basis for many of our own in Europe. Did she think that the Etruscans (and hence the Romans) may have originated from one of these early tribes, or were the Pelasgi, the forerunners of the early Greeks, descended from the Iberians (the people of the west Caucasus)? What was her opinion on those who linked the Basques and Celts with the Caucasians, perhaps explaining why the term 'white Caucasian' connects people of European extraction to these Asiatic mountains?

'Yes, these are interesting theories,' she said above the noise, but I could tell she saw them as no more than theories. 'The modern Georgian tribes are the descendants of these people,' she said more practically.

I pressed her for more details. And, with a 'you asked for it' look, she said: 'The people you see today are a blend of Mingrelians, Svans, Karts, Gurians, Adjarians, Kakhetians, Imeretians, Khevsurians, Pshavians, Mokhevians, Meskhians, Rachineans.' She smiled at my befuddled look. 'This is why the Arabs called Georgia "the mountain of languages". We are a mixture of tribes like those Khevsurs here. But many years ago the largest of our tribes, the Karts, began to rule the others, and their language is what we now call Georgian. Hence today's Georgian word for Georgia, Sa*kart*velo.'

Meanwhile, the march had turned a corner and arrived in what was then Tbilisi's Lenin Square (now 'Freedom Square'). A huge domineering statue of the Bolshevik leader stood with its fingers pointing ambiguously up into the sky. The moment the crowd saw it their cries of '*Gau-mar-jos, Gau-mar-jos*' doubled in volume, directed straight at Lenin's brow.

'*Gau-mar-jos* is a Georgian toast,' Marika explained. 'It also means "to victory".'

As she said it I glanced at my watch and noticed the hands approaching 3.30 – the time set by the government for its ten minutes of sanctimonious silence: an idea with eerie similarity to George Orwell's 'two minutes hate' in '1984'. I watched the minute-hand clip past the half-hour and as it did, almost to the second, came the sound of a single car-horn, followed by another, then another. Within fifteen seconds just about every car, bus and motor-cycle klaxon in the city rattled furiously on its mountings. As the perfidious, ear-splitting din drilled into my head, I reflected on the absolute stupidity of the Communist authorities' decree. By attempting to hijack the demonstrators' cause in calling for this silence, they'd demanded of the people the same speechless compliance of the past seventy years. No wonder the cacophony.

From Lenin Square we proceeded down Baratashvili Street with its old town wall and elegant wooden balconies bulging out from the nineteenth-century town inside, and went on to the Mtkvari River and walked along its bank. The Sioni Cathedral was afloat in a lake of demonstrators. Above the faces the flags still waved, but all shouting had ceased. We'd arrived at the nerve-centre of the tragedy – the memorial to honour the dead. Its presence damped down the crowd's anger.

Marika and I moved through the thousands of faces, some with black sashes tied round their foreheads, others clutching handkerchiefs. Their expressions had taken on an uncertain air, as if encountering something stronger than rebellion. On the brick wall surrounding the cathedral, numerous letter-sized papers fluttered in the wind: the messages and poems of the mothers, fathers, brothers, sisters and friends of the dead. We stopped before a large sheet of paper with its curling Georgian script composed around a detailed pencil drawing of a teenage girl's face. Underneath it three of her small shoe-prints had been dipped in red paint and walked across the paper. Carefully handwritten words encircled each of the prints. I asked Marika to translate, but she just stared at the paper without responding, Suddenly I felt ashamed of my curiosity. Did I really need the words? These private words of grief, many written in large, childish script, spoke with more eloquence than any translation.

Pushing our way inside the cathedral precinct, we came up to a huge shrine of flowers spreading across the paving stones. Scores of wreaths, made up of pink, red and white carnations and roses, had been worked into elaborate shapes. Some spelt out the names of the dead, some the date 9 April, others had been turned into crosses, or the flag of free Georgia. Before these, a pile of literally thousands of individual red carnations was growing by the minute, dropped by the citizens of Tbilisi, Georgian, Armenian, Azerbaijani, Russian (the local Russian population deplored the massacre no less than the Georgians). Above the flowers a row of twenty black-and-white photographs were pinned to the ivy of the old city wall.

As we arrived, a slow procession of mourners made their way along the small path forged between the mounds of wreaths. They walked slowly, stopping every so often, placing a flower or a keepsake next to a photograph and then moving on. I watched a girl with deathly pale face escorted away sobbing from the photograph of a young man; I guessed he had been her fiancé.

I asked Marika if it would be all right for me to join this queue.

'Of course,' she said, surprised at my question.

'A few minutes later I found myself just inches away from the faces of the dead, most of them young women, no more than teenagers. Their eyes looked back with the same bright hope for the future, as I'd seen just a few minutes earlier in the demonstration. It seemed impossible to understand how any sentient human being could deliberately kill these children – the youngest was just sixteen.

Later, making my way back to the hotel alone, I bumped into Georgi and Tamoona by pure chance, not far from the Sioni shrine. They looked very relieved to see me.

'We looked for you everywhere,' Tamoona said, speaking for the first time, again in good English. 'We're on our way to Sioni now to pay our respects. Come with us.'

I joined them and returned to the cathedral. As we descended the steps, Georgi pointed up at the elegant pepper-pot dome of the cathedral looming above the old town.

'This is the cathedral of the Patriarch of all Georgia,' he said solemnly. 'It's our most holy church.'

The interior of the cathedral thronged with people holding candles. The hundreds of tiny lights reflected on the gold patterns climbing the walls towards the dome, where a giant figure of the Almighty looked down as if from heaven. He gazed at us sadly, his face slightly obscured by shafts of smoky blue light. He too seemed to deplore the action of the Soviet authorities. We joined the hundreds of mourners walking from icon to icon, lighting candles, whispering prayers. With the faces of those twenty dead so fresh in my mind, I found myself also wishing to light a candle. Tamoona had already bought a large bunch and she handed me a couple. I looked around for a suitable icon. The walls and pillars were clustered with the sombre, glowing faces of Georgian Orthodoxy, whose saints date back to AD 337.

Noticing a press of people adding to a forest of candles surrounding a free-standing icon on the floor, I walked over to find a strange modern painting of a smart, nineteenth-century man wearing an every-day jacket and collar but with the peculiar addition of a halo round his head. Who could this secular-looking man be?

'This is our new saint, Ilya Chavchavadze,' Tamoona whispered. 'He was a great poet and writer of the last century.'

Then Georgi added, 'He was a great Georgian nationalist.'

I sensed in Georgi's voice just a hint of the anger lurking within the nationalist call now filling the streets of Tbilisi. I asked if the phenomenon of nationalism might not be dangerous when seen in the

85

light of history's other great nationalist movements?

'You mustn't criticize our nationalism because of what you in the West have seen before,' he replied firmly. 'You must think about *us*, what we've been through. The Soviet system has tried to take away not only our nationality, they've tried to take away "us" from us. Our own individuality. It's not surprising now we have a little freedom that we want back the first thing they tried to take away, our country.'

I looked at Tamoona for her response, but she said nothing. I detected a sense of unease. Could this be a note of hesitation within this great common cry? I made a mental note to ask her about this later. Instead, I asked why they chose Sioni Cathedral for the shrine, and not the Kashveti church right across the road from the Government Building steps.

'Because this place is more important to us. It's the heart of Tbilisi,' Tamoona said. 'We have here Georgia's most sacred icon, Saint Nino's cross.'

She pointed to a recess in one of the church's pillars. Behind a sheet of glass I saw a strange wooden cross, its horizontal arms sloping downwards, made up of interwoven vine branches.

'This is a replica of it,' she said. 'We'll light our candles here.' She added our flames to the others flickering before the icon, then crossed herself. We stood silently for a moment. I began to feel the presence of the brimming emotion permitted by this building. No wonder Georgians always stuck by their Church; where else could they go with such deep feeling? What a different atmosphere to the steely clamp of the chilling Communist world outside. As the people busied themselves between the icons, so more hurried in, and the building took on the quality of a huge heart, the inner muscle of Georgia, with all these faces flowing among the arches like corpuscles of blood pumping through the core of the system, then out again.

'The real cross is here too, behind there,' Tamoona said eventually, gesturing towards the iconostasis.

I asked her why Saint Nino had been so important to Georgians.

'Because she brought the Christian faith to Georgia,' she said baldly, and then explained that Nino had journeyed all the way from her Jerusalem home guided by a vision of the Virgin Mary that told her Christ's crucifixion coat could be found in the pagan land of Iberia (Georgia). According to legend, she arrived among the local Karts – by then the largest Georgian tribe – armed with a cross made out of vine-rods bound by her own hair. Described in ancient texts as a 'captive girl', she then performed a number of miracles, eventually converting the Kart King Mirian to Christianity.

'We feel the original spirit of the faith is still living inside this cross,' Tamoona said quietly.

Trying to grasp the difference between Tamoona's relationship with this building and Georgi's firmer, nationalist vision of Georgia, I asked him about the importance of the Church in resurrecting the spirit of independent Georgia.

'It's very important,' he replied, and gestured to the icon of Saint Ilya Chavchavadze. 'We now have a new political party named the "Society of Saint Ilya the Righteous" [led by Zviadi Gamsakhurdia, who in 1991 became Georgia's first non-Commmunist president]. Religion is stronger than ever in Georgia now. Young people are going to the churches again. The Church wants independence as much as we do. You see the frescoes in this church?' He pointed up to the ceiling. 'They're Russian. The Russian Church painted over old Georgian frescoes last century. Then afterwards the Russians brought the Soviets here who tried to take God away from us completely.' He looked at me incredulously. 'It was like trying to separate our bodies from our heads. They told us we could only be married by their bureaucrats, that we had to go to their office, or that horrible building they built near here and sign the book. Then afterwards we would go in secret to the church to be blessed.' Then his voice hardened. 'Many things have changed and will change in Georgia, but our God never will.'

Tamoona nodded silently.

A few days later I came across a poster In Tbilisi's Ajaria Hotel advertising Georgi's 'horrible building'. It caught my eye as it seemed to resemble a cathedral, doubling as a rocket-launcher. Underneath it were written the English words:

COME AND SEE THE PALACE OF HAPPINESS
AND THE NEW CEREMONIES DESCENDING
FROM THE CENTURIES-OLD TRADITIONS OF
THE GEORGIAN PEOPLE.

Curious as to just how the Soviets, with their theology of materialism, were creating 'new ceremonies', I decided to do just that. Never before had I come across an attempt to replace the rituals of religion in the USSR. To supply a purpose-built cathedral for the job . . . this had to be a first.

The palace stood on a hillside a couple of kilometres down the Mtkvari from the Sioni Cathedral. It was in fact a highly glorified registry office that BBC Television News had once dubbed 'the Cathedral of Atheism' during Margaret Thatcher's 1987 visit to Tbilisi.

Palace of Rituals.

Arriving before its strange, semi-organic towers of tubular concrete, I reached for my notebook and scrawled the first words entering my head. I entered only two, 'blatantly phallic'. The central tower rose up out of two concrete swirls on either side – mimicking, one supposed, the central column of a church. Yet the tower also carried suspicious chimneyish or factory-like overtones.

Climbing the steps into its impressive, airy ante-chamber, I realized to what lengths the designers had gone in trying to seduce the Georgians away from their 'primitive' religious habits. The abundance of light, pastel stained glass and marble flooring did everything in its power to convey the theme of a 'Palace of Happiness'. It may even have succeeded but for the building's thinly disguised duplicitous intent, as well as the enormous failure of Soviet Communism to understand (or even accept) a religious instinct.

Threading my way through two separate wedding parties, I sensed the awkwardness among the smartly dressed families. Everyone seemed twitchy, awaiting the moment when the gleaming black Moskovitch limousine waiting outside would hustle the couple back to their Orthodox Church and the real ceremony. I walked up into the wedding chamber and slunk around the pillars as an Armenian couple prepared to be married. Above them the ceiling lifted up a good 30 metres, with its light focusing down on to a small marble desk draped in velvet cloth. Behind this substitute altar stood the substitute priest – the local registrar. I watched her lift the ceremonial pen from its stand and scratch her mark in the official ledger. The couple had now become man and wife.

But did they feel it? To me the building seemed a Palace more of Bureaucracy than of Happiness, and the only trace of happiness I saw showed in the self-important face of the registrar.

To help sanctify the event, a giant candy-coloured mural reached up above the desk some 25 metres or so into the concrete heaven: a sickly medieval landscape depicting an idealized marriage ceremony between a naked man and woman, beneath a colossal 'Mother Georgia' figure, who dropped flowers of good fortune on their heads. But to my mind this 'Mother Georgia', with her peasant scarf and blonde features, smacked suspiciously of her rival, 'Mother Russia'.

I watched another couple and their families approach in the backgound. The rewound taped music began to twinkle down anew from the public-address system as the next 'new ceremony' was prepared. The Armenian couple were quickly hustled away into a smaller chamber to the side, and the next party stepped forward.

Standing discretely to the side with my camera, my secret eye was suddenly spotted by a Palace official. To my surprise he beckoned eagerly for me to step up and join the wedding party. With nothing but the best intentions in the world, he wished a better view for my camera – much to my, and everybody elses' embarrassment. Taking my place right next to the relations, I stood there feeling nobody quite understood what might be and what might not be appropriate in this building – I imagined a christening in a bingo hall, and waited for this humiliation to be over.

As the ceremony progressed, I remembered the film *Repentance*, made by the Georgian direrctor Tenghiz Abuladze. The film, made in the early 1980s, amounted to a powerful denouncement of Stalinism. Its final line was spoken by an old Georgian woman of the generation before Stalin. Approaching a younger woman on a modern Tbilisi street, she asked for directions to the street's church. The younger woman replied the street no longer contained its church and had now been renamed Varlaam Street (after the Stalinist mayor). To this the old woman replied 'What use is a street if it doesn't lead to a church?'

Suddenly this statement seemed to answer one of the enormous question marks hanging over Georgian society; why the religious revival? As history prepared to turn everything on its head yet again, Georgians still had a ceremony to return to. The confusing version of modernity supplied by the Soviets had only annoyed everyone. The new variant from the West, just around the corner, remained equally baffling. Georgia would need some help in the transition; it would need a genuine 'age-old ceremony'. No wonder Georgians, even young Georgians, flocked to the churches. This at least they could understand.

Hurrying for the door along with the bride's relations, my pictures taken, it struck me as not a little ironic that the days when the hypocrisy of the Church had shocked a whole class into the Russian Revolution had now turned full circle. Now the even grander hypocrisy of the post-revolutionary zealots had shocked a population back to the Church.

Café Society

I sat at a café table at the caravanserai on Sioni Street waiting for Tamoona. Before we'd parted I'd managed to extricate a promise from her to show me Tbilisi's old town. All around, the former hotel's three floors of balconies rose towards a giant arched ceiling. To my right a small fountain lifted a fine spray of water into the air, giving out more than a whisper of the time when camel trains and not Ladas dominated Tbilisi streets. Today this seventeenth-century hostelry for travellers and their animals remains more or less as it has done since its reconstruction after the Aga Khan's demolition of Tbilisi in 1795. The only changes were its central drinking pool, now replaced by a fountain, and its thirty-three rooms, recently remodelled into shops, cafés and an art gallery.

I'd arrived half an hour early, bringing with me examples of that rare commodity, English translations of Georgian poetry. I wanted to try and climb inside the strange quasi-medieval self-image of the modern Georgians, that combination of Byronic chivalry intermixed with materialist Soviet zeal. When I'd asked Georgi where to hunt out these origins, at first he said, 'Try the Byron Society in Tbilisi, they've just reinaugurated it'. Then he changed his mind. 'But actually it would be better just to read Shota Rustaveli's *The Knight in the Panther Skin*. It's probably even more relevant for us today.'

As the delicious aroma of Turkish coffee heated in hot sand swam into my nostrils, I reflected on those others who, down through the centuries, must also have reached for this twelfth-century text seeking a hand-hold on the Georgian character – and more often than not in places just like this. Men like Gurdjieff, Chekhov, Lermontov, Tolstoy, Pushkin, Tchaikovsky, Alexandre Dumas and even Dostoyevsky (I'm reliably assured) had all sat by fountains like this one in Tbilisi, deep in the shade of an ancient courtyard. I pictured them in their turn, savouring the atmosphere of other bygone Georgian centuries, when the likes of Marco Polo had done exactly the same.

Reaching towards the volume of Rustaveli, an impulse made me pick up another book first – the anthology of Georgian poetry given to me by Marika. This book contained the more recent followers of Byron, and inside it I found names such as Alexander Chavchavadze, Nico Baratashvili, Raphael Eristavi, Vazha Pshavela and Galaktyon Tabidze, with elaborate praises attached to their work. Their poems were saturated with those ineffable, soul-searching perceptions typical of the nineteenth-century Romantic Movement, as well as many violently over-the-top phrases dedicated to the heroes of remote Georgian tribes like the Khevsurs and Svans. But try as I might, the grandiloquence washed right over me. I turned to the later, twentieth-century poets like Paolo Yashvili and Titian Tabidze – much praised by Boris Pasternak, who translated their work into Russian – but experienced more of the same bombastic English. Then I noticed the date of the book's publication – 1958, only five years after Stalin's death and issued by the Soviet Publishing House, Tbilisi. Could my lack of interest have anything to do with the translation?

Flipping back to the book's introduction, I encountered a thought-provoking line to sum up any collection of a nation's poetry: 'Their voices rise in a mighty roar to glorify friendship among nations, the cause of peace throughout the world and the building up of Communist society.'

Smelling a horrible rat I turned to the biography section at the end and sought out the reference under Titian Tabidze (Pasternak's close friend). It blithely stated that, before the 'Socialist Revolution', Tabidze was influenced by the 'decadent symbolism' of Tbilisi's 'Blue Horn' group, the movement that 'attempted to introduce into Georgian literature traits characteristic of putrescent West European art'. But after the Revolution 'the pessimistic, depressive strains of his poetry gradually gave place to enthusiastic songs that rose in beautiful melodies of happiness and joy'. This, I assumed, would have been around the time the socialist regime had him shot for subversion – 1937.

I found myself stunned by the brazenness of these lies and wondered if any of us, growing up in the Western 1960s and 1970s, could ever understand the extent of terror and helplessness experienced by writers living under this regime. I thought of Pasternak himself, a man excessively sensitive to all this – as his letters reveal – who only escaped execution himself due to his shared affection for Georgia and its poetry (along with Stalin). The novelist who, in 1956, submitted his *Dr Zhivago* to a leading Moscow monthly, only to receive its rejection as a 'libel of the October Revolution' and then, within a year and a half, watched it published in eighteen Western languages.

The poets whose mistranslated idylls I now read had been published in English here in Tbilisi, in 1958, the year their Russian translator, Boris Pasternak, was awarded the Nobel Prize for Literature – which he was forced to decline. At times like this I began to feel my carefully maintained ironic distance shrinking to zero.

Yet I knew a stain of this still lingered even in some Soviet publishing houses. I remembered the English writer John Michell explaining how, after granting permission for one of his books to be published in Russian, he finally came across a copy.

'They'd translated it surprisingly well,' he said, 'except that at the end of every chapter they'd written another one, like good Marxists, explaining away and refuting just about everything I said.'

Surely this anthology stood guilty of the same approach. I put the book down and turned to Rustaveli. The first translation into English of *The Knight in the Panther Skin* had been pre-Soviet, by the Englishwoman Marjory Wardrop, sister of Oliver Wardrop, the 1919 British Chief Commissioner of Trans-Caucasia. Since then several other translations had appeared.

Reading the first few pages of Rustaveli's poem raised quite different emotions. The prologue of this enormous text amounted to the poet's unashamed declaration of spiritual and earthly love for his country's queen, Tamara. The wholehearted intent of his language immediately sank in the hook. It also gave a sharp reminder of the French and English tradition of chivalric poetry of the same period. He proceeded to describe his political leader as 'a beautiful, merciless panther', and ardently declared:

I who am maddened by love for she whom armies call mistress,
Am deprived of my life and reason.

That sickness for which there is no cure,
Save by her.

I found myself intrigued. The plot cleverly traps the reader with an emotional description of a mysterious grief-stricken knight sitting beside a stream, his armour studded with pearls, his shoulders wrapped by a panther skin, tears and blood streaming from his eyes. Yet he is also a man of immense will and strength, for he then slaughters all his challengers and disappears. The next 1,500 verses of the poem tell of a hero-prince called Avtandil who sets out to find this superhumanly tragic knight. Finally the two meet, become lasting friends and together set out to right the wrongs that caused the knight his enormous sorrow.

Written 100 years before Chaucer, these verses showed themselves fully familiar with Platonic ideas, referring to God as a universal force rather than a Christian one (to the extent that the Georgian Orthodox Church has, in the past, destroyed copies of the poem and some critics have even declared Rustaveli a Muslim). They also espoused the doctrine of perfect love or the cult of friendship, still prominent in modern Georgian culture – and indisputably linked with the convention of hospitality.

I began to realize why, when asked to explain that difficult phenomenon 'the true spirit of Georgia', Georgians often refer to this poem. Disguised within the depths of the text lay a purposeful code of chivalry espoused during Georgia's Golden Age – a period of enlightenment in full bloom at the very time that most European nations were hurling themselves into the dubiously motivated Crusades. As Christian sword sought Muslim throat in the Holy Land, so in Tbilisi Georgians, Armenians, Jews and Muslims lived side by side in relative harmony. One of Georgia's traditions had always been that Georgian brides at every level of society were expected to learn much of this poem, and even today their trousseaus usually contain a copy.

The appearance of a shadow over the book made me look up. Tamoona had arrived. We exchanged greetings and she immediately suggested we leave for the old town. As we stepped out on to Sioni Street she glanced down at my books.

'Do you like Rustaveli?' she asked.

'It's a great pity you can't read it in the Georgian,' she said in a serious voice. 'Then it's something else entirely. Really about a noble way to live, to treat other people.'

She led me down to the Mtkvari River towards the dramatic Metekhi Church perched on top of a cliff above the boiling current.

'This used to be a prison, then a theatre,' she said, 'but now it's about to become a church again.'

She spoke in a quiet, unassuming voice and I wondered if I'd been right in thinking – after her brief remark beside the icon of Ilya Chavchavadze – that here walked a Georgian who loved Georgia without the nationalism.

We crossed the road and entered the low-lying Gorgasali Square, where she explained some of the local history.

'This used to be Tbilisi's main market. The camel-trains and traders would come up the Mtkvari and stop in Tbilisi for the hot baths, then they would trade in this square.'

I tried to imagine the furious business taking place here. The bartering voices in Georgian, Armenian, Azerbaijani, Persian, Turkish and Yiddish, as the bales of brocades, spices and silk were unloaded and traded for rugs, guns and Georgian wines, sold in their large wineskins.

Today, tarmacked over and marketless, it offered only a further opportunity for Georgian drivers to scare each other. We walked on and she pointed out the names of the surrounding streets – Silversmith, Blacksmith, Bath-house, Dyer, Wine Rise – all indications of the professions formerly thriving there. Then suddenly she stopped walking and asked, 'This information is interesting for you?'

I think she sensed we hadn't just met to play the 'city tour'. I confessed my interest in her background and opinions on modern Georgia. She looked relieved, telling me she had studied English literature and language at university, and now vaguely pursued an urge to write. So what had she written?

'Some poems and short stories,' she said, but added dismissively, 'They're only fairy-tales. I would never get my stories published here. Anyway, they're no good. I think they're wrong.'

I asked what she meant by wrong.

'I don't know. I'm not saying what I should be saying.' She looked at me earnestly. 'There's something very important here to be said now. It's about Georgia, some central, crucial part that is being lost, that nobody is talking about. And I don't mean a physical part. It's in our soul, and I really mean "our", because I fear it's also a part of myself. I feel Georgia is dying – is losing itself for ever.' Then she said more quietly, 'The louder those nationalists shout, the harder they wave their flags, the further away they push from this place that seventy years has made them forget. I think this is why my stories are not correct. I'm already forgetting this place.'

She lowered her eyes to the road and I realized this troubled her very deeply. 'It's like a great craziness what's happening now,' she added, gazing at her feet.

I looked at her walking beside me, ashamed at not being able to say what she felt. Here was an intelligent woman, a couple of years out of university, yet filled with a childish shyness and lack of confidence, too sensitive, too contained within herself for the new society she saw forming around her. She felt herself cut off, unable to integrate with the noise and histrionics of Georgia's new politics.

I wondered if she, and the others like her, were experiencing the sense of alienation for the first time; the phenomenon we in the West accept as normal. Georgian culture had until recently been fused together by the single focused quest for 'freedom', with any real likelihood of its arriving prevented by the almighty Soviet obstruction. Now everything had changed; the barrier had simply rolled away and there it stood, or something stood, straight ahead, a kind of blinding blur. The nation now faced something it couldn't quite define.

I felt for these Soviet-educated women like Tamoona. Statistically, the Soviet population has been more widely educated than the British. Practically, it is infinitely more restricted in the application of this knowledge. Well into *glasnost*, students still face chiefs and professors of the old regime, all clinging jealously to their positions. Graduates come up against a terrible debilitating dilemma – educated for what?

We walked on up the hill in silence. The streets on either side began chopping, swerving and changing direction, narrowing and widening according to the houses they encountered. Here homes came before roads, and no two were alike. We walked past fine old Persian-style galleried balconies, their paint peeling, their supports sagging, daring only the foolhardy to walk, although washing had been strung gaily across the arches. There were houses with courtyards, their front walls built entirely from uneven panes of glass, filling the rooms beyond with light; above them the first-floor balconies opened out with their intricately carved railings, ready for those cool Caucasian summer evenings. This was a part of town where Georgians, Tartars, Azerbaijanis, Jews, Kurds and Armenians lived next door to each other. The place felt friendly and the higgledy-piggledy houses, although seeming on the verge of collapse, looked clean and lovingly maintained.

I began to sense the Georgia Tamoona feared might disappear – not so much the houses, as the spirit within them, the indefinable quality of life that all Georgians found impossible to articulate.

A couple of young children, aged three and four at most, walked towards us, unaccompanied. They stopped still and stared. Then just as we passed, the older one turned to me and shouted out shrilly, '*Gamajoba!*' – the Georgian for 'hello'. He almost seemed to be

95

welcoming us into his home.

Unlike in so many other shanty-type towns around the world, the greeting was not followed by some request or demand. Here they just received the stranger automatically – as, no doubt, did their parents.

I suggested to Tamoona that they wandered the streets because their houses threatened to fall down, but she just laughed.

'These houses are strong and always repaired. People like living here very much. Living in the old town means something to Georgians. This is real; *this* is Georgia.'

As we climbed higher towards the Narikala Fortress, so the streets became more cobbled and crooked, sinking ever further back into time. Then, as if deliberately to sabotage the illusion, I noticed the giant silvery figure of a woman, flashing between the roof-tops, high on the Sololaki ridge. This 20-metre-high representation of 'Mother Georgia', constructed by the Soviets in 1958, now stood above the lovingly maintained old homes like a severe, Space Age matron. She carried a cup of wine in one hand and a sword in the other, half threatening, half welcoming the city. To me it seemed like another example of that serious Soviet addiction to sword-bearing women statues. I asked Tamoona if she didn't resent this attempt to woo Georgians into the steely orbit of a Communist future, by appropriating this much-loved symbol.

'I don't know,' she said politely, 'but I don't mind this statue.'

Obviously, I'd been mistaken in thinking that all Georgians believed all things Soviet were 'wrong'. This symbol – not a Lenin, Ordzhonikidze or some other colonist – was Georgian, and for this she tolerated it, just as Georgians, in spite of all their clamouring against imperialists, learned also to tolerate them in some degree. Georgia operated – more than most countries – under the maxim 'The best way to master your enemy is to make him your friend.' After all, the Russians, then the Soviets after them, had also brought some very real benefits to the nation. Without the Russian Army, Georgia might still be a part of the Persian or Ottoman empire. Without the Soviet's hydro-electric power, air and rail links, hospital facilities and subsidized oil, they'd almost certainly be less economically developed. On top of this came the extensive educational facilities, the scholarships in Moscow and that most beloved of all illustrations, the Tbilisi Dynamo Football Stadium.

Finally, reaching a dead end, we descended back down the hill, passing the mosque, then the Chreli Bath-house – whose mosaic-tiled front and twin minarets made it even more mosque-like than the mosque itself. Below this stood Tbilisi's popular sulphur baths, their

96

sealed, domed heads poking above the ground like buried old men.

'This is where the tourists go now,' said Tamoona flatly.

These baths had served as the city's main attraction for over 1,000 years. In the twelfth century, Tbilisi possessed sixty-five bath-houses and since that day had found many people, including Pushkin and Tolstoy who liked lounging in their elegant marble pools, as Tolstoy put it, 'imagining oneself a Pompey or Lucullus'.

Eager to glimpse this haunt of poets, I stepped into the entrance and begged Tamoona to ask the burly attendant if I could take a photograph.

'*Ara*,' he said flatly – the Georgian for 'no'. Then I placed a packet of Marlboro on the counter-top. He held up two fingers. I put down another. He then said in exactly the same voice, only in English this time: 'Pushkin cubicle three.'

I pushed open the door to be bowled over by the blast of sticky air, and a barrage of German voices – the foreign tourists. The room appeared just as Tolstoy had suggested: white marble, with jet-black statues beside a murky, odorous water. But the sight of noisy, naked Germans, drinking Georgian champagne and singing loudly drove me quickly back to the street. I told Tamoona about the bath's occupants.

'Yes, I saw them yesterday,' she said. 'They were wearing shorts. Everybody was laughing about them.'

'Why?' I asked.

'Only foreign men wear short trousers in Georgia,' she said with a trace of amusement.

We walked away up the refurbished Leselidze Street, past Georgian Orthodox and then Armenian churches, with the synagogue and the mosque only a stone's throw away from each other, and a slick-looking new building with the words 'Advertising Agency' printed across it in English. I stopped to take a photograph and began explaining how this might be just the tip of the looming Western invasion of Georgia, but Tamoona just nodded politely as if she already knew.

'Would you like a drink of coffee now?' she suggested.

A couple of minutes later we sat opposite each other in an elaborate designer café called The Argo (after the ship carrying Jason and his Argonauts to Colchis), only a couple of hundred metres from the Sioni Street caravanserai. Sitting in this fashionable, new meeting-place for the re-emerging Tbilisi café society, I realized we'd come full circle: from the seventeenth-century courtyard to these dimly lit cubicles, cleverly constructed over a real fishpond.

Concealed within the shadows and candlelight Tamoona relaxed. I began trying to encourage her about her writing. She received my words with a tiny smile, as if touched, but I couldn't decide if she really believed me or not. Finally she interrupted.

'It's not just my writing that's the problem.' she said. 'It's how rapidly everything is changing here in Georgia. I don't think we can understand it. I think we've given up, just surrendered ourselves to the instincts of the moment. We're out of control, our culture is approaching...' She paused. 'Yours, I think. Not that yours is wrong. It's just too big for us to see.'

I asked her for an example.

'Look at us, the Georgian women. We've been told one thing for centuries: about chivalry, modesty, purity. Now we're being told we're liberated, we're free. So who are we?' She looked at me, as if expecting the answer.

If you look at some young Georgian girls now, they're more confused than ever. They listen to Western rock music. It tells them to do what they feel. They now have many men, not even boyfriends. For them it's the great release from the centuries of tradition. But afterwards does it help them? Do they know who they are? I don't know. Sometimes I fear they are just losing everything, and are taking us with them.'

I asked if she could see an alternative.

She lowered her eyes. 'No, I can't see an alternative,' she said, 'but there is one. I feel it. We still have something but we're missing it.'

I asked about Georgian men. She looked back painfully.

'For Georgian men, it's different. They don't have to behave. For them all this revolution is a great pleasure. And they've always got the Russian girls. Nobody's telling them to be pure any more. Then they turn to us to be good wives.'

I told her I couldn't believe all Georgian women still fell for this one.

'No,' she admitted. 'Things are changing. A few wives aren't so pure any more, and some, in fact a lot of women now, aren't getting married. We're waiting for men to catch up...' In the dimness I caught the trace of a despairing look. I asked if a huge world of secret sensuality didn't exist here, as it did everywhere else.

'Yes.' She said in a matter-of-fact voice.

I asked how this could be when most single women and men still lived with their families.

'It's possible. There are places to go. Georgian families have two houses, one closed up in the country. We Georgians are craft.'

I looked puzzled. She took a piece of paper wrote down the letters C – R – A – F – T. When I added the 'Y' her eyes lit up.

'Yes,' she said. 'That's what we are!'

'And you too?' I asked.

'No,' she replied. 'I'm not crafty.'

Then she looked sad again. 'I shouldn't tell you,' she said, 'but I'm twenty-five now and I've not yet kissed a boy.'

The Bright-White Touch-Paper

Tamoona's urgent but forlorn reaction to her country stuck in my mind. Unlike any other Georgian I'd met she seemed to detect something dark, looming beyond the radiant ambitions of the nationalists, but felt her voice drowned by the political hysteria sweeping the streets. Until then I had only sensed an unnatural charge to the electricity in the passing faces, hoping, like most, the imminent non-Communist government would harness it to good effect. (The fact it would lead to the election in 1991 of a naively nationalistic president, Zviadi Gamsakhurdia, a blood-bath in Ossetia, then the mini-civil war of 1991–2, lay beyond the scope of my imagination). But Tamoona's profound despondency had awakened a curiosity. Perhaps such pessimism also found an airing amid the Georgian arts? Then the phone rang.

'There's a performance at the Rustaveli Theatre tonight. It's quite unique. You *must* see it.' These words came to me in a clipped Oxbridge accent in between the crackles on Tbilisi's dying and reviving telephone system. I had met their speaker, Zura, a few evenings earlier in one of the city's hotel bars. At the time, I had watched him speaking, wondering why this educated Englishman had made such an in-depth study of Georgian history and culture. Finally I had put it down to his eccentric personality – the sudden, unBritish bursts of enthusiasm, the proximity of deep emotion strangely lurking beneath his words.

Discovering him to be a Georgian came as a profound shock. I retreated to the bar for a stiff drink and some soul-searching on my ability to discern character. Zura's profession as an English teacher had endowed him with the correct English but not the accent. However, his second job, as translator for Tbilisi's Rustaveli Theatre Company – one of the few companies in the world to impress the English with Shakespeare – may have explained it. I accepted his invitation and he told me to wait outside the entrance on Rustaveli Avenue.

Peering in through the glass I saw a spacious pre-Revolutionary vestibule: elaborate gilded arches, marble staircases, Greco-Roman statues – an example of Russian Classicism at its most opulent. The theatre had been purpose-built in 1899. Beyond the vestibule, an 850-seat galleried theatre awaited the appeciative Tbilisi audiences, who regularly packed the house.

It has been said that nations of dramatic temperament (like the Georgians) are less inclined to life's falsified, secondhand versions on the stage. Because they indulge feverishly in the everyday drama, they lack the kind of fascination that so drives us English to the theatre. But the Georgians are an exception to this rule, adoring drama so exorbitantly it makes no difference whether it is on or off the stage. Around me on the street came further proof. A large crowd of other invitees steadily collected beside the door. I watched a couple of girls in their early twenties walk down the street together, their fingers touching like children, then stop and stand a few metres away. Guessing they spoke English, I leaned over and asked the subject of tonight's performance. They gave me a dark look. It seemed to say 'This is no performance for a tourist'. Then after a long pause one said quietly, '*Dievatoye Aprely*' (9 April in Russian) and turned away, continuing her conversation in Georgian. I began to feel the weight behind Zura's words.

A few minutes later he arrived. We shook hands swiftly and after some earnest discussion with the *babushka* behind the stage-door desk – who looked me over as she would a serial-killer – I slipped through and into the gilded inner sanctum.

'Tonight it's the unofficial performance,' Zura explained. 'Or, as they say, the official rehearsal of tomorrow's performance. It's a theatrical requiem to the 9 April. A one-off event, designed for Georgian people, not the international audience. It's something very personal to us.'

Under the theatre's splendid walls, gold cornices and sparkling chandeliers, the grim tone of his words didn't fit. He led me into the main auditorium, where, under an even more fabulously ornate ceiling – with cherubs dancing around a massive mandala-like light cluster – stood a single, lifeless tree centre-stage, its branches hanging limply down. From its sticks hung two red bandages, of the kind attached to the fence now surrounding the Government Building steps. I asked him to explain.

'In the Georgian countryside we have many sacred trees,' he said, unable to disguise a rising emotion. 'Some call them wishing trees. The local people tie small prayers on to their branches so they blow in the wind, in the hope they'll come true. This tree is like one of those, a kind of tree of life, but as you see, all its branches are dead, and the wishes have turned into blood. The tree also symbolizes the Georgian people. Our culture is one so full of growth, fecundity, yet so often in its history it has had all its new growth stripped away.'

I asked who had written this theatrical 'requiem'.

'It has no words,' he replied. 'It's a series of enactments to a piece of music by the Georgian composer Gia Kancheli. Our theatre's director, Robert Sturua, created stage drama to go with it.'

Then he looked at me quietly. 'It will be a strong performance.'

I already knew of Robert Sturua's work. His burlesque-style production of Richard III had deeply impressed Peter Brook, Vanessa Redgrave and most of England's critics when it toured Europe. Since then his productions have often appeared in London's West End. The Novosti Press Agency, in their 1987 official guide to Georgia, credited him with an entire chapter, entitled 'Robert Sturua's Phenomenon', citing his theatre's worldwide success with Shakespeare as a fine example of how 'Soviet' artists can make deep impressions into the domains Westerners exclusively believe their own.

Zura led me down a rabbit warren of rooms and corridors, away from the backstage area, then abandoned me amid a feverish community of actors squeezing themselves into costumes, to hunt the director. Standing alone among priests, nuns, noblemen and common folk of the Georgian nineteenth century, I experienced a moment of eerie dissociation, as if just stepping into a living corner of the old town I'd visited earlier on with Tamoona. Now trader and customer pulled on boots, straightened their jackets, talked earnestly in Georgian. These modern men and women had now metamorphosed into their proud, pre-Soviet selves, donning the clothing of their great-great-grandfathers and grandmothers.

Then, walking through the nineteenth-century bustle, came a distinctly twentieth-century man, with casual open sweater, middle-age paunch and immensely round, hamster-like face. Robert Sturua had arrived. Shaking hands, I apologized for the bad timing of my arrival – only twenty minutes before curtain-up and asked him to suggest a time when we could chat.

'What about right now, if it suits you?' he replied politely.

To my amazement he then found us a bench just inside a buzzing wing of the stage, where we sat talking right up until the moment the lights dimmed.

'This play is about the history of Georgia from the start of the nineteenth century to the present day,' he said in deep and slowly pronounced English. 'It's about our partnership with the Russians. On 9 April our nation received a slap in the face which woke us up from a sleep that had been going on since 1956. This is the touch-paper to a flame that now is catching on in republics all over Russia.'

He spoke with all the composure of someone sitting in their own living-room. I constantly expected to be interrupted by nervous actors,

101

stage-managers or technicians in the final crucial countdown to curtain, but nobody disturbed us once. His voice seemed fully in tune with his private thoughts.

'Until now the feeling in Georgia has been a confused type of dissatisfaction. This event has purified our emotion. It makes us feel more noble, more chivalrous. Georgians prefer this and would rather fall in love with tragedy than worry about every little consequence of their actions.' Then he looked at me. 'This is like a Mediterranean zone here. All the emotions of life and death are taken more dramatically than elsewhere.'

But surely such carelessness for the future might be dangerous, I suggested.

'It's true,' he said more gravely. 'Some people are very caught up in this emotion, but not everybody. The question we all wait to see answered is, who will dominate?' He took a deep breath, and glanced at the actors bustling around us.

I asked how Georgians related to his 'elsewhere', which they would soon have to deal with as an independent nation. What had he, as a Georgian, detected in us when he toured the capitals of Europe? He thought for a second.

'I detected many things, but one thing I feel is, in developed Western countries people are struggling towards something that we, in a way, have born into us here in Georgia. Qualities of direct emotion, an instinct for genuine chivalry, qualities we've deliberately held on to from our history.'

I felt the blossom of a fine conversation just beginning to open when suddenly the lights faded. But before his face completely disappeared I quickly asked if this Georgian idea of self might not be slightly inflated?

'Oh yes, it's inflated!' came a cheerful reply out of the gloom. For the first time I wondered if the enormous, swashbuckling ego of the Georgians might also be capable of great practicality and vision – when blended with an appropriate discipline. I wanted desperately to ask Robert Sturua for his opinion on this, but a hush had already descended on the auditorium and the air around us was filling with a ponderous, deep silence.

It may have been only symbolic, but that night I watched the performance from backstage, witnessing the actors re-create Georgia's tragic history from behind the scenes. The following night I took my place with the public in the stalls. I sat among a dignified Georgian audience which included many senior public figures. Looking at those silvery, bushy moustaches and heavy-eyebrowed faces of the not-so-forgotten Georgian nobility – many with prominent positions in the Communist regime – I saw how, to this proud gentry, the Rustaveli Theatre had always worn the mantle of liberal respectability. I could also sense the 2,000 kilometres between this theatre and Moscow, a distance often facilitating the passage of Georgian theatre and film productions more easily past the censor's nose. Several times in Moscow I'd heard jealous film-makers claim the celebrated films from Tbilisi's Gruzia Film Studios had been shown only 'because the censor couldn't understand Georgian'.

But this performance never saw the shadow of a censor. To a surging orchestral soundtrack the lights dimmed and a sinister white gas (dry ice) crept ominously across the stage towards the audience – a quite unambiguous reference to the gas used by the Special Forces on 9 April. For just a split second a wave of irrational panic overcame me – perhaps this was not dry ice at all! It took a firm, mental slap to snap me out of it, as I realized I too had been overwhelmed by the spirit of 9 April. Instead of witnessing the front row of the stalls clutching their throats and gasping for breath, I watched a man step forward through the stage mists holding an infant in his arms – I assumed the symbol of the emerging nation of Georgia. The music then crashed, the lights flipped to red and he collapsed – the Russians had arrived. The stage flooded with women covered in black Arab-like head-dresses, standing in the background, hands stuffed into their mouths in the gesture of enforced silence – a reference to the period after 1801 when the Georgian royal family were sent packing and Russian law superseded the code of the Georgian kings.

I heard someone sniffing a couple of rows ahead. For this audience these ghostly mementoes of the past wedded perfectly with the symbols of the present – a symbolism everyone instinctively understood. The history of Russian calumny in Georgia is drilled into every Georgian child at home (making up for school, where Georgian history – until recently – was hardly taught at all).

After some dramatic struggles, symbolizing the Red Army's conquest of Georgia in 1922, a man in a black-vinyl jacket – typical of today's KGB, and formerly of Beria's dreaded Cheka (secret police) – rose up through a trap in the floor to announce the arrival of the first Stalinist purge of 1922–4. Crowds of women were rounded up and bundled away, and a priest was handcuffed (the suppression of the Orthodox Church). During the second purge of 1936–7, the priest was shot and not only intellectuals but also many prominent Bolsheviks and former allies of Stalin were led away. (During this terrible period many fine writers were liquidated. In 1936 Boris Pasternak had written to his close friend the Georgian symbolist poet Titian Tabidze, praising his recent book of poetry as 'a reminder of the time when people such as poets survived in the Soviet Union'. A few months later Tabidze was shot – at the hands of Beria's thugs. His death, along with that of the poet Paolo Yashvili, profoundly influenced Pasternak's *Dr Zhivago*.)

Then came sincerely gesturing bureaucrats (the Communist Party) strutting across the stage, quietly ordering generals, in less obvious areas, to attack. A giant black jackboot was placed centre-stage (symbolizing the Red Army's presence). Then, as a trembling crescendo of strings scaled the heights of what seemed like saccharine sentimentality, a woman dressed in white held out her baby before an evil bureaucrat. The lights snapped again into deep red and she fell to the ground, dead.

For me, the drama had entered the realms of cliché, swinging far too heavily to one side of Georgian history. But for the audience, the truth was at last being told. To them the rewritten history books from their school-days stood boldly corrected. They hadn't come for intellectual stimulation; the spectacle had been intended to re-create a sense of collective emotion, the reawakening Robert Sturua had mentioned in our talk.

At the final, climatic moment of the drama, amid a great din from the orchestra, the entire lighting rig descended low over the stage, every one of its filaments burning brilliantly, to announce the brash arrival of the tanks in Tbilisi on 9 April. Then suddenly, every one of the lights swivelled to glare painfully into our eyes – an indication not only of the 9 April massacre but of the threat still remaining. Everyone knew the tanks had simply retreated to their bases just outside Tbilisi, or on the Turkish border. They could return at any time.

Thus the performance ended, none too soon for me. I wondered vaguely why I'd never heard a Georgian mention the benefits of the Russian Caucasian Army in the nineteenth century – saving Tbilisi from further ruin at the hands of the Turks and Persians. But the many sniffles told me now was not the time to acknowledge any benefits from the Russian Army. As we stood up several men energetically blew their noses. The performance, with all the tricks and devices of theatre, had presented a dream of Georgia for the last 200 years, the 'universally forgotten land' as their much-praised poet Ilya Chavchavadze described it. The play told the endless tale of an inferiority complex, drilled into this proud people again and again. Georgia, it said, had been the vassal state of a cruel and sinister overlord for too long and, in that final, climatic blast of light, it seemed to me, the onlooker received the glare of a clear challenge to respond.

I rose from my seat with the audience. Had the touch-paper been lit? All around the faces streamed out on to the street: the elegantly dressed women in their black dresses and gold jewellery, next to their well-established husbands, the senior Georgians, the grander intellectuals, and surely even some politicians. No. Here one felt the political message more or less safely contained. The long-tied knot of power between the Georgian government, the KGB and the mafia would continue to hold together for some time yet.

But as the cold air of Rustaveli Avenue touched my face, so a hysterical, horn-blasting, flag-waving Lada screamed past the theatre entrance, its cargo of wild-eyed nationalists revelling in the new identity of 'independence'. I began to feel again this huge head of youthful steam aiming itself towards adventure and 'freedom'. I changed my mind. The touch-paper was already fizzing. The question was simply, which way would the rocket now shoot?

The Symbol of a Nation

I'd already visited Tbilisi's Art Museum once but Tamoona insisted on taking me again.

'I want to show you the museum's treasury,' she said. 'It's important. You should look at it not like a tourist.'

I asked her what she meant, but she didn't reply. However, having already seen its sumptuous collection of icons from all periods and areas of Georgia, and the powerful guard mounted around its entrance, I guessed the exhibition served more as a church than a museum – a kind of super-reliquary or Holy of Holies, open to the public.

The building stood on the diminutive Pushkin Square, next to Tbilisi's Freedom Square, its grand Ionic portico grinning back at the bustling traffic. It seemed a fully appropriate setting for art, yet until 1905 the building served quite a different purpose, housing Tbilisi's seething Theological Seminary. This establishment can claim direct responsibility for Georgia's two greatest revolutionaries, educating the democratic socialist politician Noe Zhordania, who led the heroic but brief government of independent Georgia between 1918 and 1921, and the not-so-democratic Joseph Stalin. Besides these two, the school produced numerous Bolsheviks, socialists and Georgian nationalists who never became priests due, all too often, to their expulsion. One of these, Lado Ketskhoveli, a militant Marxist revolutionary, met and then took under his wing the nineteen-year-old Joseph Dzhugashvili (who later renamed himself Stalin), then installed him as a leader among the secret ring of workers' discussion groups in Tbilisi. From

Queen Tamar's Cross.

this point, Stalin quickly rose to become a leader among the radicals. A small plaque on its outside wall announced Stalin's presence in this building between 1894 and 1898 (it has since been removed).

Looking up at this writing on the wall, I asked Tamoona for her opinion on the great Joseph.

'We have a saying in Georgia,' she said, ' "Don't expect heaven from the parish priest". Stalin set out to be that priest, but along the way he forgot this because he thought he could supply heaven. A great and foolish man and still a large shadow inside the Georgian character.' She glanced at me. 'He's still hard for many to look at properly.'

We entered the museum and deposited every conceivable item that might be used to steal an icon at the cloakroom, then submitted ourselves to the armed police-guard at the treasury entrance. Safely vetted, we stepped into an intimately carpeted chamber, with numerous well-lit exhibits set inside sturdy glass cabinets. The atmosphere was hushed, more akin to a church than a museum. Even today I've yet to come across a plusher or better-guarded museum in all the Soviet Union. The treasury also functioned as a much-needed bank vault for Georgia's most valuable relics. Most had been rescued from the churches throughout the Caucasus, as well as from Western Europe. When the Bolsheviks ousted the Georgian Menshevik government in 1921, Zhordania and his ministers fled with a portion of Georgia's transportable heritage, fearing for its safety. This may have been a wise decision, bearing in mind the subsequent purges in the north, where icons were chopped up to make potato crates, burnt as firewood or painted over with Stalin's face. But now, with the circular irony of history, Georgian icons are in danger of disappearing again, this time via the West's voracious underground art market.

Tamoona beckoned to me from beside a small, heavily built cabinet.

'This for me is Georgia's finest icon,' she said earnestly.

I looked into the cabinet and recognized Queen Tamara's small pectoral cross.

'This is her only known relic,' she explained, then stood silently before it in deep admiration.

Following her gaze I saw a simple cross, a few centimetres long at most, composed of six pearls, four emeralds and five rubies, set within a thin gold frame. The emeralds, roughly cut into oblongs, formed the arms of a cross, with a ruby at each tip and one in the middle. I could see why the smallness of this relic might be appropriate for this modest-sized nation, a country that, under its Muslim rulers, had worn its cross hidden beneath clothing. But what else? Tamoona's motionless face told me I'd missed something far more significant.

Then I remembered how on my first visit to this museum I had watched as a middle-aged Georgian woman burst into tears the moment she first saw this cross. What did Georgians see here? I tried to imagine this pendant hanging around the bare shoulders of a young twelfth-century woman, tall, slim, and large-eyed, of the kind endlessly portrayed in Georgian art. Standing here, did they feel the presence of the noble queen, a nearness to that bygone Golden Age?

Tamoona stood before it for a long time, then touched my arm in an uncharacteristically confident gesture.

'I wanted you to come here so I could tell you about this cross,' she said quietly. 'If you *really* look at it, you can feel what it's like to live in our country. You know this spot here for me is the very heart of our nation.'

She fell silent and I had to ask what she meant.

'When I look at this cross,' she said, staring right at it, 'I think how wonderful it is that right here in the middle of Tbilisi we have a museum of our history, and right in the centre of this museum is this cross, and in the heart of this cross is a single red ruby stone! This ruby is like a drop of the blood that used to run in the Georgian people.'

She glanced at me, then gazed back at the cross. 'For me this is the most beautiful cross in the world.'

Her voice betrayed her emotion. I could see now that Tamoona was telling me something about herself through this icon.

Perhaps here, before this cross she felt part of that 'nation' again; the noble lineage running far back into the past. She became part of this ancestral line of identity that would continue to exist long after her, still displaying all the ideas of art, beauty and courage she admired in her idealized Georgia. Might this visit to the museum be an attempt to show me an alternative, more reflective nationalism?

I thought of the power of the cross as a symbol among the other rebelling Soviet republics. Who could ever forget the extraordinary Hill of Crosses in Lithuania – the small hillock bristling with over a million wooden hand-carved crosses, reaching out of the earth like a vast crop of human hands stretching towards God and independence. The Communists had bulldozed the hill twice, but each time it grew back more vigorously than before, as if from an indestructible seed deep inside the soil.

The same held true in Georgia. The red cross of Saint George (also the English part of the Union Jack) had been readopted by some of the nationalist groups and printed on to flags. These red-on-white designs were a favourite with the Monarchist Party, a highly vocal section of Georgia's independence movement since the 1830s, which called for a constitutional monarch and the restoration of that intermediary between heaven and political man, the king (the monarchy had been abolished by the Russians in 1801).

'The cross in Georgia,' said Tamoona, 'is the most important sign for us. It means unity and nearly all Caucasian cultures have it at their centre. Even in the different languages it's the same. In Georgian *djvari* means "cross"; in Khevsuretian it's *djurri*; and in Ossetian, which is from another language group entirely, *djvar* means "cross". The symbols are everywhere around us.'

I looked around the museum chamber and noticed for the first time just how many crosses it contained. They stood everywhere in cabinets or embedded in icons like marker-buoys in the long, embattled history of this nation, from the tiniest eighth-century bronze medallions and tenth-, eleventh- and twelfth-century processional crosses, to the splendid fifteenth-century 2-metre ante-altar cross from Goridjvari.

As we walked towards this cross, Tamoona stopped me beside some eleventh-century cloisonné enamel encolpoins (breast pendants).

'Look at this dragon,' she said, pointing to an exquisite plaque of Saint George the victorious, spearing his dragon with great ardour. Every scale on its back had been separately created with an extraordinary attention to detail.

'You can see how this artist loved this icon,' she said, adding, 'It's as if he wanted to draw attention to the dragon.'

At the Goridjvari cross, we found the dragon again, but this time as one of many scenes from Saint George's life. This enormous wooden cross, encased in a skin of sixteen silver plaques, carries some of the most intricate reliefs in all Georgia, each plaque depicting either a miracle or one of the tortures he endured during his trials of faith.

As we looked I could sense Tamoona debating whether to say something. Finally I asked her what it was.

'These illustrated crosses are not only icons to be worshipped as the Church would like you to,' she said more quietly. 'You know, they're like secret messages, if you can understand them. If you take them seriously they're like guides, because they show the step-by-step development of the psychology of holy men and saints.' Then her face showed a moment of uncertainty. 'But our Church doesn't like this kind of analysis. It doesn't understand it'.

Feeling a little confused, I looked at the silver plaques of the cross. They showed Saint George undergoing a horrific series of tortures: boiled in a cauldron, flayed with bull-whips, tied and stretched around a wheel. It also presented him carrying out miracles, bringing a farmer's bull back to life, slaying of the dragon. Yet I could make no sense of it. I asked Tamoona to explain.

'I can't really,' she said apologetically, 'but anyone who thinks must realize the Saint George story is purely an allegory. Every icon tells us this because, of course, dragons don't exist.' She smiled faintly.

I knew even the Roman Catholic Church had guessed as much when they decanonized Saint George in 1961, for lack of any solid evidence proving his existence.

She continued: 'To me it's the story of a saint's struggle against different parts of his personality. You can see two opposite sides of Saint George's character in this icon: 'Saint George as the martyr and Saint George as the victorious.' Suddenly she looked crestfallen. 'But I know so little about this, I can't really talk about it.'

I suggested it might have something to do with the actual tale of Saint

George's slaying the dragon. I went through it in my mind. The terrible fanged monster devours beautiful maiden after beautiful maiden, until finally the king's daughter is led out to the beast. Then from nowhere rides a youth on a white horse, his cloak billowing in the wind. The youth stabs the dragon through the eye and blinds it. The king's daughter then binds the dragon with her girdle, and the beast is mysteriously tamed. Together they lead it to the market, where Saint George kills it before a crowd of pagan townsfolk and in so doing immediately converts them to Christianity.

'Yes, it's also an allegory,' she said. 'But to me it's like a dream. I can't fit it in with myself.'

I knew the feeling, remembering how once I'd scoured religious texts for any kind of practical guide that seemed to fill the gap in my European religious background. In my case the search had narrowed on to the Buddhist Wheel of Life in Dharamsala, north India. How earnestly I'd wanted to believe that these bright images carried a crucial message for me. How doggedly I'd tried to 'understand' them, without any success. Standing with Tamoona before that cross I suddenly wondered if I hadn't given up my quest too quickly? For after Dharamsala came that flight back from Delhi to Europe (via Moscow), and its moment of grim realization that I could no longer think my way out of such dilemmas, that thinking itself might be the worst dilemma of all. There, at 10,000 metres, I had decided the only solution was to attack those huge chunks of trapped consciousness with raw experience, and thus my travel addiction had resumed.

Looking at Tamoona's puzzled face I realized she approached that icon of our own English Saint George, 'Protector of the Realm', with a good deal more hope than I'd ever been able to muster before him in England.

Tamoona spoke again, with just a trace of guilt: 'You know, I think I love Saint George. I know I shouldn't because it's really worship.' Then she added, more shyly, 'But you know, I also feel for that poor king's daughter.'

After the treasury, Tamoona had one more room to show me.

'You must see Pirosmani,' she said more brightly.

We skirted the museum's Iranian rooms, with their fine paintings of nineteenth-century Persian courtesans and dancers – costumes strikingly similar to those of the dancers I would see later at the Pioneer Palace – then climbed up the stairs to two low-ceilinged rooms filled by light, childlike paintings – the largest space given over to any one painter in Georgia.

'This is Niko Pirosmani,' she said. 'He's a Primitivist or Naïve-style artist.'

Across the walls stood strange, bold animals and scenes of nineteenth-century Georgia, with men in national dress, drinking-horns raised, picnicking amid wineskins and great spreads of food. Every part of his works, the food, the animals, the human beings, had been presented in the same stark lack of detail.

'I love these pictures,' Tamoona said in one of her mysterious fits of enthusiasm.

I began to realize that for all the gloom and sadness in her life, she found genuine companionship, even a kind of friendship, among these icons and works of art. No wonder she wanted to take me to this museum.

She led me straight across the room to a painting simply called *Janitor*. It presented a bearded old man holding a staff. He wore an apron round his waist and a cap jammed on to his head, as he stared blankly out of the canvas, like a tramp kitted out in a uniform he didn't understand. The writing on the Georgian old-timer's cap was in Russian, but has face was anything but.

'We know very little about Pirosmani's life,' Tamoona said, gazing at the painting. 'He seems to have left almost no mark at all. Nobody knows where he was born, where he travelled. He is said to have lived in woodsheds, under stairs, and made all his own paints. I think of him as a silent man, a kind of holy man who just painted and nothing else. A real poet. You know, when they found him dead, nobody even knew he was a painter.'

I could see how Pirosmani played a role in her life almost equivalent to that of Queen Tamara. Yet I found her enthusiasms were echoed in most Georgians I met. Pirosmani drew almost universal praise, not so much as Georgia's only significant modern painter, but more due to the qualities of bold childishness and innocence his work and life represented.

Tamoona produced a book of his work – borrowed from the gallery guard – and held open a page showing a very strange picture: a giraffe, painted in a completely unrealistic style, its neck too short and thick, its head disproportionately large and coloured in black and white.

'This is my favourite picture,' she said. 'It's a great pity it's not here in this museum. Pirosmani painted many animals without ever seeing them. He just loved the idea of the giraffe. He was like those icon painters of the fourteenth century – he saw with big eyes, he felt everything and tried to paint the myths inside them.'

In her words I could sense the artist, now seventy years after his death, slowly transforming into legend. The Georgian film-director Eldar Shengeleya had already begun the process in his excellent film *Pirosmani*, a depiction of his life in the same style of colourful unsophistication as his paintings.

Standing surrounded by the artist's work I too found myself taken by his bright, guileless pictures. Like the odd remarks of a child, they seemed to cast an immensely simple but clear light on all they touched. Tamoona then pointed to another of her favourites, this time a huge, hairy camel with a Mona Lisa smile standing solemnly above his owner, an equally hairy Tartar trader. The two were thinly connected by a string. The picture seemed to ask the question, who controlled whom? Did the big animal emotions rule the nation of Georgia or the smaller guiding force of the man.

Pirosmani's Giraffe.

Back outside on the street, walking back to the bus-stop, I thought of that picture and Tamoona's statement – about painting the myths within events. All around us rushed busy Georgians, in the full flood of daily life. For a minute our passage became blocked by a couple of chanting Georgian women, one wearing a modern knee-length dress of bright vermillion and white stripes, the other the plain black cloth of traditional mountain dress. I thought of that modern Georgian woman now walking next to me, the one who'd confided in me with such candour, who'd told me of her own fairy-tale, the one she feared she'd 'got wrong'. It seemed so many different myths now walked the streets of Tbilisi, each one increasingly right for itself, and increasingly less right for the nation as a whole. These citizens were living close to their twelfth century – as Marika had put it – their minds filled, like Georgi's, with images of icons, freedom flags and the huge yearning desire for liberation . . . along with a Western standard of life.

I asked Tamoona what kinds of subjects she thought the simple Pirosmani might want to paint today.

'I don't think Pirosmani could exist today,' she said flatly.

The Gift from God

I was staying at the house of my Georgian friend Ilya and his family. Their set-up was typical of the Caucasus, with grandparents, parents, parent's sister and children all cluttered together in one large, antique-crammed Tbilisi flat.

Ilya invited me to stay at the drop of a hat and, at a second drop of the hat, rearranged the whole household on my behalf. The sister moved out of her room, which became mine, and the kitchen geared itself up to handle 'the guest'. But, unlike most household kitchens around the world, my vegetarianism was greeted with a casual nod – instead of the usual protestation and panic. Georgia's 3,000-year history had not limited itself just to rebellion and Rustaveli.

On my second evening, a dinner was prepared that matched any I have ever eaten. In a nation (the USSR) that six months later would undergo food-rationing and a year later had the West handing it food aid like a Third World state, Georgia stood mysteriously well stocked. No sooner had I finished one delicious and unknown item than another would appear. After that ominous beginning with the 'Kazbegi potato', the nation now unlocked another of its secrets.

In between mouthfuls I attempted to note down the dishes before they disappeared. The first and most common was *khachapuri*, a speciality in every Georgian household. This distinctive bread of unleavened dough wrapped around cheese and baked into round flat tablets or shallow pies has been a staple in the Caucasus for centuries, and is a truly portable meal.

'A toast,' Ilya then pronounced solemnly, and the whole table waited in silence as he filled everyone's glass to the brim. 'To our friendship,' he said, rising to his feet gesturing to me to stand also. 'I hope with all my heart yours is a deeply enriching stay with us in Tbilisi. That our personal friendship will grow and that you will come to love Georgia. That you will find everything you want while you're here and you will return to England to bring the friendship between our two countries closer.'

He then downed his glass in one gulp. Covering my embarrassment I did the same – the correct response. The tradition of 'friendship', as expounded by Rustaveli, still held its central part in Georgian daily life. The guest *was*, in the chivalric sense, 'a gift from God', even to my liberal doctor friend Ilya, lover of Japanese electronic goods, Pink Floyd and The Grateful Dead.

Like most foreigners, at first I found this tradition awkward. But by the end of a fifth visit to Georgia I came to enjoy this formalized opportunity to express affection or deep, underriding emotion. As one Georgian friend asked me after returning from London, 'Where in your culture are the moments every day to speak about your important friendship, your serious thoughts, your deep hopes?'

I couldn't think of any.

'Be careful,' he warned cheerfully. 'You'll become too sophisticated!'

He then went on to admit that this old Georgian tradition of speech-making via a *tamada*, or 'toastmaker', could sometimes overwhelm the meal; that their glowing emotional speeches occasionally drowned out most normal social behaviour. I told him the tale of a West German friend who once arrived at a Georgian's house for a sumptuous feast, only to find every time he reached out to put something on his plate somebody proposed a toast. He said he spent so much of the time standing up and sitting down again that he arrived back at his hotel starving and had to beg the kitchen for food.

But at Ilya's this was never a problem. In fact, it was the reverse. My neighbours at the table kept slipping new items of food on to my plate. I speared a piece of what looked like white meat with my fork and held it up inquiringly.

'*Sulguni*. Roasted cheese from the mountains. Eat it!' I was told.

I did so and found it delicious. I was then told that Georgia produced numerous cheeses in its mountain regions – at least as many varieties as there were tribes. But my stomach had already reached overload. I asked my hosts to teach me the word I was to find probably the most useful on all subsequent trips – *kmara* – the Georgian for 'enough'. On this occasion it produced only hoots of laughter and more exotic vegetable pâtés were thrust my way: excellent combinations of aubergines, courgettes, carrots, beetroots, fennel, ground walnuts and peppers. On another occasion, I managed to pin one down reliably in my notes – *pkhali* – a mixture of finely chopped spinach or beetroot leaves, blended with walnut paste, pomegranate seeds and aromatic herbs.

Then finally there came *khinkali*, pasta envelopes stuffed with meat, shaped like little money bags. These received much praise from my neighbours, and kept mysteriously appearing on my plate, along with declarations that I'd reached the appropriate moment to abandon years of vegetarianism.

In the meantime, Ilya proposed another toast, announcing with all the gravity of a priest, 'To the cook'. As a male I rose to my feet and downed in one gulp another full glass of delicious Kvanchkara red wine. Sitting down again, I complained that such a fine wine should be sipped, not instantly drained. But Ilya simply replied, 'Don't worry. We have more . . .' and immediately another bottle was produced, opened and my glass refilled right to the brim.

As the bottles came and went, it almost seemed that a meal in Georgia was an excuse simply to open as many bottles as possible. I asked about the wine's point of origin.

'Stalin's favourite,' Ilya replied, not answering my question. I asked again.

'It's from Kvanchkara!' He looked at me amazed, then explained that nearly all Georgian wines bore the name of their village of origin – this one in West Georgia.

On another occasion Ilya and his wife took me out to the Aragvi restaurant, beside the Mtkvari, for yet another gastronomic experience. But nothing I tasted in any Tbilisi restaurant compared with the cooking of his family. Indeed, most of the best traditional items still struggled to find their way on to the menus of the new cooperative restaurants. Competition and sabbotage from the corrupt state restaurants accounted for some of this – as did the soaring prices of meat and vegetables at the new private markets.

At the Aragvi, the table beside ours had been laid for another party. At the head of the table sat another remarkable dish, right out of an Arthurian banquet – a grinning piglet's head on a silver platter. I asked Ilya to explain this Georgian delicacy.

'It's not for eating,' he said emphatically.

'What's it for, then?' I asked.

'The pig is for the *tamada*,' he said, then reached over to top up my sixth glass of champagne.

'Hey, Pete, why you're not drinking?' he asked.

The Future Belongs to Us

Over successive visits to Georgia I began to detect the presence of a new brand of young Georgian growing up within the society, one enormously different to anything before and yet fully familiar to us in the West. It had something to do with an alliance between personalized ambition and a liberalization of the traditional ideas of nationalism, chivalry and manners, a character more common among women than men – and one rarely encountered up north among the more enterprise-damaged Soviets. The secret of its success – if one could call it that – grew very simply out of Georgia's well-maintained and historic school of rebellion.

My first meeting with Manana took place in London, a sure sign of her membership of this new clan of the 'independent' citizen. For, at twenty-four she'd managed to engineer this trip entirely by herself.

'Tell me how can I help your visit to Tbilisi,' were her first words to me in Tbilisi. (She spoke excellent English, which always homed in straight to the point.)

I mentioned a desire to meet people of her age and see the renowned Georgian dance. I'd recently heard Georgian traditionalists criticize the work of the Georgian State Dance Company – one of the country's chief cultural exports – as a sensationalized version of former indigenous dances, yet I knew these dances still touched on many qualities of the old unified culture.

'OK, I'll arrange it,' she said, almost before I'd stopped speaking. 'I'll pick you up tomorrow lunch-time.'

Although more or less the same age as Tamoona, the similarity between the two girls ended here. While Tamoona watched and listened helplessly to the events taking place all around her, Manana effected them, in her case bombarding Tbilisi with a sparkling, green-eyed whirlwind of energy and ambition. She arrived at Ilya's house driving her mother's car, its back seat ready-crammed with girls of her age.

'We're going to a restaurant now,' she announced, following it, as always, with a disarming smile. 'It's a place where we go.' She gestured to her friends in the back seat and promptly raced the Lada across the city as lawlessly as any Georgian man.

As we walked down the steps into a smart pre-Revolutionary building, I asked what class of people frequented this café.

'It's café for lonely people,' she smiled enigmatically.

As I rightly guessed, Manana herself didn't suffer from this affliction. 'I'll be meeting my boyfriend later,' she said at the table. Then leaning forward, she added in a conspiratorial voice, 'But you mustn't tell anyone. Not even your hosts. You see, my parents don't know. They won't allow me to have a boyfriend, especially not this one, and we have to meet secretly. My parents think I'll be with you all morning.'

I promised not to tell, and glancing around the room saw groups of girls and boys gathered at separate tables, huddled over tea or coffee, dark secret looks flashing around the room. Many of the girls had plastered themselves with make-up – almost certainly from the black-market – in a fashion that seemed to favour warlike dashes of cherry blusher across the cheeks. Their ages varied between seventeen and perhaps twenty-five, yet all wore the clothing of women twice their age in Europe – interlinking gold-chain belts and below-the-knee dresses. The boys also presented themselves smartly in new black-market jeans and clean-cut jackets. As the familiar sounds of Madonna, The Pet Shop Boys and Bronski Beat throbbed from the expensive Sony sound system, I sensed the intense electricity of teenage sexuality fizzing through the air.

A full plate of cheese *khinkali* then landed before me unordered. I protested to Manana that I had only just eaten (or rather fended off as gallantly as I could) another huge and delicious lunch at Ilya's.

'Don't worry, they're very good here,' she replied, refusing to hear the word 'No'. She then focused her eyes on me, ready for another revelation in the romantic conspiracy, her voice increasing in volume all the time. Suddenly I had the distinct impression that Manana knew foreigners found this type of story particularly fascinating, and also that several of her middle-class friends found it correspondingly shocking.

'You mustn't tell anyone this but I'm going to run away from home with my boyfriend. In two months we're getting married. You know, I'm fed up with this secret life. Now some people are spreading rumours I'm pregnant. It's not fair, because I'm a virgin.'

The last word was spoken so brazenly that several of her girlfriends around the table blushed visibly.

'What will you do then?' I asked.

'When everyone and my parents have quietened down, I'll come home again,' she said calmly.

It struck me that Manana, at the age of twenty-four was going through the same rebellion most European girls undergo at sixteen or seventeen. It also struck me that several of these faces around our table would probably never go through this troubled stage, slipping easily into the well-worn tradition of Georgian courtship and marriage. But Manana's future proceeded apace, her green eyes shining with all the determination and zeal of the new youth. She'd entered the glorious fray against dogged traditionalism, Soviet and Georgian. Like a female Saint George, she would slay the old dictatorship of her family, who still tried – heaven knows why – to find her the right man.

I glanced at those other faces in the café, all fully conversant with the new rhythms of British rock music, the new siren call of pan-culturalism. Had not the rebellion of these Mananas, like that of the Georgian nation as a whole, finally entered its adolescence? The brimming qualities of rock 'n roll narcissism and 'independence' now dropped on to the Tbilisi streets like manna from heaven.

'What will happen after you're home?' I asked her.

'Oh, it will be all right. I'm getting a job in television,' she said casually. 'Excuse me a second, I've just seen a friend.'

As she hurried over to another table, I glanced at the expressions on her friends' faces. Throughout Manana's confessions I'd watched them vacillate between outrage, jealousy and pride. When she stepped away from the table one of the more smartly dressed girls turned to me and said, as if to reassure me: 'Not all of us believe in what Manana does.'

But the moral disapproval in her voice was belied by the envy in her eyes.

That afternoon Manana fulfilled the second part of my request by taking me, true to her word, to view Georgian dance in the making – this time in the form of the generation rising up beneath hers.

'I'm taking you to the Pioneer Palace on Rustaveli Avenue,' she explained. 'It's where we go to learn our hobbies.'

The Pioneers were then the Soviet equivalent of a large and compulsory brigade of Boy and Girl Scouts, and one of the rare Soviet institutions with a wide popularity (unlike that other youth organization, the Komsomol or Young Communist League, which in April 1990 gave up the ghost in Georgia). After the 1917 Revolution, when the Tsar together with the Governor of the Caucasus had been sent packing, his elegant Renaissance-style palace on Rustaveli Avenue had been turned over to those who would build the bright new future of Georgia, its Pioneers.

Our Lada zeroed in on the grand entrance of the Pioneer Palace like a guided missile. We arrived in time to see dozens of blue-uniformed boys

118

and girls streaming in and out of the front door. Inside I found it pleasantly converted into a school, with its central courtyard dominated by a genuine Soviet Sputnik suspended from a steel arm, undoubtedly to inspire the young Yuri Gagarins of tomorrow.

I asked Manana which of all the 'hobbies' was the most popular.

'I think, certainly, traditional Georgian dance,' she said, and her friends backed her up.

To prove it, we were suddenly surrounded by dozens of excited fifteen- and sixteen-year-olds, recently transformed into princes and princesses of Georgia's beloved bygone years. With squeals, giggles and shouts the boys adjusted their silver cartridge-belts, and the girls straightened their jewelled head-dresses ready for the acrobatics in one of the world's most energetic dance traditions.

Following the sound of determined drumming, we eventually stepped into a long mirrored dance-studio just in time to see several red-tunicked male legs fly up into the air, then land again accompanied by loud war-cries. I watched these boys' burning eyes as they climbed shoulder upon shoulder to create a human pyramid, then just as rapidly leap back down to the floor.

The brooding sexual energy of the café had here transformed itself into vigorous gymnastics. We stood pressing ourselves against the wall as, in the next dance, older boys in bright-blue tunics suddenly unsheathed their daggers and began hurling them, one after the other, into the wooden floor. Several failed to bite into the wood and skidded across the floor to where the audience would normally have sat.

'This is a dance designed to prepare for the enemy,' Manana said calmly.

Who could miss the connection between these wild dervishes and the kamikaze nationalist cars screeching down Rustaveli Avenue?

In the next dance, the tempo of the drums picked up, the passion rose, dancers yelled, separated into pairs, then, grasping long cutlasses, twirled round and around, clashing the blades together on every turn until sparks flew between their faces.

'This dance is called Mtiuluri,' Manana shouted more excitedly. 'It's from the mountains.'

Then one of the group broke free, dropped on to his knees right before me and, spinning like a top, sank dagger after quivering dagger into the parquet a few centimetres from my feet.

Manana grinned at me. 'Are you afraid?' she asked.

I felt it could have been her in the black tunic hurling the knives.

Then quite suddenly the atmosphere of the performance changed completely. The girls entered the dance. Stepping out on to the floor, they glided across the parquet in a smooth motion of white floor-length dresses and slim figures. They drifted into the male frenzy like swans wafting into a hurricane. They appeared not so much to dance as to float across the stage, the long pigtails, part of their costume and dangling to their waists, hardly swaying. The contrast between these graceful, passive females and the wound-up springs of male aggression, could hardly have been greater. I sensed something here of the idealized, well-defined roles of men and women in Georgian society: enormous activity set against queenly tranquility; the pre-set roles that the Soviet urbanization of Georgia had only slightly ruffled but that now, as Tamoona sensed, might disappear in the course of a single generation.

In the next dance three girl-queens glided around the room wearing long headscarves and floor-length dresses covered in imitation pearls, rubies and emeralds. On each serene head perched a coloured crown also covered in gems. The girls floated across the floor like three separate incarnations of Queen Tamara, gradually spiralling into the centre to merge as a single, six-armed, rotating queen. The costumes and movements seemed entirely Oriental, the headscarves similar to those of the Persian court. I asked Manana what she could tell me of this dance.

'It's called Samaya,' she said but knew no more.

Again I sensed the profound blending of Near Eastern or Muslim motifs with this highly Christianized culture. Later, when I questioned an authority on Georgian dance, he vigorously denied any 'Muslim' links with the Samaya dance and connected these gracious spiralling dances with the circle dances of the mountain region of Svaneti, in West Georgia. But my own untrained eyes told me otherwise.

I asked Manana if she still danced.

'Yes, of course,' she said, 'but not like this, just ordinary dancing at the discos. This takes a lot of practice.' Then she suddenly added, 'But I sing,' and her eyes lit up. 'Would you like to hear us?'

I'd already heard several of the male Georgian choirs and their robust polyphonic harmonies, but never the women. I asked her what she meant by 'sing'. She smiled.

'I will arrange a party. Then you will see.'

As I suspected, this new opportunity to organize a dinner also provided a chance for another evening with her boyfriend. But this time I would meet him too.

When Manana's boyfriend arrived to pick me up, the car's bonnet shimmered with heat. He grasped my hand firmly but looked away as we shook. He was a lean, handsome man, with dangerous eyes and a hoarse, mafioso voice that knew no English. His eyes didn't so much look at the world as flash at it. His movements and actions were swift, succinct and restless, abrim with the emotion of Georgia's semi-legitimate underworld.

The party was to take place in one of the new housing tracts on the outskirts of Tbilisi, and we immediately shot off across the city towards it. He drove with one arm on the window-ledge, the other holding a cigarette. His words and actions seemed the result of sudden deep convictions, but unlike Manana, the good middle-class rebel, I sensed this boy could very easily go too far.

As the Lada greased its way down the avenues, I noticed the central dividing line flicking past the car on either side. He drove into an empty space on the road if it speeded our passage. A traffic-light turning red meant only slow down slightly because the way ahead may contain more traffic. 'No Entry' signs were interpreted as two-way traffic. At one roundabout, when a traffic policeman gestured us to halt and let the other traffic pass, he simply ignored him. The furious officer waved his hand aggressively, instructing us to pull over, but Manana's boyfriend continued on, talking casually as if nothing had happened.

It made me remember Marika's remark about Georgian driving: 'My grandfather always used to say Georgians drive their cars like they used to drive their horses, but they forget that, unlike the horse, the car has no brain.'

As for the speed limit along the Mtkvari embankment, speed limits were plainly a Soviet invention; most Georgians simply drove as fast as the road surface would allow, and preferably faster than anyone else.

On the Mtskheta dual carriageway he achieved such a manic velocity that we missed our turning. But instead of continuing on to the next turn-off, he simply U-turned and drove straight back down the fast lane towards the oncoming traffic to the missed exit. Cars came racing towards us, lights blazing and horns blaring, deliberately skimming past only centimetres away.

'Are you afraid, Peter?' Manana asked excitedly from the back seat.

'No,' I lied. To admit it would only encourage this madness.

But for her the performance amounted to sheer delight and I began to imagine this marriage to be: she, the queen of her mighty kingdom of ambition and naughtiness, in love with the prince of the underworld, 'living fast, dying young', suffused with disobedience and honour. Manana had fallen for a hero of Georgia's warrior class; he for one of its new Westernized heroines. But I decided this urban jousting between Ladas was one of the weaknesses of Georgian chivalry – the horrific road-death statistics in Tbilisi backed this up.

By now the red-hot Lada clattered up a dirt-track towards a thicket of new, unfinished concrete high-rises. We all had to dismount due to the terrible state of the access roads. Walking across the mud, looking up at the ghostly white towers rising out of this wasteland, I began to feel the surreal quality of these young Georgians' lives: their days and nights spent in glorious, terrible deeds one after the other; the quests for honour, independence and self-gain; waving the flags for independence; driving their cars just like horsemen in the Georgian army hundreds of years ago; discovering an ecstacy in resisting 'the Reds'; hunger-striking, refusing their compulsory Soviet military service (80 per cent at the time); and disobeying every petty Soviet law they could find. In between these raids on the Soviet world they returned to twenty-storey concrete cliffsides, briefly to recharge their batteries before launching out on the next jaunt. (Later I was to realize, here walked the raw, lawless, lust for adventure; the force of anarchy contained within every socio-political structure the world over that Gamsakhurdia's government of independent Georgia unwisely fed with guns in 1991. It did so ostensibly for its own security in the 'war' against Ossetia, but later could only watch as these same weapons were used to oust it from power in January 1992.)

Yet inside that cliffside, order and harmony found themselves temporarily restored within the table ritual. Carried out with no less solemnity that at any middle-class Georgian table, our *tamada* pronounced the toast proudly and with dignity. The food was spread before us and shortly afterwards, true to their promise, the girls launched into song.

I listened in amazement as they broke into complicated three- and four-part harmonies as easily as if they practised every day. At the end of the first song, a Russian ballad, I asked if they could perhaps sing me a 'typical Georgian folk song'? They all laughed and proceeded to sing whole-heartedly almost without stopping for the next hour and a half.

I sat before those piles of food enchanted, not eating, thinking I'd just hit it lucky with this particular group of gifted girls. Yet a few days later, at another party, this time among students from Tbilisi's Foreign Languages Institute, I found myself amazed yet again at more polyphonic harmonies from an entirely different set of girls. This other group told me that none of them had ever received a singing lesson, that they sang purely for pleasure.

After one full-throated song, in which heads were thrown back and all shyness overcome, I asked for a translation.

'Oh, it's Mingrelian, we don't know,' they shouted back, whereupon they launched themselves into a Beatles' hit, followed by 'It's a Long Way to Tipperary', which ended in a fit of laughter as nobody knew more than the first two lines. But everyone remembered the melody and could create a three-part harmony for any tune I named.

The men just sat round the table and listened appreciatively, never joining in. One of the girls explained that several of them sang particularly well. When I asked why they didn't join in, she said: 'In the old traditional Georgian singing, the men and women never sing together, always separately.'

I remember leaving that evening wondering how much longer this polarization between the sexes would last. A single generation full of Mananas could wipe it out completely, but would they really take everything with them as Tamoona feared? The looks of enormous pleasure on everyone's faces in that room suddenly made me think not.

CHAPTER SIX
MTSKHETA

I'd come to Mtskheta, the former Georgian capital, with Tamoona. It would be our last trip together. She said she had two friends in the town to visit, one from her university days and the other . . .

'You probably think I'm sentimental,' she said, 'but I feel its cathedral is a kind of older relation. I always learn something from it.'

For the twenty-minute drive up the Mtkvari River from Tbilisi, a taxi hadn't been difficult to find. The problem came in the driver's baffling refusal to accept my money.

'*Ara*,' the severe Georgian face responded to every diminishing bundle of roubles held before him.

'*Ara*,' to the packs of Marlboro, the rouble's parallel currency and in Moscow an absolute necessity for a taxi.

'Come on, let's leave,' Tamoona repeated. 'You're insulting him. The ride was his gift to you.'

But my upset British standards of behaviour had frozen me to the seat. How could the normal financial transaction between strangers become a gift? Overcome by guilt, I hesitated in the car. What had I done to deserve such generosity? Why could *I* never be so generous myself? Deeply touched, it seemed my only way out of this moral dilemma would be to give in return, but what? I carried nothing but my pen, notebook, cameras and film. Tamoona shuffled awkwardly outside.

'Let's go!' she said with unusual insistence.

Hoping a second *faux pas* would forgive the first, I reached into my pocket and handed him my 79p British Museum pen and opened the car door. He accepted the gift with a sharp nod, engaged the gears noisily and roared off in a cloud of dust. Tamoona gave me one of her rare smiles.

'You English don't understand generosity, do you?'

I admitted that in this case I didn't.

'He liked us. He wanted to show his friendship back,' she said. 'In

Georgia we often do it. It's far more important than money. It was his pride to refuse your money, and I think he was right.'

With a feeling of shame, I confessed he may have been, and wondered why the English almost never expressed affection in this way. What did *I* have to learn here? But Tamoona had already turned away and was looking up at the cathedral keep's crenellated walls. I followed her gaze. Over the wall, the giant eleventh-century basilica of the cathedral lifted into the sky, far more my idea of a 'cathedral' than the others I'd seen in Georgia. Closer to, it gave the impression of the usual Byzantine-style Georgian church but placed in an enlarger – or maybe the people streaming towards it had been shrunk down to Lilliputian size.

'To me Mtskheta is still the capital of Georgia,' Tamoona said quietly, a curious statement since Mtskheta had abdicated that title 1,500 years before and had since reduced itself down to little more than a large village. 'Tbilisi is just the administrative centre,' she elaborated. 'It's got nothing like this cathedral. This building here is placed at the central point of our country.'

Noticing my quizzical look, she added, 'I don't think you know the history of this area.'

But I did have some idea. I knew that Mtskheta had been the capital of Kartli, the kingdom which the Greeks and Romans referred to as Iberia, from the third century BC to the fifth century AD; that this nexus of two valleys had served as a major cult and religious centre for many centuries before this, with Persian, Zoroastrian, Hittite and possibly even Sumerian influences, that there were more pagan temples and shrines here than in any other part of Georgia.

Looking up, I noticed the surrounding hills dotted with churches, each one almost certainly claiming the site of a pre-Christian cult. I also noticed how this huge cathedral seemed to dominate the crucial triangle of land between the confluence of Georgia's two main rivers, the Mtkvari (Kura) and the Aragvi. The cathedral's present-day name, Sveti Tskhoveli (Cathedral of the Life-giving Pillar), could hardly be more pagan. The myths, memories and rich religious heritage of Georgia dripped off every cornice and cliffside in this valley. The mountain overlooking the town, Mount Kartli, still apparently housed the spirit of King Kartlos, the legendary father of the Georgian people and supposed descendant of Noah's son Japhet. According to Strabo (in the first century BC), the area of today's cathedral precinct contained the palace of the former Iberian kings and close by a copper statue of the Zoroastrian fire god, Armazi (the Georgian version of the Persian god, Ormazd), flanked by numerous gold and silver idols. Other reports tell of a colossal pagan statue of Armazi (possibly the same one) dominating the summit of Mount Kartli. The statue has long gone but its Christian replacement still survives, perched high on a rock above the Aragvi River – the sixth-century Djvari Church (Church of the Cross). The rounded dome of this church stood up like an erect nipple, 150 metres above Mtskheta, ready to be suckled by the renewed Christian eye of independent Georgia.

As we stepped into the cathedral precinct, Tamoona crossed herself solemnly. Before us the cathedral lifted its arches from the middle of an open lawn, like a towering Gothic ship moored in a green harbour. Beneath its massive stone cupola and almost windowless stone walls, a stream of tiny Georgian figures poured in and out of the entrance, like shiftworkers in a strange factory of emotions. For me, stepping inside its cavernous, vaulted belly was like descending from the twentieth century to the time of Armazi. Tiny lights flickered in the darkness against luminous icons, while echoing voices bustled around in the gloom. It took some time for my eyes to adjust. When eventually everything came clear, we stood before an elaborate white marble iconostasis, on a floor patched with irregular slabs of stone, engraved with crests.

'These mark the tombs of former Georgian kings,' Tamoona explained. 'The royal blood of our Bagrat family is buried under this cathedral here, and also Jesus' crucifixion robe, which is what Saint Nino came looking for when she brought our faith to Georgia. *Everything* is in this cathedral,' she said quietly, but with heartfelt conviction.

I began to understand why so many Georgians visited the building. They could feel the pumping heart-beat of their 'homeland' throbbing reassuringly just beneath this floor. The Bagrat dynasty had produced Georgia's kings from AD 888 right up until the Russians expelled the royal family in the nineteenth-century. Above the slabs, pious faces, old and young, came to light candles and honour the memory of their last Georgian political sovereign. I remarked on the number of young people among the crowds – many more than in churches I'd visited in Russia.

'There's a religious revival in Georgia,' Tamoona replied. 'Churches and monsteries are opening up, being reconsecrated everywhere. Young people always used to come to church in Georgia to rebel against Komsomol (the youth league of the Communist Party) but the religion stayed with them. Now with independence so close, they come even more.'

As she spoke, I found my eyes fixing on the south wall and an old fresco peeping out from the whitewash. It was almost certainly a vision of the Apocalypse.

Recognizing my attention, Tamoona said, 'Yes. I love this fresco too. It's a seventeenth-century Apocalypse, and I think if it were fully visible it would be one of the most important frescoes in Georgia. Look how peacefully they painted the scene.'

It came across certainly as one of the more sublime versions of the great débâcle, although parts of the picture had been lost. I saw human-headed lions, friendly sea-monsters, cherubs puffing inside the clouds, dancers, lute-players, kings and bugle-blowing knights. To the right a Wheel of Apostles radiated out of the central Christ figure. I asked Tamoona if she'd ever studied the symbolism of this deeply cryptic Christian event.

'No,' she said. 'I want to very much, but it's impossible. But I like to come and stand here because I feel everything they wanted to take away from us is still there.' ('They' referred to the Communist Party.) Then she glanced at me. 'Is that why you're interested in Georgia? You want to see how much can survive our politics?'

For the first time she voiced curiosity about my motives, advancing an unusually percipient suggestion for someone who had never left the Soviet bloc. I remembered when the first stream of post-*glasnost* Westerners arrived in the USSR, many Soviets had been baffled as to why we wanted to visit their crippled economy, save perhaps to see Red Square, Saint Basil's, or the Caucasus mountains. When the tourists kept returning, however, and Sotheby's began selling modern Soviet art for five-figure sums, some cottoned on to the fact that their culture possessed some quality unavailable in the West. I remember one Russian with almost no interest in art arriving in London and informing me, 'I can organize the best art of Moscow's finest artists to be exported to London for the English to buy.' I asked him to describe this art, to explain what it had that might appeal to the Western public. 'We Russians have something you've lost,' he answered boldly, 'and you need it. You want to buy it.' Then he added, 'If you organize the venue I'll give you 10 per cent.'

But Tamoona's sensibility had taken this several steps further. She already guessed that the Soviet (or Georgian) 'forbidden culture' would quickly exhaust its charm in Western eyes; that the curiosity we visitors expressed was partly curiosity about our own culture; that we used the Soviet world as an inverted mirror to see ourselves and, in some cases, as a means of merely boosting our self-esteem at their expense.

It seemed a great shame that people like Tamoona, whose intelligence and insight outshone these jet-setting Soviet officials so many times over, still hardly dared to present their 'fairy-tales' to their friends.

As we made our way around the cathedral's icons she told me we would then visit her friend 'just for a moment'. But I declined – already knowing that, under the protocols of Georgian hospitality, it was impossible to enter someone's house 'just for a moment'. It would end up as a four-hour drinking and toasting festival.

Making the excuse that I needed to take some photographs, I suggested instead that we meet in an hour, after she'd seen her friend.

'I won't visit my friend,' she said emphatically.

But I insisted, telling her I needed to be alone while photographing. Eventually she nodded and a tiny flicker of hurt crossed her eyes.

As I turned away towards the burning blast of sunlight at the cathedral entrance, I was hit by a wave of guilt, that feeling of taking unfair advantage, in my privileged position as drop-in voyeur on her life. Did I really deserve all the time and attention she gave me in return?

Half an hour later, queuing up alone at the cathedral's souvenirs kiosk hoping to replace my pen, I heard a Georgian voice addressing me in heavily accented but good English.

'Pentax are good cameras . . .'

I looked into the face of a clean-shaven, long-nosed man in his mid-thirties, well dressed, apparently addressing my camera not me. 'Could I have a quick look?' he asked.

I decided it would do no harm and handed him the camera. He turned it over in his hands as if appreciating an antique.

'Very, very nice camera, Pentax.' He looked up. 'How much do you want?'

My heart sank. 'It's not for sale,' I said gruffly.

'OK, no problem,' he said and handed the camera back with a lop-sided grin. 'But join us for a toast to our countries – England, yes?'

The idea of a glass of wine appealed. Noticing the group of picnicking Georgians spread nearby on the grass, I realized that the escape route from hospitality would be easy and so I accepted his offer. Within seconds, that instant quality of friendship characteristic of nearly all Georgians had asserted itself. We drank a toast to our respective countries and quickly became embroiled in, as I realized later, a particularly revealing conversation on the new economics about to confront Georgia.

Guessing that he might in some way be linked to the small- or medium-time mafia (as so many people were), I brought up the subject of the 'I'll do you a favour if you do me a favour' system of Georgian business.

'Yes, I know this system we have now is the Soviet corruption system,' he admitted, 'but in Georgia, as you see, we're not poor like the Russians. We know how to use their system better than they do. When we have independence, then we'll start a better system, more like the West.'

'Do you know what our system is?' I asked.

'Yes, it is a normal system, like our black-market.'

I tried to explain that the international economy was vastly more complicated and attempted to present some of the more basic ideas of long-term investment. He started to look puzzled, so I tried another tack.

'The main difference between our economy and yours is that we've legalized your corruption. We've made the middle-man into an honest broker. We've given him a straightforward percentage.'

A crease suddenly appeared on his brow and I saw his mind imagining his freewheeling profits coming under regulation. He grinned nervously.

'Legal corruption, but that's what we've had in Georgia for the last seventy years! Perhaps we will do things a little different from you in the West.' He smiled and put his hand on my shoulder. 'Give me your glass!'

I began to feel myself in the hands of what the Georgians call a *merikipe*, or assistant to the *tamada* – the man who fills the glasses, stokes the conversation, but remains sober. Stalin had apparently been one of the finest and used the spilled-out secrets to orchestrate his dastardly coups against his rivals.

But I also detected a gathering incomprehensibility on the part of the *merikipe*. Like so many, he'd spent his life operating within an economy which bypassed the fundamentals of supply and demand. He would never quite understand my explanation without seeing it in operation.

His argument brought to mind a conversation I had once had in 1988, with Tiit Made, one of Estonia's senior economists. He had told me that Estonia then contained only four economists capable of understanding the international economy. He said that they needed more of such people as much as they needed independence itself, and that this applied equally to all the republics.

One of the great problems encountered by many Western–Soviet joint ventures is that all too often Soviets just cannot trust a system not based on corruption – ironic though it sounds. This is only because they have known no other system that benefited them personally. Long-term investment projects that took five years to make personal profit stretched the imagination too far. All five-year plans still belonged to the state not to individuals or companies.

My camera, I rightly suspected, lay beneath all his argument.

'I'll give you 2,000 roubles for that Pentax,' he finally said. I told him it didn't even warrant discussion. Yet I could tell that as long as it remained before him, so hope remained. Changing the subject, I asked what Georgia would do when, with independence, they cut themselves off completely from the Russians and their subsidized oil, steel, power, technology, etc.

He looked wistfully up towards the Djvari Church. 'It will be hard at first, but we'll succeed.' Then he looked back sharply. 'You see, we have the *will*.'

I asked about the Soviet Army. What would happen when Georgia abandoned this historic protection of its borders against its Muslim foe, the Turks and the Iranians? I'd heard talk of the growing friendship between Georgia's Muslim neighbour Azerbaijan and the militarily powerful Iran. When the Berlin Wall came down, so too, briefly, did this border – and regulations were temporarily abandoned.

He looked back determinedly.

'We are not weak. We will fight if we have to. Besides, the Americans will come to help us.

I told him not to bank on the Americans, but he just shrugged. I could tell this registered as only a minor detail beside the Holy Grail of independence.

Fortunately, I then saw Tamoona approaching and explained I had to go. He looked crestfallen; the camera was about to leave.

'Another drink, another toast!' he cried, but I declined. He opened his mouth to make a final offer on my camera, then stopped himself.

'It doesn't matter,' he said proudly. 'Georgia will soon be trading Pentaxes from Japan.' He grinned and shook my hand firmly.

Tamoona found us a ride back to Tbilisi. On the way we passed a strange picnic area, with tables and benches apparently constructed right next to slabs that looked like tombstones. I asked her to explain.

'It's a cemetery,' she replied, telling me that the tables accorded with Georgian and Armenian customs of Easter feasts on the graves of ancestors.

I asked if she could explain this non-Christian ritual.

'It's not a ritual, it's a custom,' she said. 'We just leave food and wine on the table for the ancestor, that's all.'

Graves with tables and wine.

I asked if this bore any similarity to Mexico's Day of the Dead, when spirits were said to return to the earth.

'My mother says she feels she can speak to them on Easter Sunday,' she said, 'and I suppose when I go, I do have the feeling something is watching me, that I should wear a nice dress, be on good behaviour.'

We drove on in silence. Then, when the car entered Tbilisi, she suddenly turned and asked if I wanted to see her family's grave. 'It's in the Vake district. This car is driving right past it.'

We asked the driver to drop us there. He agreed and again refused to touch any of my money. This time I accepted gracefully.

131

Walking through the grand entrance to Vake Cemetery, I instantly recognized it from Tenghiz Abuladze's film *Repentance*, the film that caused uproar in the Communist Party right up to Politburo level. Even when I'd seen it in London, it seemed to go further than its eloquent denouncement of Beria and Stalinism in Georgia. I asked Tamoona if she'd seen it.

'Of course,' she replied. 'I saw it in 1986, just after it was finished, when you could be put in prison for showing it, even on video.' Then a serious expression crossed her face. 'I think that film told some of the real truth about Georgia, the truth that's still not being told.' Then she brightened, 'But it did win six Oscars!'

Walking through the cemetery brought back the film's unforgettable imagery: the opening funeral-service scene for a high-ranking Party member; the back-handers even as the mourners paid their last respects; then the moonlit scene of a beautiful woman digging this Stalinist (bearing a remarkable resemblance to Beria) out of his grave. It was a painful reminder of the bitter suppression of Georgia by Georgians (Stalin, Beria, Ordzhonikidze were all Georgians), and revealed the desperate need to unearth this terrible past, expose its continuance into the present.

Just as in the film, the cemetery immersed us in an ivy-clad atmosphere of mausoleums, tall cypress trees and grand tombstones. Tamoona led me down its neat pathways, past the black marble with white plaques, proud moustachioed busts, to a modest tombstone enclosed by its own small fence. Next to it, as at many of the others, stood a small iron table and bench.

'This is my grandfather,' she said.

On the gravestone, a ghostly white engraving of a man's face looked back out of the black slate. On the earth covering the grave lay a couple of small crimson-painted eggs. I asked her how they had ended up there.

'They're left over from Easter,' Tamoona said. 'We put them on the earth then.'

Tamoona's mood had changed again; she appeared calmer. I asked why she'd wanted to come here.

'I like this place, I like the feeling here. People have stopped their lying here,' she said. Then she turned to me quite unexpectedly, 'And I suppose after this, now you too will disappear for good back to England.'

I didn't know what to say.

We started back for the road and the bus-stop. Suddenly she began to ask me all about Europe, wanting to know what books were available.

Could I possibly send her a copy of Milan Kundera (I'd created a huge obsession by describing his books)? As we passed the cemetery gates she asked me to tell her about my home in London.

'How far is it from Oxford Street?'

Could I tell her the names of the bookshops on Charing Cross Road? Did I still live at home with my parents (like her)? How much did the London metro cost?

I sensed the desperation in this last rush of questions, kept bottled up during all our previous meetings. I answered them as best I could, as the trolley bus slowly rumbled down the hill towards us.

'You will send me that book?' she asked again, and I saw a flicker of fear in her eyes. Her brief brush with the West was now to vanish – possibly for ever.

I promised her I would, adding that I hoped one day she might come to London and see it for herself. Immediately her eyes lit up as if I'd just handed her the plane ticket. I cursed my stupidity. To name casually the one event she dreamed about more than any other, that she wished for so violently she dared not even think about it, was like opening a wound, or offering a prisoner freedom and then laughing, saying it was only a joke.

By the time the bus door opened, her face was sad again. She said 'Goodbye,' in a quick, nervous voice, then stepped back and the door slid shut.

As the trolley bus drove off, those last words of parting repeated again and again in my mind. They took on the echo of all those millions of quiet, good Soviet citizens rarely met by tourists, the dreamy, shy multitude who stay silent, not even daring to hope for a visit to the outside. What a cruel let-down I must have been for Tamoona.

I craned my neck, and through the murky bus window saw her solitary figure standing by the side of the road, not moving, watching the bus out of sight.

CHAPTER SEVEN

GORI

Of the many cult shrines dotted around the world, the one focusing on the town of Gori in central Georgia must count among the more genuinely surreal. A smallish industrial town of about 60,000 inhabitants, 90 kilometres west of Tbilisi, Gori is a lethargic valley community with little to lift its name out of the dust, save one crumbling castle and one similarly collapsing legend. Yet to its inhabitants, this legend is all.

Gori's fame rests on the sole fact that Joseph Dzhughashvili (Stalin) uttered his first earthly demands here in 1879, born on what is now Stalin Street, to the wife of a cobbler. As the rest of the former USSR attempts to erase his personality cult from the slate of history, so the local inhabitants are still busily shoring it up.

As we drove through the suburbs I thought of all those older Soviet citizens still showing up at demonstrations across what was then the USSR, determinedly clutching posters of Stalin. (During the huge May 1989 demonstration in Tbilisi, marking the end of the forty days of mourning, the delegation from Gori arrived carrying large banners of Stalin's face – to be used, of all things, as a defiant symbol of Georgian independence from the Soviet Union. Apparently it took some persuasion before they agreed to leave their hero out.)

To Georgian intellectuals these actions are a deep embarrassment; to government officials they are an annoyance, especially now as the dreadful past bobs up ever more frequently to the surface. Yet at the same time, the world should never be allowed to forget how this one man from here in the Georgian mid-west completely changed the face of modern politics.

Arriving in the large central plaza of Gori, I looked down the triumphal walkways and gardens, all converging on one tiny shack at the bottom, and felt the first icicle running down my spine. There, lovingly constructed over the two-roomed hovel, stands a Doric-columned temple to protect the birthplace of one of history's most ruthless men. Until the 1930s, this area of the town contained nothing but ordinary streets and rows of houses, of the kind preserved under the temple, but then came the death of Lenin. During the 1930s, as Stalin set about discrediting and eliminating those who criticized his replacement as General Secretary, so the town of Gori underwent a redesign. A huge tract of land in the town centre was cleared of streets, houses and all traces of its former modesty. Several hundred homes were demolished so that this one could shine out from the centre as the glorious representative of the victory of the proletariat. This brick 'hut', as it is often described, now stands at the hub of the town's central point, a focus for the red Intourist buses turning left off the Kutaisi highway and thundering down into the suburbs.

As I wandered around this monumental open space, worthy of any capital city, I tried to imagine the feelings of the locals in the 1930s as they watched their homes being knocked down for the sake of this dictator. But of course, in those days Stalin appeared as very much the opposite, the saviour, the great leader lifting the Soviet Union up by its collar and thrusting it into the industrial age. They believed in the world-dominating master-plan of this visionary politician, understood he had no time for foolish voices of dissent or heartless capitalism. When the propaganda machinery declared Stalin to be the great general who won the Second World War on behalf of the rest of the world, they believed it. To us in the West, now thoroughly aware of the numbing epoch of totalitarian terror in the 1930s and 1940s, the man's name still sends shudders down the spine (as it frequently did to me that day). Yet those former inhabitants of Gori reacted to this redevelopment, as they still do today, with pride. Indeed, when Stalin's body was removed from the Red Square mausoleum in 1961, and all the USSR's Stalin statues came tumbling down, the people of this town mounted a round-the-clock guard on their Stalin. And he remains there to this day, standing before the District Soviet, all seventeen metres of him, the only official Stalin statue in the former Soviet Union.

Deciding that I couldn't take all this in at once, I decided to relax for a moment and buy an ice-cream at a stall behind Stalin's house. Asking for the standard (and only) ice-cream, I noticed a stack of cigarette-packet-sized photographs on the freezer top. As the vendor took out my ice-cream, I gestured towards them. He took off the pile and handed it to me with the words, 'One ice and one Stalin, one rouble sixty kopeks.'

I studied my inadvertent purchase: an immaculately groomed fully mustachioed, black-and-white photograph of the Generalissimo, his chest brimming with medals. This was obviously a souvenir of Gori for the town's many visitors. Slightly taken aback I slipped this pin-up photo, complete with dates, lists of achievements and vital statistics, into my pocket. But the surrealism had only just begun. Behind the small Stalin temple rose another, far grander Stalin temple – the Stalin Museum. With a tall Italianesque bell-tower at one end, the structure dominated the plaza more like a Tuscan seminary than the reliquary of a totalitarian dictator. Constructed in 1957, one year after Khrushchev's famous speech denouncing Stalin, this building has to be one of the Soviet world's most extraordinary legacies.

Unfortunately the irony has now been noticed by Moscow, and today, according to Intourist, the building is officially 'closed for renovation'. But just how closed remains to be seen. Since my original visit (in 1987), I have passed this museum on two separate occasions and each time have seen figures moving around inside, and once a party of schoolchildren being ushered in through the front door.

However, Moscow's directive had then yet to bite. Wandering into the stately marbled vestibule, our group expressed such an ardent desire to see the rest that an impressed official, proud of the local boy, quickly found us a guide. So up we climbed, along the grandiose, red-carpeted stairway to the first floor, which housed all the exhibits, a climb that afterwards seemed as much a descent into the rich and terrible fantasy world of a madman.

At the head of the stairs we found ourselves suddenly bathed in a royal-blue light pouring in from several church-like stained-glass windows. And there to meet us stood a life-sized statue of Stalin, carved in a spooky white marble, his gaze personally greeting every entrant from its dominating position. I could hardly believe it. With all the unconciousness of an act of devotion, the museum-designers had moulded into stone the exact presence haunting every alley of the town and, to a lesser extent, all of Georgia – Stalin's ghost.

In the rooms that followed the ghostliness gathered momentum in the presentation not of the power-craving human being, but a glorious god, whose cult rose to such heights during his lifetime that a Metropolitan of the Russian Orthodox Church once actually invoked Stalin as 'Our Father'.

To enter the building pre-fed on a Western diet of the man's ignominy, and then to find only goodness and righteousness presented, with the monster praised to the skies, is to experience a profound sense of unreality. Here, everything drilled into me as evil or demonic had been twisted around and given a smiling face. On the walls, we saw Stalin the model child, the poet, the striving son of a washerwoman who sent him to the local church-school hoping he would become a priest (a plan he exceeded, but never to her satisfaction), followed by the ideologically pure man.

Our guide, a stern middle-aged woman wielding a metal cane, then reinforced the power of messages on the walls by unleashing on us a genuine dose of Stalinist indoctrination. In her greeting she referred not to Stalin but to our instinct to run away, gesturing to the room's floor, a magnificent parquet with 2-metre-wide bright-red carpet following the walls.

'Hello. I ask you first to make sure not to deviate off the red carpet,' she said in a no-nonsense voice.

Under the extraordinary spell of the museum, her voice seemed to gather disconcerting authority. Suddenly nobody had any intention of straying from the red road. I guessed these instructions were meant as a kind of disciplinary warm-up message from the 'steel' man (the name Stalin, which Joseph Dzhughashvili chose for himself, derives from the Russian word *stal* for 'steel').

As we proceeded around the exhibition, suddenly the sound of a guttural Georgian voice speaking Russian emerged from the walls around us. With no direct point of origin, the voice almost seemed to originate in our own heads (as if we wore headphones). The museum had a hidden public-address system.

'This is the voice of Stalin,' announced our guide, then raised her cane towards one of the frames on the wall containing a poem. 'Stalin's early promise as a schoolboy was remarkable. He showed great sensitivity, vision and poetic qualities.'

Then, raising her voice above the public-address system, she quoted one of the poems:'

A rose bud has just blossomed,
To become entangled with the violet next-door.

To the background sound of the dictator's harsh voice, I wondered how she failed to notice the massive contradiction between these flowery words and the tone of his voice. By now the icicles were creeping down my back, bringing with them that sense of being openly lied to by someone whose sensitivity had been so frightened and blunted that she passed on propaganda without a second thought. Her voice, more terrifying than Stalin's, spoke of that enormous eager submission to authoritarianism that swept the Soviet Union in the 1920s and 1930s. By bombarding the population with Communist propaganda, Stalin cleverly stripped away their psychological supports, then crushed all remaining human curiosity (and independence) under the weight of the disappearances, denunciations and uncertainties about one's closest comrades.

I found myself remembering the time of my arrest in Novgorod for taking one photograph of a town monument – the first time the power of this lie had really hit me. I'd been walking alone around the city and, on an impulse, decided to take a snap of the local District Soviet display-board. No sooner had I released the shutter than a policeman had tapped me on the shoulder with his baton. He beckoned me to follow him to the nearby KGB headquarters, without any explanation.

Stepping inside that miniature Lubianka in Novgorod, two years into *glasnost*, for doing absolutely nothing made me realize with a jolt just how deep this collective paranoia had installed itself. Inside the entrance I encountered another white marble statue at the head of a stairway. This time the face belonged to Lenin, the goatee personality cult so extravagantly promoted by Stalin to divert attention from the power struggle between himself and his rivals like Zinoviev, Kamenev and Bukharin. Lenin's eyes had bored into mine with a single word, 'Guilty'. Although I had broken no known law, I felt guilty.

Not only this, but as we walked down the long marble hallway a hidden public-address system also came to life, playing, for some extraordinary reason, a drear Wagnerian aria. I felt I'd just entered the same surreal operatic tragedy as so many other Soviet citizens before me, experiencing a small taste of that huge unreality known to the millions of human beings who never emerged from these strange moments. My crime had been to walk round a city with a camera alone. The children of Big Brother Lenin did not enjoy this open expression of curiosity; theirs had died so long ago.

The officer escorted me to an interview room, sat me down beside a table bare except for a single red telephone with no dial, and locked the door. I sat there alone, contemplating my 'crime', not knowing what was planned for me. Half an hour passed, then the door swung open and the same officer stepped in and gestured for me to stand up. I was to be released, he told me. He then snapped his heels together and saluted me as he would a senior officer. Pointing at my camera, he shook his head woefully as if to tick off a wayward child. I walked out into freedom knowing I was being followed, realizing at the same time that lone sharks like myself, wandering through their cities, were like the dark unpermitted thoughts lurking in their own minds. Allow them a free, unbridled reign and heaven knows what might be dislodged.

Back in the museum I soon wearied of our guide's voice extolling Stalin's virtues and slipped away from the group, preferring to make my own way among the exhibits. I looked on in growing disbelief as frame

A shoemaker's hovel, similar to Stalin's house.

after frame recorded Stalin's departure to Tbilisi's Theological
Seminary. Here was his induction into revolutionary activities; there he
was conducting Marxist discussion groups, fomenting labour strikes in
major Caucasian towns. They praised him for his numerous arrests for
Bolshevik activities (seven times between 1902 and 1913), without any
mention of the strange brevity of his sentences and his easy escapes
(some have speculated that Stalin operated as an agent provocateur,

paid by the Tsarist police). He appeared as a glowing, cheerful revolutionary, a man of the people and the future. Completely ignored was his deteriorating ability for intimate relationships (Stalin accused his first son Jacob of being a weakling after he failed in his attempted suicide).

At the glorious 1917 Revolution, no mention was made of Lenin's dire warnings about Stalin, or the brutal purges in Georgia after the Bolshevik takeover (carried out on Stalin's instructions by Ordzhonikidze in 1922). This had led Lenin to describe Stalin as 'not merely a genuine social chauvinist but a coarse, brutish bully acting on behalf of a great power'. As for Stalin's major rival, Trotsky, he didn't exist. Instead the walls proudly displayed those now infamous retouched photographs with Trotsky and other political opponents transformed into sections of furniture or whitewash. Stalin's sudden rejection of Lenin's New Economic Policy in 1928 in favour of his own state-dominated scheme of collectivization and five-year plans was praised to the skies, even though an estimated 10 million peasants are said to have died during the enforced collectivization of farms and the terrible famine in the Ukraine, not to mention the mass deportations and creation of labour and concentration camps.

I also noticed the omission of every detail of his vicious witch-hunt after the assassination of his political rival Kirov in Leningrad – the bogus excuse for his new campaign of terror launched against the very members of the Communist Party who brought him to power (Khrushchev believed Stalin arranged Kirov's death himself) – and the 1936 show trials of Zinoviev and Kamenev, their forced and fabricated confessions and deaths.

The next room devoted itself to extolling Stalin's bravery as the victorious general defeating the Nazis in the Second World War. The cabinets were filled with trophies and captured Nazi memorabilia, of course making no mention of the cynical Molotov–Ribbentrop Pact made with Hitler in 1939. The museum had turned into a promenade inside an imaginary Soviet superman's head, passing from great statesmanship, to great victory, to indestructibility itself.

I began to wonder if the museum designers wouldn't attempt to display even this – Stalin as eternal, indestructible and deathless. Stepping into the next room, I realized with another jolt that they had. For now came a room with no exhibits at all – save one: a sombre velvet-lined chamber with a single white pillar rising up in the middle, out of a well of blackness. Placed on this plinth lay Stalin's deathmask, glowing in its own light, like an eternal ambassador from the underworld. A solitary shaft of light burned down from the ceiling to illuminate the features of this old paranoiac, as if from heaven. Finally all the pretences of the museum had dropped away and the cult stood up and revealed itself in all its macabre, cloying adoration.

The bronze mask glinted in the gloom, the face of a weary, self-consumed man, the leader who, at the end of his life, ordered the arrest of all Kremlin doctors (the only people able to cure him) on charges of attempted murder. This was also the man who almost singlehandedly inspired one of the most rapid processes of industrialization in modern history. From being the world's fifth most-powerful military industrial complex in 1913, the Soviet Union rose to the world's second by 1949, and this after a civil war and the calamitous German invasion. This success he achieved, like any clever conjurer, by redirecting people's attention, swiftly undermining their old beliefs and then handing out the crisp new alternative of Soviet socialism. Then, when the old adage about not fooling all of the people all of the time came home to roost, he set in motion his own famous adage, declaring that he didn't care to claim people's convictions any more because convictions could change; fear, on the other hand, never changed.

At the end of the tour I caught up with the group again in the final room. From their expressions of numbed disbelief I could tell that their spirits had already started to flag. All around, the room's plain glass cabinets were filled with Stalin's possessions. As the finale, our guide tapped a glass cabinet to catch everyone's attention for the last point of information.

'And *that*,' she said, pointing to a small white piece of china, 'is Stalin's teacup!' She folded up her metal pointer. The tour was finished.

'But what about the gulags?' said one of the group nervously. 'What about the show trials, Lysenko, the persecution of artists, literature?'

But our guide had little time for these sophisticated points. 'Stalin made a few mistakes too,' she said, 'but who doesn't?'

Stepping out into the light of day brought with it a strange sense of joy. The warmth of sunshine touching my cheek hinted that sanity might exist after all, that another, wiser system of social organization could yet be created somewhere in the world under all that blue sky. Their god was dead and their museum (one hoped) would never bring him back.

As we walked towards the bus I overheard one of our group saying idly, 'Somebody should turn that museum into the *real* Stalin museum, one that tells what really happened.'

It took a good meal at the Intourist hotel and several glasses of excellent local wine to shake off the feeling of having stepped into a black-magic evocation of Stalin's spirit. By the time dessert arrived, I

141

had gathered enough confidence to reach for my souvenir of Gori. Looking at it again under that fierce sunlight from the window, Stalin's retouched face and all those medals suddenly looked quite ridiculous (in fact his face was pockmarked due to a bout of smallpox as a child). Friends in London, I thought, might even find it amusing, and for the first time in my life I thanked God for kitsch.

CHAPTER EIGHT

VARDZIA

Often Georgians would ask why I liked their country; why I kept returning. Perhaps the mountains, they would say; the hospitality; the life-style? Then all too frequently would come the question, 'Have you seen Vardzia?'

Until mid-1989, to visit this cave-monastery right on Georgia's southern border required an almost-impossible-to-obtain permit from the defence ministry. Vardzia is only a few kilometres across the Iron Curtain from Turkey, and the presence of a large military base had sealed it from the public for many years. Yet the yearning tone of this question had always puzzled me. From what I'd seen of the site in a book, it amounted to no more than a tall cliff-face peppered with small man-made caves, deserted now for several hundred years. The caves contained a few frescoes, but they hardly seemed to warrant the book's claim that Vardzia was a 'masterpiece of world culture'. Then Marika, who had obtained a permit, explained that the caves carried some particularly fine twelfth-century frescoes, including a rare portrait of Queen Tamara painted during her lifetime. Then Tamoona, who'd never seen them, had told me about a pool of crystal-clear water hidden deep in the centre of the hill: 'The water is called Queen Tamar's tears. It's like holy water to us.'

I guessed that its years of Soviet military occupation had turned the monastery into a symbol of the forbidden past. Tamoona had even added, 'To really understand our history, I think you must visit Vardzia.'

By the time the Soviets reopened the monument (one wondered why they ever needed to close it) I had heard its name spoken so many times, and with such passion, that when my loyal friend from the Writer's Union, Iraklie, announced that permits were no longer required, I begged him to take me there. Very kindly he agreed, adding, 'I'd like to see it myself too.' And so with Ilya as our navigator, we set out. By the time we reached the Mtskheta junction I was forced to conclude that

Iraklie was no ordinary Georgian, for he drove his Lada with great restraint. With the cupola of the cathedral in our sights, he swung the car's squat nose away from the Military Highway and towards Kutaisi – the nation's second city and former capital of West Georgia. I asked Ilya why he had volunteered to be our navigator.

'I've been to Vardzia before,' he said bleakly. 'For two years I've been there, during my military service for the Kremlin!'

As he spoke he looked up at a craggy, eagle's nest of a structure perched on a hill above the road, then repeated with a trace of incredulity, 'Two years!'

Before the nostalgia overcame him, I asked the name of the passing castle.

'The Ksani Fortress,' he replied flatly.

Then came the beginning of successive kilometres of vines and orchards, with apple, cherry, pear, quince and walnut trees standing beside the road.

'The Ksani collective farm,' Ilya said. Cheering up slightly, he added, 'Soon it will not be collective.'

(Since the election of Georgia's non-Soviet government in 1990 some of the collective farms have begun reverting back to privately owned smallholdings, to correct the massive damage done to Georgian agriculture by Stalin's enforced collectivization.)

Shortly afterwards we sped past Stalin's home town, Gori, then on towards the Surami mountains, the range that historically split Georgia into its two halves: East and West.

'There's another fortress here,' Ilya said, 'Surami Fortress. It has a legend.'

He seemed a bit vague on the legend's details but later, back in England, I saw the film *The Surami Fortress*, by the Armenian film-maker Sergo Parajanov. It told the classic Georgian tale of a young man built into the castle walls to prevent their crumbling, a myth vividly portrayed by Parajanov's use of painterly sets and costume. Its theme – youthful sacrifice preserving the vigour of an old collapsing tradition – is one never too far from the world of Georgian politics, ancient or modern.

But before we reached Surami, Iraklie swung the Lada off the Kutaisi highway and headed south, towards the Turkish border. Suddenly mountains wrapped themselves round us again, this time the Lesser Caucasus. They lifted up furry arms on either side of the road, a more gentle mountain range than their northern cousins with trees clinging to their rocky biceps, and clouds streaking across their snowless summits. Winding between them, our road stuck doggedly to the course of the

Mtkvari River and soon arrived before a well-presented town.

'Borzhomi,' Iraklie announced. 'Where Georgia's main mineral water comes from.'

I mentioned that I'd heard Chekhov came here to take a cure for his tuberculosis towards the end of his life.

'Stalin too,' said Ilya, who then explained that Stalin had his dacha here.

From the car window we saw a narrow ribbon of buildings hugging the riverbank, penned in by the pressure of the mountains. We passed a road-sign to the ski resort of Bakuriani, some 600 metres above us. Iraklie slowed the car.

'Bakuriani is one of the best winter-sports resorts in the Soviet Union,' he said. I noticed new emotion in his voice. 'But you know what happened here . . . ? It was put forward for the Winter Olympics and the International Olympic Committee came here and approved its nomination. But then came the 9th of April and the Soviet authorities suddenly withdrew it and suggested Sochi instead! Can you believe it? Sochi is a summer resort on the Black Sea coast. It has no snow! The authorities said they feared more unrest, but all Georgians know they just wanted to punish us.'

What a cruel disappointment it must have been for Georgia. To host the games would have put the small nation on the map, and given the Georgians a perfect opportunity to charm the world with their hospitality – as is their time-honoured pleasure.

A few kilometres beyond the Borzhomi water-bottling plant came another of those typical Caucasian transformations. We rounded a corner and suddenly the mountains fell away, the cliffsides became hills, the trees disappeared and the grass converted from lucid emerald into a glorious gold pelt, its now dry mustard-coloured stalks glowing in the sun. Through the middle of this newly arid terrain ran the royal-blue shaft of the Mtkvari River, a few patches of green cultivation along its banks. In these few kilometres Georgia had suddenly presented another, entirely new face. I began to smell the presence of the parched Muslim landscape of northern Turkey, now only a few dozen kilometres to the south, and beyond that the extensive Anatolian plateau rolling out ever westward towards the Mediterranean.

With it came images of the numerous traders and camel-trains following this route when it served as part of the famous Silk Road, and of the many great armies that had rumbled through this southern gateway into Georgia – the Ottoman conquerors who swept over in the sixteenth century, then the Russian generals who swept them out again during the Russo-Turkish wars. In the 1870s, it served as the principal supply-line while the Tsar's army pushed deep into Turkey and blockaded Erzurum in 1877. This action has greatly increased confidence in the territory of Georgia, encouraging the population of Tbilisi to double during the last thirty years of the century – a trend which has continued up to the present. Until the 1917 Revolution, Georgia extended another 200 kilometres south from this spot, but today Turkey has reclaimed most of the area, although it still contains a large Georgian population and the ruins of many Georgian churches. Georgia has constantly complained of their mistreatment by the Turks, but to no avail.

At the Red Army garrison of Akhaltikhe we joined the road from Batumi (Georgia's south-western port) and with it a steady traffic of thundering supply trucks heading east towards Armenia, now just 60 kilometres away. After a few minutes Iraklie gave us the explanation in a single word.

'Leninakan.'

Every one of these enormous Soviet-built trucks carried relief for the earthquake victims, a weight of traffic proving that not all Soviet activity in the republics was malicious (a belief held by a good many Georgians who even believe that Russian atomic scientists and not God deliberately instigated the Armenian and Georgian 1991 earthquakes). Looking around at the sleepy amber hillsides, it seemed hard to imagine such a congenial landscape could produce some of the world's most vicious quakes – Vardzia itself was reduced in size by half during an earthquake in the thirteenth century.

But these hillsides had also witnessed another of those enormous, purely human catastrophies. In 1947 Stalin deported the entire local population of Meskhian Georgians – about 10,000 people – to central Asia. They remain there to this day, clamouring to be returned. (Before achieving power the leadership of Georgia's non-Communist government had called for their re-instatement. But once the magenta, white and black flag of independent Georgia flew over the Government Building they suddenly changed their tune, fearing the Muslim Meskhians would re-establish links with the Turks across the border, who still claimed the Muslim Batumi region of Georgia.)

After passing yet another dramatic walled fortress overlooking the highway at Khertvisi, we left our slot in the relief convoy and rejoined an empty road. About twenty minutes later I noticed caves dotted across a cliff to our right.

'Are these like the caves at Vardzia?' I asked Ilya, imagining them as an outlying village.

'This *is* Vardzia,' he replied.

Vardzia caves.

I couldn't believe it. These tiny openings, speckled along the rock-face like a Swiss cheese, were the object of all the yearning statements. Obviously what was once a substantial complex of caves had now been devastated — I assumed by the thirteenth-century quake. As we drew closer, so our view of the cliff improved and I counted nine tiers of caves – apparently there had originally been nineteen – but I had yet to be impressed.

We drove past a large concrete building on our left, sprawling across the hillside opposite the caves like a rogue shopping-mall. 'The

Intourist hotel,' Ilya murmured. We soon arrived at the monument's large car-park, only to find it stuffed to the gills with bus-loads of Georgian tourists. Vardzia didn't look like much but with the floodgates now open, everybody hurried to their much cherished forbidden monument, as if fearing the gates could just as quickly shut again.

A heart-pounding, sweat-drenched climb later (Vardzia stands at 1,400 metres), the three of us stood before the entrance of the old monastery, where, at last, my opinion of Vardzia began to change. We seemed to have stepped into an enormous Stone-Age high-rise. All around us the open-mouthed caves, stone ladders, secret passages and irrigation channels of a former thriving community dominated every direction and revealed a monument a good deal larger than first appearances had suggested. Stepping into the domed bell-tower, tour guides and photographers appeared out of nowhere and buzzed around us. Unfortunately none could speak English, so back they all melted into the gaping black caves and we were left in relative peace. Eventually, I separated myself from Iraklie and Ilya, and walked on unmolested, climbing up and down between the various levels. Finally I arrived in what had been the monastery winery: a long, low cave with elegantly melting window-arches and well-like storage vats carved deep into the floor. The room still contained the everyday furniture of the twelfth century, impeccably preserved as tufa-stone shelves, benches and cave cupboards. Could this be what Tamoona meant by understanding their history – simply imagining the everyday life of Georgia's Golden Age? With much of the interior design preserved in stone, this structure offered a better opportunity than most. Or did it have to do with the central cave of the complex, the Church of the Assumption?

Minutes later I arrived at what had to be its twelfth-century wooden door, with a keyhole the size of a child's hand. After several energetic shoves, it gave way and I stepped up into a large cave, its walls covered in delicately coloured frescoes from the same century. The church was certainly unique with its hollowed-out stone interior cut into the Georgian landscape, instead of perching on top. Its musty, elemental interior was filled with haloed human figures climbing from floor to ceiling, or standing in obedient rows around the walls. Their partially disintegrated forms gave the frescoes the feel of primitive art, like a Christianized Lascaux. The Turkish invaders of 1578 had tried to deface these images of the infidel, and Georgians (including Marika) had tried to restore them. Amid the flying angels and heavenly hosts, two larger-than-life figures of a king and his daughter stood stiffly side by side on the main wall. I recognized the plump, girlish face from photographs and posters all over Georgia as Queen Tamar. She wore a delicate black choker decorated with gems and a crown on her head. In her hand she held up a model of a church, signifying that she was its founder. I looked a this almond-eyed girl with long dark eyebrows and delicate fingers, wondering if it could be true a likeness of the beloved queen?

Then suddenly Ilya came up to me from nowhere.

'Tamar's tears,' he said urgently. 'Come on, quickly!'

He steered me over to what looked like the door of a gaol cell. There we were met by a guard who led us through a shallow arch into a long, low passage heading straight into the hillside.

'You're lucky,' Ilya whispered. 'Most can't come here.'

At the end of the tunnel lay Tamoona's goal: a small, simple pool of water collected under a dripping ceiling, its surface clear and colourless like a sheet of glass. The guard smiled at me kindly and I wondered what Ilya and Iraklie had told him about me. He took my arm and steered me to the pool's edge, then dipped a dirty glass under the surface and handed it to me.

'Drink,' Ilya said earnestly.

Realizing that I had no choice, I swallowed the liquid, expecting some dreadfully mineral, stomach-churning taste. But to my surprise the water tasted fine – unbelievably cool and refreshing, just as all holy water should be.

Back down at the car-park Iraklie and Ilya left me to search for lunch – never an easy task in the Soviet world. I instead decided to hunt out yet more of the Vardzia complex – the part, according to my book, known as 'Upper Vardzia'. Ilya pointed southwards along a winding dirt road, saying I would probably find it down there. An hour later, completely lost, not entirely sure I hadn't wandered across the border into Turkey – the frontier runs only a few kilometres south of Vardzia – I began asking myself just what I really hoped to find on this quest into nowhere, right up against the Iron Curtain. A magnificent surprise, a revelation, or just some old church? What was it we tourists sought as we beat our paths to the far off corners of continents? Suddenly I didn't know. Something had dragged me there, perhaps the same hope that inspired all those Georgians who insisted on my visit, not having seen Vardzia themselves. Like the image of 'freedom' they pursued, did Vardzia as they guessed it have any relation to reality? Sitting down on a stone, looking around at the dry hills I found myself remembering a moment way back in my childhood, standing next to a wall with an older friend, listening to him describe what he saw on the other side. I remembered that feeling of intense heartbreak, of unspeakable injustice that I wasn't just a few centimetres taller and able to see over the top too. It had produced floods of tears and a sense of tragedy. Life couldn't continue until I saw what he could see. Was this the same emotion these Georgians felt in their thirst for Vardzia, and I with Upper Vardzia?

At that very moment came the sound of a revving jeep driving up behind me. 'Border guards!' I thought and, turning round, saw an army-style jeep bumping up the track. I prayed they wouldn't be Turkish. The jeep skidded to a halt and a voice from the cab shouted down, 'Get in.' A thumb jerked towards the back of the jeep. I walked sheepishly around and lifted the flap, only to receive another complete shock for inside, instead of a squad of grim-faced soldiers, I found the compartment filled with smiling, jeans-wearing young Georgian women.

'Come in,' one said, again in English, making a tiny space in the cramped compartment. Another then banged on the roof and the jeep lurched forward.

'From London?' she asked.

'Yes,' I replied, astonished.

'Looking for Upper Vardzia?' asked another.

'Yes.'

'Are you taking photographs?'

Suddenly I suspected Ilya and Iraklie, and rightly so. The girls then explained they had met my companions down the track, and had been told to look out for a lost Englishman.

'So what are you doing here?' I asked.

'We're students from the Tbilisi Academy of Sciences,' said one. 'We're in Vardzia helping to construct a new village for the victims of the Ajaria mud-slide.' (This had been a recent natural disaster in Georgia, completely overshadowed by the Armenian earthquake.)

'We're going to look at a church in Upper Vardzia. We'll take you.'

And so, miraculously back on course, I clung to the roll-bars as the jeep bounced and crashed its way up the track towards my mysterious new goal, until finally it could crash no further. We all then bailed out and walked the last 300 metres to an eleventh-century chapel, the Veda Church, standing forlornly in a forest of weeds. As we closed in, one of the stems flicked back in my face; I recognized it instantly – marijuana. Furthermore, this was not just a few isolated plants but an enormous crop of the illegal herb, worth many thousands of dollars in the West. Wading through the head-high leaves, I tentatively asked one of the girls wearing jeans if she recognized the plant.

'Oh yes,' she replied breezily.

Didn't she feel tempted to return to this field to make a cool profit, I joked.

'No. Why?' she asked. I didn't answer, but instead picked one of the leaves and handed it to her.

'Not even slightly tempted?' I asked again.

She smiled back at me, 'No, not even slightly tempted,' she repeated firmly.

I knew Georgia had its collection of hippies like any other area of the Soviet Union, but these girls never even showed curiosity (or they concealed it well). Arriving at the church, we found it recently re-roofed, but with an untouched and destroyed interior. Looking at that painstakingly saved, then re-abandoned piece of Georgia's heritage, I began to think ruefully about all our varying expectations – and what we found on arrival.

At the end of my muddled symbolic trail I may actually have encountered a genuine symbol: a building whose outer shell had been shored-up to prevent the structure's further collapse, but with its interior left in confusion. Furthermore, a holy place surrounded by an encroaching forest of Westernized weeds, of the kind of consumer culture we now boldly offered the Soviet world. For all my lack of direction towards Georgia's past, could I have stumbled across an icon of its future?

CHAPTER NINE
KAKHETIA

'They say Kakhetia is the happiest, most easy-going part of Georgia' Marika said, then added: 'There is a joke revealing the character of those who live there. An American tourist is walking through the countryside of Kakhetia when he comes across a local man asleep under a tree. "What are you doing wasting your life asleep under a tree," he asks him, "when you could be out using your time more productively?" "How?" asks the Kakhetian. "You could be out working, or studying, or planting . . . " "Why?" asks the Kakhetian. "So you could be rich and then do what you wanted to do," replies the astonished American. "What do you think I'm doing right now?" asks the Kakhetian and turns over, pulling his cap back down over his eyes.' Marika smiled. 'I don't know if it's a completely fair indication of character,' she said, 'but it is where our best wine comes from.'

Either way we would soon find out. Our bus already hummed its way through the Tbilisi suburbs. To our left the rows of white 1970s tower blocks followed the city's eastern ridge like a duplicate Greater Caucasus, to be followed by the huge Red Army barracks (where the Soviet tanks of 9 April were now returned to their deceitful slumber) and on towards this hot south-east corner of Georgia.

Minutes later the bus sailed up over a ridge and suddenly the landscape made another of those abrupt Caucasian about-turns. The colour green was sucked out of the ground and, in its place, the arid Samgori steppe stretched away to a hilly horizon – an almost treeless panorama but, unusually for the Caucasus, encircled not by sparkling white peaks but just peaks. This was my first glimpse of the eastern Lesser Caucasus, the lower deck of the mountainous sandwich that is Georgia. At the end of this valley lay the border with Muslim Azerbaijan, far more of a frontier than the so-called 'Iron Curtain' with Iran some 200 kilometres further on.

Yet the brown, lifeless vista gave off a deceptive message. The huge valley is in fact one endless, well-irrigated, lovingly tended grapevine, sprawling across dozens of kilometres in all directions. At last there was an explanation for why Georgia's reputation as a wine-producer had spread far and wide across the USSR.

A little further on at Ninotsminda, the bus pulled to a halt beside a perfectly walled fortress, surrounding a church.

'This site here is fifth century, with a seventeenth-century brick bell-tower. It's worth a quick look,' Marika announced. We descended from the bus. But no sooner had the heavy fortress gate swung open than a large group of local schoolchildren appeared from nowhere and poured into the citadel all around us.

Dressed in well-starched uniforms with white shirts and vivid red sashes crossed loosely around their chests, these little anarchists immediately found a new and far more fascinating focus for their history lesson – us. Every time I raised my camera at the tower's elegant brickwork about twenty leaping, grinning boys' faces bounced up and down in the viewfinder, with the girls racing up behind holding hands and shouting, 'We luv yeeu! We luv yeeu!' at the top of their voices. Finally I gave up on the monument and turned the lens on them. The immediate squeals of delight sent the teachers into a frenzy, arranging this misbehaving throng together in terms of height for an enormous group photo. Their organization took up the rest of our visit and, as I ran for the bus, I concluded that Georgian schoolchildren were no different to the millions of other joyful hooligans peopling British and European schools.

Back on board, we hurried towards the winepress of Georgia, as vine after vine flicked by. Every so often the view slotted in another perfectly presented castle, perched either on a sylvan mountaintop or, as in the case of the Manari Fortress, on a hillock beside the road. I began to think Walt Disney may have arrived here years ago and set-designed the landscape. But the bus never stopped.

'We have an organization in Georgia called the Society of David the Builder,' Marika explained, 'named after our famous twelfth-century Georgian king. Its members often repair these fortresses now.'

I remembered the Heritage Societies in Estonia. They had been some of the most powerful movements towards independence before the arrival of the Popular Front, groups of citizens fiercely seeking out and restoring their pre-Soviet buildings as if the walls themselves contained their stifled national identity. I asked Marika if Georgians felt these old stones in any way represented the idea of their former selves that needed to be rebuilt.

'Possibly,' she said gravely.

As the altitude increased, eventually the Gombori mountains closed

153

in around us, a minor range dividing Kakhetia into two sections, inner and outer. At the small mountain market at Bakurtsikhe, the bus halted again and I found myself staring at a large shop declaring in bold English letters, 'Half Finished Product'. We asked Marika to decipher this esoteric phrase so far away from any English-speaking buyers.

'I've no idea. Maybe they're hoping for tourists,' she said.

Many Georgians believed a tourist boom would follow independence as automatically as a cart followed the horse. But from walking round the shop, clearly the explosion had not arrived. The shelves stood almost empty and apart from an elegant spear-shaped bread called *shorti*, the market outside showed a similar dearth of produce. I passed one of the most forlorn toy stands I've ever seen: a large empty table offering just four Soviet dumper trucks and four smiling plastic cats standing on their hind legs. Behind them sat a man, his expression as empty as his table. We'd just entered Georgia's 'happiest' province, yet hints of the morose, mountain gloom that prevailed in Kazbegi hung in the air.

But from here the road descended into the more genuinely cheerful valley of the Alazani River – the true Kakhetia. Plantations of roses, geraniums, basil, various fruits and wheat soon skimmed past the window, as the valley extended away to the Dagestan mountains rising up in the west. In this fertile region, once again the fields stitched themselves together with the endless pegs and wire of vines. Village after village passed by, many well known throughout Georgia for their distinctive wines. Inner Kakhetia is cherished for bearing many, if not most, of the best: Mukuzani, Tsinandali, Kardanakhi, Tibaani, Napareuli, Akhmeta and others, not forgetting the brandies such as Eniseli and Gremi.

The abundant cultivation showed no sign of the brutal history associated with this valley. The invading Persian armies had marched through it many times from the south, and from the north the nineteenth-century rebel and scourge of the Russian Army, the Imam Shamil, relentlessly harried the Caucasian Army and this valley, only to melt back invisibly into the Dagestan Caucasus, now just a few kilometres beyond the final row of vines. In 1853 he mustered an army of 10,000 mountain men and surged down into the valley in a valiant attempt to oust the infidel Russian invaders once and for all. The Russians squarely defeated him. But the Turkic tribes of Azerbaijan (Russia was then in the process of conquering large tracts of northern Turkey) sought their revenge so fiercely that he tried yet again the following year, only to be routed once more.

Looking out across this blissfully productive valley, with ears now

Kakhetian Man.

tuned to the gathering storm of political change transforming Georgia and the Soviet Union, it suddenly seemed a very fragile place.

Not far from the village of Tsinandali came another of our scheduled stops: the elegantly shaggy manor house of the poet Prince Alexander Chavchavadze, the nineteenth-century founder of the Georgian Romantic Movement. This proudly preserved Georgian stately home,

155

visited by Lermontov and the Russian playwright Griboyedov (the poet's son-in-law), stood inside a beautiful ornamental garden that included a small zoo.

At the entrance, lagging behind the group as usual, I encountered a stubbornly cantankerous Georgian police officer. In spite of my obvious foreigner's clothing, camera and accent, he simply refused to believe I belonged to the tourist group he'd just let through. All attempts to reason were met with glowering '*Ara*!'s, followed by some strange dismissive hand gestures – or so I interpreted them – towards the ticket office (now closed). I retreated, waited until he returned to his guard's hut, then quietly sneaked through.

Half an hour later, walking out of the house (now an unspectacular museum), I saw him standing in the centre of the drive staring straight at me. He beckoned and, in a stern Georgian accent, said, 'Come!' in Russian. Prudence told me to obey. He escorted me back to his guard's hut and told me to sit down at a small table. As I contemplated the likely results of my crime I saw him reach down to the floor and grasp something shiny hidden beside the door. He then turned round and, beaming ear to ear, held up a bottle of Tsinandali. 'We drink!' he said with great enthusiasm.

To my astonishment, he then filled two glasses to the brim – I noticed the bottle was already half empty – and, breaking into fluent Georgian, he proposed a toast. He gestured for me to stand. When the oration finished – I understood none of it – we both lifted our elbows in the air and down the delicious liquid flowed. A look of deep satisfaction entered his eyes. My crime, I realized, had been forgiven.

Watching him fill the glasses again, I contemplated the sublime difference between the Novgorod police and those of Kakhetia. Both arrests stemmed from imaginary crimes. In Novgorod I'd commited an act of psychological warfare against the state by using a camera unescorted. In Kakhetia I'd simply turned down police hospitality (of the genuine sort). It turned out I'd misread his original series of gestures at the gate: rather than asking for a ticket he had in fact been inviting me into the hut for a friendship toast. This non-Soviet local policeman stuck inside a Kakhetian guard-hut still managed to blend work and pleasure together. But for those officers in Novgorod, the two remained forever separate. As the second gush of liquid raced down my throat, I reflected that here in this hut I experienced that vital difference between life in Georgia and that in the Soviet north. In spite of all Stalin's attempts to institutionalize fear, the Georgians never forgot those crucial moments in life that say, 'The rules be damned', right down to the last police officer.

After the third glass I made some noisy excuses in English, which he in turn couldn't understand, and gestured urgently towards our bus. Finally he nodded and sternly held out his hand. As I stepped out the door his momentarily severe look quickly disappeared to the sound of one final *'Gau-mar-jos'*, the Georgian word for 'Cheers'. For punishment I had received friendship.

As for Alexander Chavchavadze, hero of the Romantic Age, to this day I know almost nothing about him, save he would almost certainly have approved of modern Kakhetian police methods. His renown, such as it was, has been massively eclipsed by another, unrelated, Chavchavadze, Ilya. Also a nineteenth-century poet (dying fifty-one years later in 1907), he had founded the popular nationalist newspaper *Iveria*, which flourished until the end of that century. Now the Georgian nationalist movement had elevated Prince Ilya to dizzy heights, granting him not only his own society, political party and shrine at the Sioni Cathedral but also sainthood.

As the bus lurched forward up the valley I reflected on this quest to create the perfect Georgian man, an invisible, holy, *Georgian* leader to guide the country and its people forward. During all those years of Communism, identity had been attacked furiously in preference for the new global Soviet Man. The experiment had failed. Now identity had to be reconstructed before it could move forward again towards any collectivization of the kind waiting just around the corner in the West, with the increasing federalization of Europe, or the even grander inter-continental 'Green' or 'Environmental' Man. (This call was to return loudly again in 1992, after President Gamsakhurdia's downfall. In the ensuing power vacuum many Georgians felt only a king would succeed in presiding over the country's squabbling political egos. Frantic messages were then sent to Spain where the Bagrat family's most eligible descendant now lived, requesting his return.)

Meanwhile, the bus completed the last leg of the journey into the heart of Kakhetia by climbing up the gentle Gombori slopes into the town of Telavi. As the former seat of the kings of Kakhetia, Telavi retains today's administrative throne and local council (formerly District Soviet). As we wound our way up towards the sunny town centre and its splendid fortified citadel, so a huge square shadow began intermittently to fall across the road. The bus crossed and recrossed it as we climbed the hill. Peering up through the window, I caught glimpses of an enormous, ruler-like tower block rising above the town next to the citadel, and blotting out the sun. But unlike most Soviet tower blocks, this one stood almost entirely by itself, rearing up above the quaintly tree-lined, wooden-balconied town, in an act of supreme architectural machismo. The Soviet planners, having restrained themselves and preserved Telavi's amiable, low-lying skyline, had obviously felt obliged to make up for their sensitivity by spiking the town through the heart with one single monstrosity.

I asked Marika what kind of people inhabited this desecration of all the principles of town-planning. She looked at me and said with more than a touch of irony, 'People like you! It's the Intourist Hotel.'

Up on the fourteenth floor, unwillingly transformed into one of the sinister denizens, I decided that there was only one person who could find a positive advantage in this tower of domination – the photographer. With evening already well under way, I hurried for the lift.

Over the years I'd discovered that in most Soviet hotels, as in the Soviet Union as a whole, the further one strayed from the central nerve centre (on the first floor), so the more backward management became. Usually the top floors of Intourist hotels showed the most signs of wear and neglect. Carpets would expose more threads, service-desks remain unmanned for longer and, most importantly of all, doors to the roof flapped open in the breeze. The Telavi proved no exception. Standing on top of that Kakhetian Empire States Building, surrounded by a circus of swifts diving and swooping in the wind currents, I squinted though the times-two converter on my 300-mm lens (600 mm) at the city below. As I did, I remembered the first time I crouched on a Soviet hotel roof with a long lens, in Yerevan in 1987. Then, as I focused on Mount Ararat, I expected the KGB to rush up and arrest me for spying. Until the end of the 1980s, few Soviet cities offered more than rudimentary, and often inaccurate, maps for tourists. Any map good enough for serious practical use would be good enough to pinpoint communications centres, factories and other military targets. NATO and the West still required up-to-date photographic records.

Yet apart fom that incident in Novgorod, I'd only once before come into conflict with the authorities on matters of national security. It occurred after I joined a group of American Vietnam war veterans travelling in the USSR during the Afghanistan War. Towards the end of the trip, the archetypal blonde Soviet girl had sidled up to me on our bus in Moscow (no one had ever seen her before) and asked, bold as brass, how much I would earn selling my photographic 'Russian secrets' when back in the West. At the time I didn't take her seriously. (What KGB officer, I reasoned, would be so forward?) Very stupidly I made a joke, telling her I planned an early retirement on the proceeds. I'd thought no more of it until a week later, when arriving at Soviet customs. The officer took one look at my passport, ran his finger down a list of names and stopped (I guessed at mine), then told me brusquely to open my bags. Unhappily, the first item he extracted just happened to be a packet of photographs given to me by an 'Afghantsi' soldier, who hoped to see them published in my report. Every one contained a different angle on a current Soviet weapon. Within minutes, the entire contents of my bags had been spread across the customs desk turning it into a supermarket display, and a group of at least eight officers stood around inspecting it. Every so often one would hold up an object and shake his head dolefully (I'd been given numerous military souvenirs by the Soviet soldiers). My notebook was confiscated, cameras fondled suspiciously and film canisters placed to one side. After a good twenty minutes of intense scrutiny, I was taken to one side by a more senior and, I have to say, very charming member of the border police (one of the largest branches of the KGB). He asked with an odd lack of curiosity what I was up to. I told him I'd been travelling with the veterans for three weeks, and what harm could there possibly be in that when not six months earlier the Soviet Army had flown Peter Kosminsky of Yorkshire Television up on to a battle-station in Afghanistan? He listened attentively, then responded with a question of his own.

'Are you a *correspondient*?' already knowing full well of my assignment with the *Observer*. I admitted I was. At this he'd smiled, handed me back my notebook and my film, instructed the officers to seal up my bags, then waved me through, lock, stock and, one could say, barrel. *Glasnost*, I told myself, had finally arrived.

After this, roof-tops in northern Kakhetia and elsewhere lost much of their frisson. Indeed, the only secret up here showed itself as the fantastic suffusion of evening light and clouds, settling down on to the southern flanks of the Greater Caucasus. Their multiple layers seemed to melt into each other like a sea of lifting crimson waves. Dotted across the blackness before them, the tin roofs of the city reflected back like brilliant silver rafts.

One roll of film later, I descended to the dining-room for what was left of dinner. Our group, it turned out, had been waylaid by the locals. A couple of drunken Georgian men, spotting the foreigners, had wheeled fearlessly over to our table, first applying their attentions to the women.

'Dance!' they'd declared in a gruff, grinning English. The women instantly clamped themselves to their seats. Realizing this road was thoroughly blocked, they then turned to the men.

'Come and join us at our table,' they insisted again and again, as our Intourist guide nervously assured us that the tradition of Georgian

159

hospitality fully encompassed such random invitations. Yet, as far as I could tell, the tradition of honouring the guest also seemed to include 'owning' him or her. Our refusals just wouldn't be heard.

I spent a good twenty minutes sneaking in mouthfuls of food between variations on the negative reply as an enormous Georgian hand gripped my arm as if to drag me off to their table.

Fortunately the sound of angry shouts at the host table distracted everyone's attention, quickly followed by the sound of a fist smashing on the table-top and glasses crashing to the floor. I saw several dark hands immediately grab bottles by the neck. From the intensity of the black looks flashing across that table, it seemed certain a terrible fight would begin. This put an end to the assault on our group, as our prospective hosts were persuaded to return to help restore the peace.

This sudden and impetuous passion belied a dangerous streak in the Georgian character, one I would encounter again as the long history of inter-ethnic struggles continued to flare in Abkhazia and Ossetia and then between Georgians themselves in 1991 when families split down the middle in support of or opposition to Presient Gamsakhurdia.

(It is a mistake to take at face value the wide-eyed Georgian claims that until the Soviets arrived their many tribes and internal nationalities always managed to live harmoniously together. After the grand unification of Georgia, shortly before Queen Tamara's reign, the country had de-unified again and split into squabbling princedoms, only to be quickly overwhelmed by invasions of Persians, Turks, Russians and, finally, Soviets.)

The next morning I ventured out on to the streets, past the Tevali police station, where three prisoners weeded the front garden as their guard, a single police officer, chatted idly with his back turned. Beyond it came a charming 'hang-out' café, with large shady patio and ice-cream fountain. I stopped there to open my *Morning Star* (on sale at the nearby news-stand) and read that 'the British inflation rate had risen to 8 per cent', then walked on into the central Iraklie Square, with its enormous National Theatre and high citadel walls.

Within minutes I realized that reports of the relaxed Kakhetian atmosphere had been accurate. As somebody with 'Tourist' emblazoned all over his body (camera, clothing and uncertain direction), Telavi turned out to be the only part of Georgia where nobody asked me to change money, where women and men often smiled when passing on the street, and where several of my photographic victims actually said, '*Maadlobt*' (Georgian for 'thank you') when I secretly (or so I thought) took their pictures. (Former Soviet citizens, so used to the camera as a KGB instrument, are often only too glad to tolerate the innocent snappings of tourists.)

Yet for all its passionate praises from Tbilisi, Telavi possessed another unsettling face. It first hit me during the search for a barber's shop and my souvenir haircut. I finally found one with several 'styles' displayed on the waiting room wall. Yet a quick glance left little doubt as to the preferred look in Telavi, for, dominating all the photos, in the middle hung a metre-high picture of Stalin, his swept-back, shiny locks glinting enticingly at the customers.

Deciding a hat might make a more suitable souvenir, I found a tailor's shop further down the hill and asked the store-owner for one of the distinctive felt Kakhetian caps, still widely worn. Directing me to a large pile, he suggested I try one for size. As I adjusted the cap in the mirror, so I met eyes with the watchful Uncle Joe again, this time staring up at me from a small photograph in a corner of the glass.

Like a paranoiac's fantasy, the totalitarian dictator seemed to follow me everywhere across Telavi.

Mentioning this apparition in the mirror, the store-owner smiled cheerfully and lifted it from the frame. 'Present,' he said in Russian and handed me the photograph. Then in a language I just recognized as English he wished me a 'Happy stay Georgia'.

Stalin appeared yet again in the taxi home, this time pasted against the dashboard. As the clean, 'happy' streets of Telavi drifted by, I began to sense the presence of this man hovering among the details of daily life here, like a kind of absent king. To them he appeared as the biggest, jolliest international leader of all time, who briefly corrected their sense of smallness. His fame served as a kind of adrenaline drip to this remote valley and the great force of the man had entered the inhabitants' hearts and minds as a hopeful reminder of their own unrealized greatness.

As the taxi halted beside a wall bearing the word 'Hitler' scratched in red crayon, my mind returned to Tamoona's dark fairy-tale of Georgia's future, suddenly connecting it to the Bronze-Age myth of Amirani. Is this what she feared, 'freedom' followed by the reappearance of more Georgian Amiranis? More 'big men' and women running out into the open shouting about national socialism, casually dangling Kalashnikovs lest anyone accuse them of being 'little men' or Georgia a 'little nation'? Increasingly, I understood her feeling of profound tragedy. Georgia had indeed once been a liberal, inspirational nation worthy of its poet visitors' praise. Those like Tamoona felt this very strongly, knowing it could easily be so again, if only the dream wouldn't constantly be shattered by this ever-returning, re-arming stock of deluded heroes.

A year later, back in England, I heard a song to Stalin sung at the

Kakhetian festival of Alaverdova, on a Radio 4 programme. Recorded beside the nearby cathedral of Alaverdi, several male voices emitted wild hysterical cries of praise to the glory of their great general. No matter how vehemently my intellectual friends in Tbilisi denied it, Stalin's ghost lived on, not just in isolated pockets of Georgia but in the heart of its countryside.

In the afternoon, our bus took us on a brief tour of the northern valley. We raced over to the magnificent eleventh-century Alaverdi Cathedral (at the time under repair), then on up into the deep green hills and, to my mind, the most beautifully set of all Georgia's churches, the Ikalto Monastery. Surrounded entirely by woods and tall, wistful cypress trees, the tower of the eighth-century church rises above the ruins of a former eleventh-century Academy, the place rumoured to have enrolled Shota Rustaveli as a student. Now the Academy engaged in earnest Platonic arguments only with the encroaching undergrowth.

Inside the church, on the loose with my camera, it came as no surprise to find a nineteenth-century line-engraving of Rustaveli's hero knight wrestling with the almighty panther of the poem. It hung on the wall like any other religious icon. During our short visit I caught a tantalizing whiff of that deep spirit of poetry, so admired by the Georgians as a race, the culture that used to insist that brides learn chunks of Rustaveli's poem to recite to their husbands. I could clearly sense here the unique brand of tranquility that would enable a man to sit down and create his epic verse. I felt at Ikalto one could easily spend days in the the presences of these lost, imaginary spirits of Georgia, those looked for so longingly by nineteenth-century poets. As Pushkin pleaded nostalgically in an 1828 poem:

> I beg you please sing no more,
> The songs of Georgia,
> For their mournful sounds
> Recall for me
> A distant life
> A distant shore.

But not for me on this occasion. The bus summoned me back with a rude blast of its horn. Clambering on board, I found myself greeted by the frosty stares of my companions, who patiently waited for my day-dreaming to end. Then off we flew, like a petrol-fired cannon ball, back to the electronic age.

CHAPTER TEN
SVANETI

The rusted sign beside the road read 'For the 12th Five-Year Plan You Need to Maintain Good Speed and Rhythm'. From my place in the front seat of Ilya's Lada, I watched our driver smile at this quaint tribute to Communism, used as target practice by passing locals. Beyond the car bonnet stretched a glorious sight: a green hobbit-type valley, rich with pastures, vines and citrus trees, leading the eye up to a sudden eruption of mountainside and snowy peaks – our destination.

There would be no problem in maintaining speed and rhythm, for our driver, Temur, had but a few years earlier been Formula Three champion of Georgia.

'Eighth in all the USSR!' put in Ilya from the back seat. I pulled discretely at the Lada's seat-belt. Would it make any difference? This bonding between myself and the hurtling Lada added only a commitment to faith, a faith I feared might grow to full-blown religion in the yawning canyons ahead.

Before us lay the most notorious stretch of road in all Georgia – the 117 winding kilometres up to the much-talked about region of Upper Svaneti. The road was eternally at war with the elements, blocked by the huge snowdrifts of the winter and washed out by flash floods in the spring. Yet the remoteness gave a hefty clue as to why Georgians revered this distant corner of their mountains beyond all others and also why Svaneti is frequently declared the most Georgian part of all Georgia. The dialect is said to be similar to the Georgian language of the sixth century BC. The churches still contain many of their original crosses and icons (most other regions have lost them either to thieves or to the State Art Museum in Tbilisi). The people are fierce and suspicious of foreigners – a reputation they've maintained since before Christ, when Strabo, the Greek philosopher, described the Svans as 'foremost in courage and power'. He went on: 'They have a king and a council of 300 men, and they assemble, according to report, an army of 200,000, for the whole of the people are a fighting force.'

'The Svans are traditional and very proud,' put in Ilya. 'They are also armed. Many weapons in Svaneti. We must be careful.' He smiled widely.

For a traditional Georgian (by our Western standards) to describe other Georgians as 'traditional' implied something more than merely parochial. The word had quite different connotations here to the rather conservative or ossified ones it had taken on in England. It still shone with nobility. To these men from the capital, Svans embodied something they'd lost, or feared losing; an ideal character, a cultural independence – factors well attested by the Svans' survival through the very centuries their low-land cousins had to watch Georgian cities repeatedly sacked and looted. Furthermore, they were a resiliently religious people. Nothing tells more of the modern Georgian ideal temperament than those wide-eyed bronze icons gazing up from the tenth century in the Tbilisi Art Museum, their all-seeing, righteous expressions full of purpose as they spear the dragon, trample the non-believer. Svaneti possessed more icons than any other part of Georgia.

A few kilometres down the road came the first sign of our entry into the land of the severe Svans. I'd been thinking about the horrified expressions of Tbilisi natives when describing Svan driving, particularly Marika's account of their roadside drinking houses, where rather than stop their journey to drink and relax, they'd drink the better to continue. Could it really be any worse than in Tbilisi? The first hint of verification came with a peculiar metal object standing by the side of the road, rather like a mailbox without a door. As the Lada jerked to a halt Ilya identified it.

'Svan religion,' he said ambiguously. I gave him a puzzled look. 'A shrine,' he elaborated. 'A Svan drove off the cliff here.'

The back wall of the black box carried the photograph of a young man and next to it were messages from friends, a few burnt candles and then, to my astonishment, a collection of empty glasses. Below that, halfway down the tubular-steel post came what could only be described as a miniature bar. There was a square metal platform stocked with bottles of local wine, vodka and the legendary (and horrible) Chacha – a locally brewed spirit – all in varying degrees of fullness, ready for the next passer-by.

The irony dial flicked deep into the red when I considered that drunken driving is the primary cause of fatality on this road. Yet true to tradition, Svans still encouraged drivers to stop and drink a hefty toast to the memory of one dead almost certainly as a result of drunken driving. I smiled wistfully. But the smile wore steadily thinner as the kilometres mounted up and more of these grim tributes to road-death

Bottle shrine on road to Svaneti.

flashed by. For all we knew, a heroic young Svan could be stopping at every one of these shrines, on his way towards us... I thanked Providence for the current petrol shortage and the miraculous absence of cars on all Georgia's roads.

The road continued to rise, climbing from sea-level towards its 1,500-metre goal, Mestia, the administrative capital of Svaneti. The dense, dark fir and deciduous forest either side never thinned – a clue to the lush Alpine landscape waiting ahead. I remembered my journey to Vardzia just 100 kilometres to the south, with those barren, utterly brown mountainsides of an entirely different climatic zone. What a difference to this dripping green chaos of leaves, fallen branches and ferns.

It added another tiny notch of credibility to the idea that Jason and his Argonauts may well have visited this same valley many years before Christ, that Georgia was indeed the magical, multifaceted land of Medea and the Golden Fleece. Adventurers like Tim Severin devoted years of their lives attempting to prove this. It was he who sailed a reconstructed *Argo* from Greece to Poti on the Black Sea coast and discovered evidence that the small quantities of gold still found in these mountains are collected by Svans sifting water through sheep's woollen hides staked into the rivers – hence the link with a golden fleece.

As the car switched back and forward up to the long artificial lake of the Enguri dam, so I recalled those centuries before when the road amounted to no more than a muddy track, now lost far below the water-line, its narrow gorges easily defended by the Svans. With the arrival of the Soviets and this vast hydro-electric project, the Svanian refuge finally lost its potency. As a result, the dam is much resented by the Svans, who regard it as an invasion of their sacred land and thus the source of many dilemmas and natural disasters. But they do have at least one tangible cause for concern, with the lake's unexpectedly rapid silting up and the accompanying rise in the water level. Yet, in today's changing Georgia, the greatest protest the severe Svans could muster at plans for another dam has been an occasional hunger strike.

Beyond the lake, the valley closed suddenly in on the road. The river Enguri periodically disappeared and reappeared at the bottom of a deep, guttural chasm. Every so often the road surface vanished completely, replaced by compressed landslide mud and stone. Ilya had now taken the wheel, swerving us blithely round the fallen rocks, all the while doling out more information on the dangerous Svans.

'They have a big problem of vendettas between their families, but only in Svaneti. The Svans have customs like in the middle centuries.'

He explained how the local newspaper frequently reported interfamilial murders, then began telling stories of his own experiences with other Georgian mountain people, once in particular when he joined a group of doctors in a nearby valley town.

'At night, at one in the morning, we have urgent telephone call from village up in the mountains. "Very sick, come quickly," they said.'

He employed a variety of dramatic hand gestures, and each one meant he abandoned the wheel.

'So we find driver and drive for two hours, two hours up this little road to the village, and when we get there, do you know what it was?' His eyes shone. 'You know what it *was*?' he repeated again, turning to look at me, completely forgetting the road. 'A pig! It was a big pig. We couldn't believe it!'

To emphasize his point, he then took both hands off the wheel and jerked them emphatically in the air to the great God of Absurdity, much loved by all Georgians. I waited for a crashing sound as the car hit the rocky verge, then plunged into the ravine . . .

A few kilometres later it almost did. Negotiating another mudslide amidst more heartfelt storytelling, suddenly an almighty thud under the engine stopped the narration dead. The front wheels of the car reared up and then thumped down, accompanied by hideous scrapings and crunchings that shuddered down the length of the chassis. When the car finally gound to a halt we looked at each other in stunned silence, praying that the damage would not be as bad as it sounded – for without doubt Ilya had run right over a serious boulder.

But this time my prayers failed. A quick inspection of the car revealed the left-hand rear wheel locked solid. We couldn't continue. We had a major transmission problem in the high Caucasus, 40 kilometres from the nearest village, on a road almost traffic-free, with night approaching. But my companions took the situation boldly in hand. Without a moment to lose, they'd removed the offending wheel and, finding nothing but the frozen drum, began trying to free it by hitting the casing with a heavy tyre iron.

The sight of these two earnest Georgians thrashing an innocent piece of metal induced a moment of speculation on the national character. Some instinct drove them to activity at any cost, as if this was an antidote to all the years of lassitude following the Stalinist terror, that uniquely Soviet paralysis where doing nothing is always the safest.

As the clanging grew more desperate, it seemed almost certain that our journey had now reached its end. The nearest well-equipped garage lay down the road, not up. The inevitable hitch-hiking direction would take us away from our goal, back towards Zugdidi on the plains below. After all those frantic preparations, time taken off work, searching for petrol in Tbilisi, my attempts to see this fantastic medieval kingdom had been dashed. But perhaps I, the humble guest, should take just one extra glance under the car? Might it be something as simple as the handbrake?

'No!' came the reply from the other end of the tyre iron. But ignoring the advice, a brief scrutiny revealed this to be the case. The rock had merely bent one of the brake-cable supports. Surely if I disconnected the entire handbrake, the wheel should free. The banging halted and wearily the driver/mechanic consented to look. Then came an amazing change of heart.

'Yes!' To be followed by more instantaneous action. None of those self-deprecating 'Oh, I'm sorry, You're absolutely right's, which I would have expected from the English. These Georgians simply switched from angry, frustrated mode to the opposite, without the bothersome in-between of apology.

It brought to mind another puzzling reaction. A month after the terrible 9 April slaughter of Georgian demonstrators, the nearby school on Rustaveli Avenue reopened, only to find many of the children mysteriously ill. Fearing residues of a toxic riot gas, the authorities immediately closed the building and an international delegation of doctors, already in Tbilisi, began an investigation. They found that once home, the children quickly recovered, symptom-free, and reached a unanimous verdict that the illnesses were psychosomatic, picked up fom the teachers' and parents' constant anguish at the original gas-poisoning. The illness even possessed a specific medical name and etiology. But, interestingly, not one of my Tbilisi friends (including the sensible intellectuals) had any truck with these findings – although they trusted everything else from these doctors. They preferred their own interpretation, that the Soviet gases held properties unknown to Western scientists, that their ugly effects were specifically selected to deter future separatist protest among the Georgians. I found it impossible to find anyone who did not hold this conviction.

The wheel repaired, we soon bumped cheerfully along as if nothing had happened. Below the Enguri River changed colour from muddy turquoise to boiling white, and the road's course took on an increasingly desperate air. Back and forth it crossed the Enguri, at times swinging out over the angry glacial water propped on spindly concrete struts, or slinking nervously under huge hanging bulwarks of mountainside. Occasionally it disappeared altogether into unlit, roughly hacked tunnels in the cliff, with water streaming from fissures in the walls.

Although the road seemed empty, every so often a furious, horn-honking Lada would come up against our rear bumper, a young Svan driver wearing the traditional grey felt cap, gripping the wheel determinedly. A few seconds later he would roar past, bouncing and swerving between the potholes as if Armageddon had just been announced. Even our racing champion smiled and shook his head in admiration.

Eventually the switchbacks relaxed, the forest eased off and the occasional long-haired pig sniffed its way beside the roadside – a sure sign of human habitation. Then came an open field, then another, with more space overhead, glimpses of brilliant white snow between the clouds and a growing sense of achievement inside the car. We'd finally made it, amazingly, into the high mountain grasslands of Upper Svaneti.

And very quickly the atmosphere changed completely. The landscape opened out into one huge, deep green valley, flanked by jagged peaks. The earth showed an unexpected level of husbandry. Fields of wheat, maize and livestock inserted themselves like patchwork into the universal greenness. Then the eye picked out tiny brilliant specks of colour dotted across this giant billiard cloth. The specks, slowly crossing hillsides, were women working dressed in their vivid traditional colours. As we came closer we saw flashes from the silver scythes as they sliced down hay for winter fodder. Closer yet, and snatches of their songs drifted in through the Lada's windows. Stone walls popped up at the roadside and occasionally we passed some of these women, their foreheads bound with black headscarves like nuns. In a farmyard beside the road a couple of bullocks pulled a crudely made sledge across the concrete – a reminder of the long, cruel winters never far away.

Such great change in so few kilometres. Then rounding a corner, came the startling sight for which Svaneti is renowned all over the former Soviet bloc: a sudden row of tall stone towers rearing up out of the landscape for no apparent reason. At heights of between 20 and 25 metres, they loomed over the first village of Upper Svaneti like a squad of alert warriors. This abrupt and strange new civilization coming at me so unexpectedly, and in such an inaccessible valley, set my heart pounding. The monuments seemed so distant from our own time, yet there they stood, dapper and well maintained, playing an integral part in the modern community.

Most of these towers dated back to the twelfth and thirteenth centuries, but some were as old as the first century BC. In Europe only a handful of such family towers still remain in Tuscany, but remote Svaneti possessed over 200, most still used by their owners. They

169

served as a defence against avalanches and enemies, and carried a top-floor room equipped to last out a long siege or several snowbound weeks. Around these ancient keeps, the modern family homes clustered under their tin roofs, clinging like temporary lichen to these rocks of the past.

The Lada pulled to a halt and we stepped out the better to receive this first impression. As I reached for my camera, a sudden shaft of orange sunlight sliced through the clouds and ceremonially knighted the tower-tops with a golden sword-blade. I fumbled frantically with my lenses, as images of Crusader-like inhabitants bearing broadswords and shields rushed into my head. Under that unearthly spotlight, time seemed to have bent back on itself; our Lada had turned into a time machine. We'd mistakenly driven back 400 years to stand like stunned intruders in some virginal, unspoiled epoch.

Such total enchantment is the stuff of travel; moments stepping over the rim of your own world into the fantasy realm for ever lurking just outside.

These fanciful thoughts were abruptly brought back to reality by nearby electricity pylons and a rusting Soviet caterpillar tractor left starkly in the middle of a field. Yet such a paroxysm of romanticism prompted a moment of thought on my role as ambassador from their future. The Svans had always had a reputation for distrusting visitors. Russians are even less welcome here than in the rest of Georgia. Could this vendetta-troubled people be right to suspect me too; to suspect that the culture I represented – now on the verge of taking over where the Soviets left off – might conceal even more devious intentions? In places like this one can never quite trust even one's best intentions.

Directly ahead stood the first village of Upper Svaneti, Latale, its clean towers now standing out crisply against the dark valleys beyond. As we drove towards it giant Soviet-built tractors thundered past us on the road, their trailers piled high with cut hay, spilling across the tarmac. These two epochs of man seemed to cohabit crazily side by side. In this land where the wheel and television arrived in the same human lifespan, its people had simply grabbed hold of the modern machinery and used it as an extension of their own primitive system. When the diesels broke down, the Svans simply abandoned them right there in the field, just like another old sledge.

A few kilometres later we arrived in Mestia, not so much a town but a large village of some 2,500 inhabitants, its centre one of those architecturally dead Soviet impositions – a statue of Lenin, a pathetic ornamental park now brazenly grazed by pigs, and a wide characterless square, refreshingly free of cars. On arrival, our car was the only one and my companions, leaving me behind as guard, immediately embarked on a search for the Communist Party chief, who apparently expected us. With the Lada finally parked and my two companions off and looking, the atmosphere of this mountain community began to settle in.

The only sound came from a wedding party taking place under a large clear-plastic tent directly ahead. Out of this mountain marquee a series of amplified ballads drifted nonsensically up into the evening air. The songs, occasionally punctuated by gunshots, lifted upwards like wisps of jangling smoke into the huge mountain stillness. All ceremony here seemed futile. The tinny noises of this human celebration were quickly mopped up by the huge, skimming clouds, as if by celestial blotting-paper. High above everything, poking occasionally through those drifting wet wads, the peaks glimpsed down with chilling indifference, rather like a distant heavenly government. In the face of so much eternity, of what concern was humankind? On the street a couple of girls strolled towards the music, their faces plump and pretty, hair blonde, eyes light green, cheeks apple-red due to the extra haemoglobin at this altitude. Again, this was an unusual sight as most Georgians are now dark, having mixed with the Turkish and Persian cultures to the south. Yet according to Georgian lore this blonde characteristic of the Svans is the sign of truest racial purity, achieved only by their centuries of privileged isolation.

With the Communist Party chief nowhere to be found, inevitably we ended up at Mestia's Intourist hotel, newly founded on a hillock overlooking the town. Like most modern buildings in Svaneti, it jarred uncomfortably with the old stone architecture.

Inside our room we discovered the obligatory already-playing radio and both fridge and television. Ilya was deeply impressed.

'A fridge here! My God! A TV!' He grinned at us. 'But don't work, and don't work.'

He seemed to know by instinct, for he was quite correct – neither worked. Anything Soviet, like this hotel, was in his eyes automatically damned. At the reception desk we met a couple of East German tourists being turned away from the virtually empty hotel because their visas failed to mention the word Mestia. Ilya couldn't resist poking fun at Soviet regulations.

'My God, it's so serious. No word in their visa! They are *spies*! Yes, I can tell they are spies!'

I couldn't help siding with this cheerful Georgian mockery. What a situation for these holidaymakers. As if Mestia held any Soviet secrets!

Georgians quite rightly followed their instinct for natural law and ignored as much of the outdated legislation as they could do safely. Most secretly regarded Soviet authority as a rather stupid, blunt-headed schoolmaster, his heavy discipline all the better for encouraging disobedience and delinquency. (Some observers of the new Georgian non-Communist government described it as if the students suddenly had been put in charge of the school.)

Out on the hotel balcony, the small town stretched away below, its rows of towers sticking up out of the earth like the fingertips of the long arm of Svan tradition reaching down beneath the soil. They were dotted randomly across the valley, like enormous signposts to the bottomless history of this race. Archaeologists have found evidence of Svan communities from the second millennium BC and theories abound as to their connections with the great early civilizations. Two Svanian villages bear the name of the Sumerian water god Lakhamu, and other links have been made between the languages. The pagan Svan sun god, Lile, is often paralleled with Enlil of the Sumerian sun cult and today villagers still sing songs opening with the words 'O Great White Sun'. In today's Svan churches one finds Christian crosses adorned with rams' horns, and several with pagan animals built into their walls, wholly out of keeping with their Orthodox Christianity. For a nation as invaded, conquered and intermixed as Georgia, this small community's direct link to its ancestors of 5,000 years ago is indeed a remarkable feat.

In those distant centuries the Enguri had served as a lifeline to this mountain sanctuary for the many escaping persecution below. The region's inaccessibility – almost completely cut off in the winters until this century – proved an impregnable defence and thus the villages and language survive. The only nationality to redirect the culture with any permanence has been the Soviet Russians, who brought the road, the gas pipeline, the television transmitter, the air strip and the wheel (not needed before as carts are useless in the deep snow), all since the 1920s.

Over a crude supper at the Intourist restaurant – operated by the same girls who made the beds and ran reception – we discussed the problem of depopulation now threatening the community. With the arrival of the road, television and visitors, young Svans have inevitably gathered a taste for the wider world beyond their valley, beautiful though it may be. Furthermore, the severe winter of 1987 brought down a number of terrible avalanches and over seventy people died, most of them children at a school high in the mountains. This left a bitter scar on the superstitious population and helped invoke the largest exodus of young in the region's history. In 1988 an estimated 4,000 left, dropping the population to around 12,000. Today, teenagers ask themselves what they can achieve by remaining so idyllically cut off and so apparently threatened, a fact that seemed to worry Ilya from Tbilisi.

'It's important the Svans keep one child, one brother only in the valley. The Svans feel this too. It's *very* important to preserve the tradition.'

Then the meal arrived. A bowl of murky soup concealing (for me) hideous lumps of sheep's stomach was placed in front of us – as unappetizing a sight as I'd ever wish to see. But my vegetarian palate was saved by a delicious spicy bean dish, bread and, of course, many full glasses of vodka and wine.

As Ilya succinctly put it, 'We've arrived. We must drink!'

Temur and I readily agreed and downed our glasses, toasting firstly to 'friendship', then to 'independent Georgia', then to 'all the women of the world', and finally on down to the dregs of two vodka bottles and several wine bottles, at which point even the entrails seemed to smile back. Following Ilya's gallant lead, we obeyed that time-honoured Georgian convention of gaiety at all cost. Soon Ilya was telling stories about the shortage of alcohol up north, 'in Russia', as he often called the rest of the then Soviet Union.

'The Russians have a new favourite. I read it in the newspaper. Three shots of insecticide, one of eau-de-Cologne in their beer – delicious!'

I then proposed a toast to Georgia's wine-soaked region of Kakhetian, not realizing this fell outside the domain of tradition toasts. But nobody minded. One clear difference between Georgia and its northern neighbour are the shop shelves, nearly always stocked full with cognac and wine. In Moscow, queues quickly form round the block at the merest sniff of spirits. While the Georgians like to drink, alcoholism is rarer than in the north. As a consequence, we all had the benefit of a profound night's sleep.

The next morning the search for Svaneti proper began. The trail led first to the doorstep of a cheerful, ruddy-faced official from the Mestia Museum, called Shadur. Contrary to my expectations of the Svans, he greeted us with a burst of heady Georgian good nature. This soon evolved into violent enthusiasm for our visit. He led me into his office, sat me down at a desk dominated, for some reason, by a giant green apple, and then asked me my official business.

'So you've come to discover Svaneti,' he said factually. 'You've seen Ushguli yet?' He looked at me earnestly.

'No,' I answered. Noticing my eyes straying towards the huge apple, he suddenly reached over and thrust it into my hand. Not knowing what to do and in a fit of embarrassment, I took a bite. The moment I revealed my awkwardness his eyes lit up.

'We go today!' he announced. 'Ushguli are the highest villages in Europe. You cannot visit Svaneti without visiting Ushguli. Impossible!' In the light of such determination, we surrendered willingly.

Ushguli

Back in the car, now with Shadur in the back seat, everybody agreed that celebration was in order. We drove to the car-park of Mestia's largest restaurant, dominated by a rusting sign depicting an Aryan boy and girl speaking a message in Georgian. I asked Ilya for a translation. He looked at it distastefully. 'We are friends of Lenin's business,' he said flatly. No one showed any surprise when the kitchen staff appeared not to have shown up.

His tone of voice reminded me of a Georgian friend at the Leningrad television studios who in his moments of frustration (television in the former USSR is a minefield of complexity) would explain the dilemma thus:

'There are three types of logic in this world. Logic logic; women's logic; and Russian logic. *That* is Russian logic!'

With lunch temporarily off the agenda, Shadur asked if I had any specific questions about Svaneti. So I asked about the reports I'd heard in Tbilisi of Svan snow ceremonies in the winter: tall pagan towers built of snow, to ascertain the direction of the best harvest from the direction of their fall.

'Yes, it happens in Latale and Legere villages, two days at the end of February.' Then as if purely on impulse he said, 'We go now!'

So, with Ushguli placed on hold, the car was redirected back down to the village of Latale on the border between Upper and Lower Svaneti, the place where I'd first seen the stone towers. As we drove up the track to the house of the protector of Latale Church, Shadur turned to me and with some pride said, 'Latale is an important village. Latale means "guard". This is where the feudal system of Lower Svaneti used to end. Svaneti has always been free. Svanetia is pure Georgia; no Persian influence, no collective farms.'

I began to wonder if a method lay behind his apparent impulsiveness. We would begin my tour right at the border of Upper Svaneti, and then proceed in ever deeper and deeper. Or was it simpler than that? To begin at someone's home in Svaneti would, of absolute dire necessity, involve a major dose of hospitality, and in our case this would be lunch.

At the gate of the house, Shadur introduced us to a mustachioed man of about sixty. 'This is Marlen Tamliani. He is the head of the family,' he said with some gravity. The institution of the family stood at the centre of Svanian life and, at its centre, stood the proud figure of the father. But this hierarchy also applied to the village. The family entrusted to guard the church, the village's most holy place, was ranked close to the top. Furthermore, with the recent epidemic of thievery most churches could no longer leave their icons inside. Svaneti's unconquered valleys meant their churches still possessed many old and highly valuable icons, that anywhere else would end up in museums. It also meant the guard's families would have to be well armed. It didn't take long to click that Svaneti's official Soviet police force played a secondary role in these traditional twelfth-century forces.

Before lunch Marlen produced several of Latale's icons and allowed me to photograph a beautiful tenth-century silver processional cross with cloisonné enamel faces. Ilya whispered to me, 'Pete, you are lucky. This is very valuable. Maybe we are trusted.'

At the table, several plates full of cheese, tomatoes, cucumbers and meat quickly appeared. I also noticed three jugs of local wine, one of vodka and another of the dreaded Chacha. Before I had a chance to line my stomach with any protection, the toasting began. First, as was traditional in Svaneti, came 'The Great God', second 'The archangel Gabriel' and third 'Saint George'. After that they resumed, Tbilisi-style, with toasts to 'Friendship', 'Our nations' and 'Independent Georgia'. Marlen then introduced the topic of the Second World War, speaking about his own role in the battle against the Nazis in 1942, when their southern front advanced towards the oil fields of Baku, to be 'stopped' just over the mountains from Svaneti. Making the point, he took off his felt Svan hat and shook it in the air as he spoke. Thus a toast was called for, partly to diffuse the emotion, partly to enshrine it in the halo of this great victory. He rose to his feet and we all stood with him. 'To Stalin, our great General!' he said. By then I simply raised my glass with everyone else. Ilya then explained that Stalin's mother had never let him forget his Georgian roots and he'd always carried a soft spot for the Svans.

Meanwhile, Shadur and Ilya began to toast earnestly to their new friendship, and it came to me that in Svaneti this ceremonial descent into drunkenness amounted to a formal treaty between strangers. And in the valley of vendettas trust, for a stranger like me interested in their priceless icons and treasures, could hardly be more valuable. As Ilya was to say later, 'Pete, Svaneti is Wild West. Nobody protect you. If we disappear . . . God save us!'

After this, in the end, largely liquid lunch, we stumbled our way up the adjacent hill to Latale's Maksvarisi Church. The picturesque chapel is renowned for its twelfth-century frescoes, but tragically all I remember are a number of magnificent blurs, plus a pagan-like cross covered with rams' horns. Far too much vodka and Chacha swam between me and any discerning faculties. After I had photographed Marlen in his splendid traditional dress, we stumbled back down the hill and into the car.

With Shadur, Ilya and me unashamedly drunk, the driving fell to the faithful Temur. He steered the Lada at Shadur's directions, back to Mestia then up on to a dirt road heading straight for the massive but invisible, 4,990-metre shoulder of Tetnuldi mountain, at the head of the valley.

'Ushguli, this way!' Shadur pointed drunkenly towards the cloud concealing this snowy giant. But, as we found out later, the upward angle of his finger hardly exaggerated.

As the fields rattled by, I tried to make conversation with Temur, asking him about his life and profession as a psychiatrist in Tbilisi. However, I experienced serious alcohol-inspired language difficulties. Noticing my problems, Ilya helped out. 'Temur is a *Tartar*. A Tartar from California!'

The car splashed through fresh puddles, crunched over gravel, dipped and lurched into potholes, in another severe test on the Lada. As the damp valley passed by, the landscape appeared not unlike Switzerland before the arrival of tarmac: fields laced with dirt-tracks, in turn leading to balconied and well-eaved houses, politely dotting themselves across hillsides, each one a self-supporting unit; meadows that in the spring could be found carpeted in wild bluebells, cornflowers, and anemones. But all comparisons with the Alps instantly evaporated at the sight of another Svan village with its remarkable cluster of medieval towers. Such a fantastically intact twelfth-century presence, returning kilometre after kilometre, could belong to only one region on earth, even within the Caucasus. The towers of other districts, like Ossetia just over the mountains, were now mostly crumbled and of a different design to the crenellated Svan tower.

Meanwhile, the road began to climb up steeply, out of this valley towards the next. At the top we looked down into another deep-green gully containing a small village, a few towers, some more raggedly cultivated fields, all dominated by a church sitting on a hillock. There were no more obvious Soviet-built edifices and the road began to fulfil its promise of winding us back through time. 'Nakipari,' Shadur said to me, indicating the church, 'the Church of Saint George. Twelfth century. We will see it now.'

We arrived in the village at the same time as a violent mountain downpour and an East German film-maker called Rolf. Rolf had heard about our mission and decided to tag along in his own jeep, in the hope of opportunities to film. Meanwhile, Shadur hurried off, seemingly undaunted, into the torrent and returned, dripping from head to foot, with a man clutching an enormous bunch of keys.

'This is David,' he said, introducing the man. 'He is the church protector.' I looked at the keys, some at least 15 centimetres long, not only pre-Revolutionary but possibly pre-Russian as well. He spent a good fifteen minutes sorting out how to undo the numerous chains, locks and devices barring thieves from the church. While we waited, I asked Rolf about his luck trying to film the suspicious Svans.

'It's been very hard,' he admitted. 'I've been coming here for four years and still need more.'

He said gaining permission to film often involved long drinking sessions and such permission could be revoked on a whim. 'In one village they wouldn't let me take the Saint George icon out of the church because they said it would rain for a month.'

We walked round the building and he pointed out the pagan symbols of a stag's head, deer and a mountain goat carved prominently on to the outer walls: symbols most other Christian churches had long since removed. There could be no denying that here the two religions thrived side by side, with Christian gods doubling up as their pagan predecessors: Saint George also spoke for the moon god; Saint Barbara for the sun god, Lile; and the archangels for the protective spirits of the mountains.

Finally the doors gave way and we stepped into an almost completely dark chamber. As my eyes gradually acclimatized to the gloom, so holy figures and strange deep-red areas loomed out of the blackness. First I noticed a spread of silver halos dancing across the firmament, then the saintly faces slowly filled in beneath. Finally the figure of a huge seated man, dominating the entire dome of the church – the Great God – emerged to gaze at us from his heavenly chair like a mountain king. Dressed in shadowy greys and burgundies, he held up one hand for attention, while the other spread open a copy of the Bible. Behind his head, the haloed saints receded back towards infinity.

For the first time in a Georgian church the totality of the art struck home. For here, unlike in other fine centres of fresco art — say, Vardzia – the paintings remained virtually unmolested since their day of creation in 1130. The images stood faithful to the vision of their creator – Theodore, the court painter of Georgia's celebrated King David the Builder. These little-known 900-year-old frescoes must rank among the best-preserved examples in Christendom. I saw again the vivid depiction of the tortures of Saint George, with the image of a human body stretched across a wheel, a grim illustration of the torments of faith, his inner and outer persecutions elegantly represented by an imperiously robed Diocletian commanding his torture. Next to this came two wonderfully fluid portraits of Saint George and Saint Theodore heroically slaying both Diocletian and a dynamic-looking dragon – the symbolic vanquishing of wild pagan emotions. But in this church I couldn't help but feel the stern overhanging presence of the non-Christian mountain gods. The background colours of the frescoes had been painted a primitive dark green and black, with edges outlined in Arabesque red-and-white geometric patterns. I could sense the influence of the distinctly pagan ceremonies still held outside the church at weddings, funerals and some saint's days. As in most Svan churches, I stood immersed in a magnificent, three-dimensional, cave-like portrayal of an ongoing pagan Christianity.

Looking up at it all made me think of the churches of my childhood in England. How slender was the connection with the religious feelings I had experienced at that age. In our churches the iconography of God had refined itself away deep into the walls, far too remote and adult an image for the child to grasp. But here, in this mountain church the forces of nature glared back full of their resolute purpose – to overwhelm their viewer. Up here I felt God had not yet been tamed by man, something almighty hung over everything. God was indeed still 'great'.

As if to prove it, David then unlocked the church safe and pulled out a solid golden chalice along with a bottle of milky liquid. He poured this ominous fluid into the chalice, then pronounced a long toast in Svan language, 'To the Great God', praising his power and domination. With a sense of foreboding I began to realize what would come next, and dreaded the end of his speech. Finally he stopped speaking, lifted the chalice into the air and, gazing at the great figure in the ceiling, downed the stuff in one gulp. Then, with eyes rekindled, he filled it again and handed it straight to me.

Holding the solid gold chalice, staring at the terrible bleach-like liquid, listening to another long toast in the strange, soft-sounding language, my mind raced through every possible excuse to avoid this horrible refreshment. Take a sip, not swallow, then hand it back ... and faint? The demons of invention span in hopeless circles and, too late, for he finished his speech and immediately two sets of fierce Svan eyes glared at me. A swift glance at Ilya's face brought back memories of vendettas, the easily offended Svans, and informed me I had no choice. Lifting the chalice briefly towards the Great God, I tipped the contents into my mouth and gulped. My throat roared out as burning red-hot knives seemed to shoot down to my stomach, then fire out tiny missiles and bomblets throughout my abdomen. With eyes watering, I concluded it definitely tasted like bleach. Then to my horror David refilled the cup and handed it back to me. Accepting defeat, I closed my eyes, prayed deliverance and knocked this one back too.

Perhaps the Great God heard my prayer because David then turned to Ilya, who, with the dedication of a true friend, took over my duties as guest. Quickly I pleaded the excuse of photography and, stepping outside the church, found myself instantly drunk – again. Dimly I noticed the rain bouncing off my head in joyful splashes but realized, like a true Svan, that water didn't matter any more. I'd lost all fear for my health, which was just as well, for the damage had already been done.

Back in the car, I asked a noisy Ilya how many gold cups he'd drunk in the end.

'Five,' he shouted, then grabbed my Walkman, slotted in Miles Davis, and began thumping his feet loudly on the Lada's floor. A couple of minutes later he removed the headphones. 'Pete,' he said with a look of sudden enlightenment, 'I think that liquid was also twelfth century.'

Nevertheless, he survived it, while I, one day later, came down with a mysterious, gut-gipping fever – for which I hold this supercharged holy water totally responsible.

Night approached and the Lada splashed on through heavy rain up the valley to the village of Lalhor. Here we pulled into the drive of a large private house with a balcony. 'We stay here,' said Shadur emphatically.

'But they're not expecting us,' I whispered to Ilya.

'Don't matter. This is Georgia. No problem,' he replied, then added more quietly, 'I think.'

I'd already detected a hint of anxiety in this boisterous doctor from the capital. Even for him Svan customs were a little strange.

At the house we were greeted by a number of children's faces peering round door-frames, up over windowsills. As far as I could judge, the building housed a family which included at least six children, plus attendant relations. Inquiries into the size of Lalhor only produced the answer, 'Tilty-three families'. Stepping into the ground-floor kitchen area, the senses immediately filled with the rich smells of baking *khajapuri*, emanating from a metal wood-fired stove in the room's centre.

As the young faces gathered up courage and approached, I reached into my bag for my standard stock of electronic trinkets, now an integral part of visits to the former USSR. To the eldest girl of about ten I offered a Donald Duck calculator. 'Pull his neck and he'll play a tune,' I started to say, but before I could explain the calculator function, she snatched it from my hand, and ran over to the corner, where her brothers, sisters and relations all scrummed around, pulling it open again and again, just to hear the tune. I doubted if they ever found out what it really was.

In the corner of the room I noticed a Soviet television tuned to the Moscow channel, its picture snowy and its sound turned down. The Soviets had been quick to give this other electronic miracle to Svaneti, mounting their transmitter on Svaneti's prominent Queen Tamara's Tower as 'a gesture to symbolize the link between epochs'. What, I wondered, did this new generation of Svans think when they looked at me and my electronics? Was this what came after the transmitter?

At table that evening, spread with more brimming jugs of Chacha, more cucumbers, mutton soup and 'serpent's cheese' – a long braided cheese special to Svaneti – I sat next to a young man of twenty-four with pale skin and red cheeks. He shook hands firmly and sat down next to me, eager to practise the few words of English he had learned at school. But more than this, I soon discovered, he wanted to find out all about the life-style of another young man like him.

'How old are you? Do you like Georgia? Where is your wife?' The questions came thick and fast.

I told him I wasn't married and he just nodded.

'So when will you marry?'

I explained marriage wasn't always necessary in our culture, that a man and a woman could live together without it.

'I feel the same way,' he said earnestly. I could tell he'd already thought deeply on this issue.

When I asked what he did for a living, he announced simply, 'Work.'

Plainly he did everything it took to keep the village running. But at this point our conversation was interrupted by an emotional toast from Ilya – roaring drunk for the third time that day – directed to an independent Georgia. At the end of the speech, my young neighbour lifted his glass, looked at me fervently and said: 'I'm ready to die.'

His tone left no doubt of it. The 'freedom' of his country was as important as his own life and any declared threat to this (as say from a trusted politician on the family television) would be met with the greatest sacrifice. (This fact was exploited at the end of 1991 by independent Georgia's beleaguered and paranoid first President, Zviadi Gamsakhurdia. Before his opposition's military assault he broadcast a nationwide appeal for help, and a number of Svans just like this boy, arrived in the capital to fight their fellow Georgians, believing Gamsakhurdia's description of the opposition as 'agents of the Kremlin'.) Yet no sooner had he lowered his glass than the emotion was forgotten and his intensive interrogation of my life continued.

'You can choose a woman when you want, not have to marry her? You too decide when you have children? Why did you come here to Svaneti?'

I could sense the earnest comparisons he was making with his own life. What about this other culture that allowed a single young man, not unlike himself, to travel alone all the way to his village just to look around and then return; or to choose a woman, and not have children? At the end of the meal he stood up, shook my hand firmly and said with a look of intense gratitude: 'You the first foreigner I've spoken to. Thank you!'

The memory of that grateful look haunted me for some time. What had I said or done? How had I affected him? I thought of my tawdry calculator sitting treasured in some little girl's pocket, planting its own irreversible seed into the community. I argued with myself that if not my calculator then somebody else's; that my good-quality boots and windcheater spoke as many volumes as anything I said, that these and my footloose bachelor life-style were simply the fruits of natural human evolution – and that I should shut up.

But I couldn't avoid that lingering feeling of responsibility.

The next morning arrived to the sound of a crashing mountain river and the tinkle of cow-bells on the road. Stepping out on to the balcony I looked at the dripping village, its scattering of houses and towers hemmed in by two enormous mountainsides disappearing into the cloud. Around the muddy lanes, collapsing stone barns stood like battered old rooks, their stones falling back to the earth like spent feathers, a clear sign of Svaneti's depopulation. On the main street, a couple of cows strolled nonchalantly towards new steep green pastures, old car pistons tied round their necks as bells. I noticed the snowline had crept several metres down the hillside.

After breakfast the owner of the house offered to take us the final 10 kilometres up to Ushguli in his jeep.

'My car will live!' announced Ilya, lacking any prophetic skills (the ongoing series of minor accidents mounted up, forcing him to sell the car shortly after our return to Tbilisi). We all climbed aboard and our host directed his jeep with an astonishing un-Svanlike sedateness up the dangerous road towards the 2,500-metre-high hills surrounding Ushguli.

181

Ushguli.

As we climbed higher so the snowline grew closer. Trees fell away, leaving just shrubs and then they vanished too, to be replaced by the monotonous green turf of a landscape accustomed to deep snow. Then, just as I began to wonder how anything more than a few itinerant sheep could possibly live up here, I spotted a tower standing high on a hilltop, hundreds of metres above the valley. This distant black sentinel seemed to scratch the bottom of the clouds like a guard-house to heaven itself. The jeep continued on under its gaze, switchbacking to and fro up a steep incline until finally we crept over the rim and into a shallow, treeless valley.

'Ushguli' Shadur announced emphatically.

Directly ahead of us stood three incredible Stone-Age-looking villages, their haggard beige and black towers clustering together like old men before their gaunt leader – another solitary black tower standing on a hilltop. The four villages of Ushguli (the furthest, Gvibiani, lay concealed beyond the hill) still contained about 1,000

182

inhabitants. The villages now had electricity, yet the air surrounding them was saturated with the feel of an earlier age. The roofs of the towers were covered with shaggy black slates and below them the rendered skin of their walls flaked off to show the dark flesh of granite stones beneath. Unlike the towers of Mestia that seemed to rise up as something apart from the earth, these belonged to it, as if whittled out by some fantastical primitive wind. Not only the highest villages in Svanetia, they were also among the oldest. Archaeologists have dated the bases of some Ushguli towers to the time of Christ – which is another possible explanation for why these stone uprights command almost the same respect among Georgians as the mountains themselves.

The villages followed the course of the Enguri valley as it approached its source. The dominating black tower stood over the second village, Chazash, which also contained Ushguli's famous museum, and not-so-famous new hotel. Ushguli's school also used to stand at its foot, but now the site lies as a ruin, after the terrible avalanche of 1987 that buried so many children. They say not a single family in Ushguli remained unmarked that terrible winter.

As for the hotel, I asked our jeep driver, through Ilya, how much it cost for a night, and whether it had been constructed to encourage new industry in the region.

'It's closed,' came the brusque translation from Ilya as they chatted on among themselves.

At the same time I detected a reluctance on Ilya's part to translate some of my questions, as if he worried that I'd upset the carefully constructed house of cards he now balanced around our visit. Later on, during a lull in one of the drinking parties to follow, he turned his red face to me and admitted as much. Clutching a beaker full of sloshing vodka ready for the next toast, he said: 'Pete, I too am working now like you, I'm working hard. The Svan mafia is terrible – like Colombia! You know someone said you are English mafia? I deny that for you!'

I realized his primary concern was for me, since I was his guest. On this count he certainly 'worked' to make up for my own unguestlike moderate drinking. On one occasion I watched him down a two-litre bottle of wine (the equivalent of one of the enormous Svan drinking horns) in a single, endless gulp. Admittedly, this was followed by his taking up residence in 'the hospital', as we renamed the Lada's back seat. About half an hour later, wailing to Leonard Cohen's song 'Everybody Knows', with the words 'Everybody's nose . . .' he suddenly ripped the headphones off his ears.

'Stop the car!' he shouted.

'What's the matter?' Temur asked, driving on.

'Stop the car!' he shouted again, then added, 'I'm dying!'

He then leaned forward, grasped me by the wrist and said pleadingly: 'Help me. I'm dying.'

We kept asking him what was the matter; but all he would say was, 'I'm dying . . . the pain . . . I'm dying!'

Temur stopped the car, whereupon Ilya flung open the door and staggered to the roadside just in time to release most of the two litres of wine back to the soil. After this he slept like a child, his work complete.

At Chazash, the jeep skidded to a halt in the mud next to the museum. Shadur and our host then disappeared to hunt down the museum's guard. With no sign of their return, I strolled around the village, photographing the buildings and people. After about an hour Ilya suddenly hurried up to me.

'We go to lunch now,' he said.

'Where?' I asked him, remembering no mention of a restaurant.

'Here.' He simply pointed to a nearby two-storeyed home. It turned out that the wife of the house had seen me wandering round the village and invited the strangers in for a feast.

Leaving our muddy boots by the door, we stepped into the stone structure and a long, low room, lit with intermittent bursts of electricity. The moment we entered the room the host directed me to the place of honour at the top of the table and began a toast in Georgian. He insisted that Ilya translate every line (all too often the *tamada*, or hosts, preferred the flow of their oratory to be uninterrupted).

'Your feet bless our house,' he said with a solemn nod to me. 'You are the first foreigner to enter here.'

I acknowledged the honour and the meal commenced. Although some vegetables (such as tomatoes) found in the valleys below were lacking – possibly due to the absence of sun in Ushguli – his wife served a quite delicious fresh *khajapuri*. The Svans called it *teeshdvar* and baked it with fresh local cheeses and spices.

On the wall behind the table hung a faded picture of a young man with a black band round the outside – in the former USSR this is the symbol of death. This was their son, who had died of appendicitis, too far from the hospital in Mestia – a stark reminder of the bitter winters these mountain villages endured.

Eventually word came that Shadur had returned. And so, taking our leave, we walked back to the museum to find him there, standing next to a small, steely-eyed man.

'This is the museum's guard, Pridon,' said Shadur. 'Shake hands.'

I did as he said, only to find that this stern man refused to let go of my hand. I remained trapped before him at arm's length as he stared back at me, scrutinizing my every reaction. Like Shadur's apple, I seemed to be undergoing another test, and a pristine dose of the legendary Svan suspicion. But they did have something to protect. Rumour had it that many pieces in the Ushguli Museum rivalled those in Tbilisi's Art Museum. The Svans had lost so many of their treasures they now refused to let them leave their valleys, trusting no one, and hardly themselves. Intuition still played a major role in their defence.

He finally released my hand and turned to Shadur, saying in Georgian, 'The Museum will open,' qualifying this statement with 'when the priest arrives.'

My heart sank. This was surely a diplomatic refusal. But to my surprise I noticed a tall, bearded man strolling up the road in full robes – a priest, looking ready to conduct a service.

After more formal introductions and speeches during another downpour – the Svans never moved, as if standing in full sunshine – Pridon finally unlocked the museum door. No sooner had we stepped on to the dirt floor of the tower's first level than the door swung shut again and I heard the sound of the lock being turned. He put the key into his pocket.

Before us under a single dingy bulb stood two giant bronze processional crosses, a nineteenth-century wooden crossbow and a pike. The priest then intoned a long prayer before the cross. Plainly we had not entered a museum so much as a centralized holy of holies for the icons of most of the Ushguli churches. The prayers were also to let everyone know that entry amounted to a privilege. I later discovered how true this was, meeting several tourists who had travelled all the way up to Ushguli only to be refused entry by Pridon. The objects here were still treated as if they maintained their rightful positions – back in the churches.

After the ceremony we climbed up to the main first-floor chamber. Poking my head up through the floor, I felt suddenly I'd been propelled back to the Tbilisi Art Museum. The room was plush and carpeted, the exhibits on its burlap-lined walls well laid out, the cabinets as predicted, full of icons. As we walked round, so the hushed, reverent atmosphere followed, and I noticed many new faces in the crowd – locals who had heard of the museum's opening just before Pridon locked the door. They stood before some of the icons, crossing themselves or just gazing, their personal relationship with these objects still very much alive. Among the exhibits I saw an eleventh-century icon of Mary breast-feeding Jesus, a particularly fierce, Svan-looking Jesus from the eleventh century and a collection of European altar cups given to Svaneti by visitors, one with a man carrying an axe climbing up the stem.

'He cut off the branches of the tree of life, including the one he was sitting on,' I was told proudly. Up on the top floor, the cabinets displayed some graceful pieces of ancient Svan jewellery.

As we made our way back down the ladder the priest spoke to me: 'Fifty per cent of Ushguli's treasures have been stolen,' he said, and I began to understand why the villagers begrudged showing their treasures. It was as if by so doing the objects not only lost some of their power but also risked being stolen altogether. Yet the alternative now was to place them in the new museum being built in Mestia – its aim to protect all Svaneti's religious wealth. But could the atheist Communists or indeed Georgia's new, independent leaders be trusted? And did any good come of allowing more, dare one say it, atheist foreigners to photograph them up here? In the end it just added up to more of the same belittlement. (I'd heard several Georgians express doubts, in more candid moments, that God could still properly exist in Europe and America.)

As we stepped outside, I noticed a sonic alarm system tacked up against the twelfth-century stone, silently blinking to our departure – working, I assumed, whenever the electricity did. Once outside the door, we met the enigmatic figure of Rolf the film-maker again. Hoping for another filming opportunity, he'd shadowed our progress all the way up, but now stood outside the locked door, thwarted again. Pridon had forbidden him to film in the museum and the rain forbade filming outside.

'This English friend of yours,' he said cheerfully to Ilya, referring to me, 'has seen as much in one day as it took me a year to see.'

This was a hearty compliment to Ilya, his relentless good humour and Svan-like drinking. Certainly I had now received a whirlwind tour right into the heart of the Svan culture, and, with the icons seen and photographed, I could now leave, just like any other self-satisfied tourist.

Yet walking to the jeep, looking back at these old walls sprouting grass and lichen, these sturdily built towers, the men and women moving slowly between them, I knew I'd already missed something, in some way abused my privilege. In these rare places where antiquity still walked the street, where culture had remained stable for 2,000 years, for all their vendettas and drinking, the Svans had still achieved something we in the West hadn't. I wondered about this luxury of mine – travel – this gigantic enchanted kingdom appealing to those strangely trapped within their free-time in the West. Nobody had ever yet taught us how to use it. I stared at those majestic bending towers feeling lost. I seemed to have forgotten the purpose of my journey. If I didn't discipline myself to keep a careful track, these magnificent moments would simply revert back to just more experiences, consumed events rather than edifying, self-revealing events. Without including one's own active imagination as a part of any journey, the gift of travel, with all its opportunities, its experimentation with self, reverts back to another automatic, consumer recreation.

When I shook hands with Pridon to say goodbye, he gripped my hand and stared back as long and determinedly as before. Looking at his bushy, focused features I wondered how often he had visited Tbilisi, if he'd even seen Moscow or had any concept of London at all.

As we stopped at one of the roadside crosses on the way down and drank another toast to Saint George and independent Georgia, as Ilya and Shadur descended into one more bout of holy drunkenness, I asked myself again, what was it that seemed so important about this place? Had it to do with the purposes of this religious treasure, or 'art' as we increasingly called it in the West? The generation I knew in London visited art galleries in much the same way that the same generation here hurried to see icons at the Ushguli Museum. Both sets of imagery evoked profound emotional responses. Here the viewers looked at fine old enamels, bronze crosses and silver plaques. In the halls of New York and London, the icons of our new secular religion could be anything from a movie star to a cutely captioned vacuum cleaner in a perspex case. The price tags now started to resemble each other.

We photographers and film-makers, the art-makers of the West, now arrived here under the wizened towers of Svaneti hunting out more material, more far-off treasures to bring back and display.

Standing outside the museum in the rain I asked Rolf if, after these four years, he'd now seen enough of Svaneti for his satisfaction. Had he gathered sufficient material, filmed enough of the treasure to be able to put together his documentary?

'Not yet,' he replied. 'Svaneti is like a large, spread-out goldmine.' Then he smiled. 'You know about the Tartar treasure?' He glanced at me casually.

'What Tartar treasure?' I asked.

He gave a look as if to say, 'You've honestly never heard of it?' Then his face resumed its impassive expression. 'The Svans say they have a huge treasure hidden up in the snow. That the Tartars stole it, hid it and then were killed.'

A week later, back in Tbilisi, Rolf came over to show us the first part

187

of his film, to give us a fuller picture of the magnificence of this region (which it did). In one of the spectacular pans, taking in the mountainsides of Ushba and Tetnuldi, he paused the video on a large area of white snowfield and cliff.

'The treasure's somewhere in here,' he said in an almost offhand way.

'How do you know?' Ilya asked keenly.

'Because I'm going to look for it,' he replied.

CHAPTER ELEVEN
KHEVSURETI, IN CONVERSATION

Making Soviet friends in what is now the former USSR comes with an automatic warning tag for foreigners. The tag reads, 'Why does this person like me? Is he/she simply after currency goods, a personal invitation, marriage in the West, etc. or is it *real?*' It is the same paranoia of the rich mingling with poor wondering just how many friendships are directed at their wallets.

With the same deep programming of suspicion, I found myself groping for a ringing phone at 7.45 a.m. and listening to a female voice at the end of the line.

'Hello, I am Lela. I'm in the hotel reception. We can meet now?' Even at the hinterlands of consciousness, the warning signs flashed.

I vaguely remembered her name as someone with a letter to send to the West. But why so early and why so urgent? And what earthly reason could justify ripping me from my dreams only five hours after their start. With the callousness of the rich, I told her to call back at 10.00 a.m., when it suited me better, and went back to sleep.

She did so, on the dot. A few minutes later we stood in the dingy opulence of the Tbilisi Hotel lobby, shaking hands. I found myself connected to a fashionably dressed young woman of twenty-eight, her clothes stylishly Western yet almost certainly home-made. As we studied each other under those forlorn and dusty chandeliers, I wondered if this might be another Soviet citizen enamoured with European consumer culture? Was I to hear more moving tales of sadness, injustice and, by our standards, poverty, and all so impossible for me to rectify? As a journalist one learns that self-insulation – the shameful skill of shutting off from ordinary human reactions and the guilt of not aiding those about whom you report. As we made our way to the snack bar I thought to myself, 'A quick Turkish coffee, a quick listen, then a firm goodbye. Ten minutes at the most.'

Three hours later the batteries on my tape-recorder had exhausted themselves back in my room, as I sought to capture every word of her unrefined English. After just two minutes in the snack bar I realized I'd just met the person I should have met on my first days in Georgia. Here sat the voice of frustrated intelligence, very much alive, full of curiosity and driven by the need to communicate.

Lela's tale and everything in her life stemmed from Georgia's neglected region of Khevsureti, the remote mountainous district in the north, just across the mountains from Kazbegi. Khevsureti, like Svaneti, had inspired volumes of romantic praise (literary and now film) from Georgians and visitors down through the centuries. But unlike Svaneti, it no longer flourished as a cultural unity. In the 1920s its population totalled over 4,000, spread among several thriving villages close to the source of the Black Aragvi. But, today, the numbers stood closer to 400, with the population still declining. Every winter more families abandoned their frosty villages in favour of centrally heated flats in Tbilisi. They returned for the summer months, but with every departure, the ancient family residences took another step closer to becoming holiday homes.

Lela had been a child of this new Khevsur double-life. Her intellect had matured in the capital, courtesy of a solid Soviet education, including the study of philosophy and literature at the State University, while her soul received its soaring education during those four summer months in the mountains, staying with her family's relations (her village had now been abandoned). Thus she imbibed two sets of values: the custom, language and ritual of her Khevsuretian ancestors, against a background of the strict educational disciplines of a Tbilisi schooling. As a direct result, she attempted to combine both these worlds by teaching the Khevsuretian theory of weaving and embroidery to students at the university – exactly the same skills she'd learned as a girl from her mother. Her main purpose in life had become to keep these old skills and ideas alive in any way she could. And here the anguish began.

Sitting upright on her stool before my tape-recorder, she spoke with all the passionate sincerity of one having to watch her intention fail and the old life slip steadily away into nothing. For Lela the culture existed not just as a rich ethnographic entity but as something deeply instilled in her own personality.

'Khevsureti is such a special and unique place,' she said to me, pronouncing the words slowly, as if indulging in a secret pleasure. 'When I was a girl living up there every summer, something happened that will never leave me. There in the dark houses, with no electricity, sitting in the evenings with musical instruments by the fire, making bread, singing in this special language, special verses about ordinary events, wedding-songs, folk-songs about everything around you. Without any philosophy I came to feel the world around me was complete, perfect as it was. Perfect.' She repeated the word as if it meant infinitely more. 'It's a feeling I've never felt anywhere else, not in Tbilisi, Svanetia, Mingrelia.'

Immediately I detected a note in her voice different from those many others who praised Khevsureti. Furthermore, unlike the Georgian poets, film-makers and artists who also lavished their attention on the region, her's lacked the sense of a passing artistic ecstasy. It still breathed life into her every day.

'I've always tried to understand what this feeling really is,' she said, 'because I think it's not only to do with Khevsureti, but a more general psychological sense for life. A way of life that deals more with essences . . .'. She paused, then her voice gathered a plaintive edge. 'You know, I always want to talk about this to people, but sense most don't feel it as strongly . . .'.

I found myself thinking how strongly this lingering sense of isolation reminded me of Tamoona.

' . . . in Khevsuretian culture there existed something very unique . . .' She stopped to give me a searching look. 'Perhaps like the eternal values stored in Shakespeare, because, you see, we too had our own way of recording it, in our embroidery.'

She reached into her bag and pulled out several pieces of finely embroidered cloth and laid them carefully on the table.

'You can read it here right on our old clothing. You can find *everything* in these patterns.'

'If you understand these, you can restore the religion and character of their culture. I see it as a kind of writing. These colours and shapes represent the essences, both of the people who made them and of the tribe they belonged to. They are like banks of ideas or information stored here in code.'

She ran her finger down the intricately sewn rows. 'These patterns are so important,' she said more softly, 'because you see the Khevsuretian religion allowed no icons, no images of God. This is all there is. It's not a Christian religion. They have an invisible God, a kind of mathematical harmony that's hard to explain. But you can feel it here, sense this harmony they worship in these colours and motifs.'

I looked closely at the hundreds of tiny interlocking crosses and geometric patterns flowing across the cloth. I'd never seen designs quite like these, yet found them pleasing to the eye, as if each motif somehow prepared you for the next. (Back in London their unique style was confirmed to me by a specialist in Near Eastern carpets.)

Khevsuretian dress.

'If you look at the crosses,' she said carefully, 'you can see how they seem to emerge out of the star motif. The starburst is an early symbol for the sun.'

I knew the worship of the sun had been put forward as one of the earliest religions in the Caucasus.

She picked up one of the embroideries covered in the small, multipointed crosses. 'These are perhaps closer to the original cross. See how its many spines are like the sun's rays. Later they simplified it down to four.'

Noticing my interest, she then reached into her bag and extracted some battered photographs showing men and women wearing this traditional dress. They stood before a primitive, fortress-like village, its old walls growing out of the rock like a ragged brown crystal. Their embroidered shirts and dresses were covered with these same crosses and stars, large and small, none of them the Christian Latin cross, but all the so-called pagan (or Greek) cross, with each of its arms equidistant from the centre; the symbol adopted by some early Christians, the Crusaders – and later by the Nazis in the 1930s. They stood out in brilliant white and reds, or in yellow outline, sewn acoss the black tunic, and worn across the foreheads of women. In the centre of some larger crosses, coins had been attached, flashing back their bronze CCCP lettering like strange new cult symbols.

'These people are from the village of Shatili,' she said. 'The crosses are created over areas of the body they want to protect, both physically and psychologically.'

I pictured a human back criss-crossed with points of light, drawn in from the sun by the crosses, for the first time making a connection with this motif as a symbol of health, used by organizations like the Red Cross.

I asked her about the reports from foreigners in the 1930s who spoke of Khevsuretians walking round Tbilisi dressed in chain-mail and the large red crosses of the Crusaders.

'I don't think that the Crusaders brought this design to Khevsureti,' she said firmly. 'It's simply when the Khevsurs saw these crosses on the soldiers' armour they found them similar to their own. This is why Crusader-like crosses used to be found up here, even in this century. The design still shielded people.'

She spoke the last sentence as if the invisible Khevsuetian religion still existed, even here in the modern capital.

'This is me,' she said suddenly, holding up a photograph showing a large picnic held in what looked like a forest car-park. She pointed to the twelve-year-old girl, sitting on the ground, wearing the same traditional dress and looking towards the camera.

I tried to imagine her sitting outside the stone houses of Shatili overshadowed by the shaggy white peaks, watching the women weaving these threads together, creating these symbols of their 2,000-year-old community. No wonder, with all the social upheavals in Georgia, that the symbol had undergone a major renaissance, adopted both by the Round Table Coalition (the political opposition that finally ousted the Communists in the 1990 election) and the Monarchist Party, who hoisted it on to their flag, now boldly flying from the rebuilt Narikala Fortress above Tbilisi.

I began to wonder if I hadn't come across a more Georgian part of Georgia than even Svaneti. Certainly it was an utterly unique corner of the Caucasus (I was told later these designs are peculiar only to these villages). Speaking to two foreigners who had visited the valley, I discovered that most of the villages had been abandoned, the people more or less vanished. But why had nobody mentioned the real meaning of the embroideries until now? Tamoona had hinted as much without ever being able to say it, feeling herself haunted by 'fairy-tales' she couldn't define. Lela too seemed touched by the same undefinable sense of loss, but in her case it fuelled her way forward. I could see from her face the pleasure she gained from talking about her mother's homeland of Khevsureti.

Eager to hear more, I asked if she could explain how the individual characters of people or villages showed themselves through the various embroideries.

Her enthusiasm was instantly rekindled. 'If you look at them *closely*,' she said, and her eyes demanded that I did, 'you'll see how the Khevsuretian character is in fact a great synthesis. On one side, they follow a very strict, severe way of life and habit, and, on the other, they contain a very poetic, lyric, romantic nature. The Khevsurs are known as wonderful poets, they have a strong oral tradition and are among Georgia's best. You can see it in the dark cloth and then the sparse but brilliantly coloured patterns. You can see the character there too. If you look at the pattern on these leggings...' She lifted up an elegantly woven tube of blue swirls, geometric spirals and crosses set against a black-knit background. '...you know from the austere, rich feel to this design that it's from Khevsureti. But this other design...' She picked up a fragment of brighter, more cheerful embroidery. '...is from Pshavi, the next valley over from Khevsureti. You can see it here, the lighter, less severe style.'

I noticed how its lighter, cleverly intersecting white and yellow crosses did indeed convey a different mood.

'You see,' she continued, 'if you look at the dark Khevsur colours, you get a feel for the Khevsuretian woman who wasn't even allowed to cry if she lost her child. It would be a shame; it would show lack of strength. Because of their hard life they also tended not to get married until twenty-eight or thirty. Then, immediately after their marriage, she wasn't allowed to sit near her husband or, on their first night, even sleep on the same floor as him. Here life was very severe, strict.' Then she suddenly smiled. 'But, you know, even within this austerity they allowed freedoms. Due to their late marriage they were allowed to have what you might call "boyfriends". These would be official and formally accepted by the village. Couples could behave like lovers in every way except of course make children, which only happened after marriage.'

Then she picked up the Pshavi embroidery. 'But in Pshavi the same system operated much more freely. And you can see all these things in the colours and patterns. The Pshavian colours are more bright, yellow, happy. You can find this illustration of character throughout all Georgian traditional dress.' She looked at me curiously. 'You may also have noticed that traditional Georgian dress doesn't have pockets.'

I confessed that I hadn't.

'Well, this is because, before, we didn't like to keep money with ourselves, to be always thinking about it. Even today money isn't the main thing for us. We're not mercantile. We're very romantic in this matter.'

I remembered those numerous taxi-drivers who refused to take my money with their wide, proud smiles.

'But what about the cartridge-pockets?' I taunted. 'Are these romantic too?'

'Maybe.' She smiled. But the sound of a police-car's megaphone outside on the street made the smile quickly fade as we both suddenly remembered the latest romantic Georgian 'war' for independence on the streets below.

'What do you think about what's going on now?' I gestured towards the sound of the demonstration now shouting its way down Rustaveli Avenue. Her face suddenly looked strained.

'I want Georgia to be independent but I'm also afraid,' she said. 'No matter how loud anybody shouts, everybody is secretly frightened of what may happen.'

I wondered if this new great hunger on the streets, with the increase in crime and almost pathological nationalism, didn't also represent the cry of a people fearing the end of a former way of life and, with it, their national character. I remembered meeting the night before with one of the Monarchist Party leaders. He'd told me of his deep depression

195

immediately following the massacre of 9 April, almost to the point of suicide. Then at its darkest moment the idea of the Monarchist Party had suddenly 'dropped' on him like a beam of light from heaven.

'Everything became clear,' he said. 'I realized Georgia could refind itself with a king, with a constitutional monarchy.' (Some have agreed this is what Georgia became in late 1991, under Gamsakhurdia.)

I'd come away feeling he wanted to simplify the image of lost Georgia (and himself) into one almighty person or saviour, then re-create him as its leader, to project this wonderful, crown-wearing guiding light riding into the future like a modern Saint George. Only the pre-tried path of simplified nationalism had offered this desperate man any way forward. I asked Lela if she agreed with my interpretation.

'Perhaps,' she said. 'But I'm not sure if it's even possible to preserve our national character now, even in modified form. I think these processes now coming together are too different. Sometimes it seems to me that we're jumping from a very traditional place to a very advanced place too quickly. In the last ten years so much has changed here in Georgia. People are finding it harder and harder to understand their old self, their former way of life. Many of the eighteen-year-old girls I talk to now are so different to those just one generation removed. At school many don't have that sense of delicacy, sensitivity any more; their feel for the old embroidery patterns and colour is gone. It's terrible. I think to myself, these people will get older and die, without ever knowing this true sense of the Georgia of their parents and grandparents.'

Then she gave me an apologetic look. 'If you will forgive me, it seems we're now taking on a more Western, commercial valuation of our life. Our psychology has started to change on a fundamental level. Part of this new process has been to give people choice: the American easy-life choices; the don't worry, be happy, life – without the intellectual suffering, the wondering what to do, what to think. Unfortunately the reason many Khevsuretians left their mountains is simply because they wanted the electricity, the television, the radio, the modern products only available in the valleys. Now an easier life exists, and I know many Khevsurs who, when they finished their education in Tbilisi, decided to stay on and live here in great hardship rather than return.'

Watching her speak, I began to sense those same two conflicting Georgias in her: the Tamoonas and the Mananas; the older part in her slower more thoughtful words and eyes; the new in her tone of voice, European clothing and Soviet education. She could no more resist the trend towards finer material and intellectual acquisition than her fellow Khevsurs. Yet her energetic need to talk about this I found quite exceptional. Then suddenly her expression changed.

'But what can *I* do? I can just sit and hope. My only ambition now is to put together a proper record or book, so that these wonderful traditions of Khevsureti can be preserved. But I can't find anybody here interested to do it. Nobody is progressive enough now. I'm thinking the only place to get it published might be in the West.'

Looking at her crestfallen expression, it seemed to me incredible that Georgia, a nation so enamoured with its past, so keen to preserve its traditions, would fail to acknowledge its most obvious loss and not fund one properly researched and colour-illustrated book, while the costumes and their makers still survived.

The following day, at the house of a Khevsuretian artist, helping Lela photograph some costumes, I discovered part of the urgency behind our meeting. As I placed one of the magnificent embroidered tunics up against the wall, a maggot crawled out and hurried across the backdrop. The most valuable part of the Khevsuretian history, it seemed, having barely survived Stalinism, would now be finished off by moths! Lela said her own family's costumes suffered in the same way and asked if I could send her moth-killer when I returned to London.

As I pressed the shutter, I wondered if I stood before the shrinking candle-flame of yet another of the world's finest cultural traditions, about to extinguish itself for ever. Khevsuretian religion produced no images of their God and almost no ritual objects; these clothes were all they had.

'Sometimes I think that foreigners understand better why this custom of ours must be protected,' she said sadly. 'How very important it is not to lose it. I hope perhaps someone will want to publish this book. It might give me some more possibility here to do more.'

She paused for a moment, reached into her bag and pulled out a thick white envelope. 'I'm sorry I've taken up so much of your time, but please, this is a letter I've written to a friend in London who said she would deliver it to the Victoria and Albert Museum. Could you possibly give it to her with those photographs you took?'

I promised her I would.

CHAPTER TWELVE

SUKHUMI

Farewells in Georgia, as with arrivals, are when all the irritations of excessive hospitality melt away. At my departure from Tbilisi, a large collection of new friends, old friends and friends of friends arrived to send me off at the railway station – a posse of earnest, God-speeding faces for the benefits of one who'd boldly declared his intention to prise out all the secrets and then run.

Ilya's final word of advice came as I stepped into the carriage.

'Have you ever been on a Soviet train before? Be warned!'

The implication, as with all things Soviet, was that it might not make it or, if it did, would be late, uncomfortable, unhappy and any other negative you could imagine. Yet I wondered how the purified, techni-colour trains of independent Georgia ran in his imagination. To my eye, this Soviet-built train running on Moscow time (the timetables at stations across the USSR still operated according to centralized time) presented itself as clean and well supplied. The crisp, new sheets, pillow cases and blankets matched anything British Rail could produce. But I thanked him for his warning – Ilya had been a true friend.

As the train juddered out of the station, I watched the smiling faces and waving hands, shrinking away on the platfom. Who could not feel affected by this time-honoured sense of concern for the guest. It may have been a Georgian tradition, it may simply have been the thing to do, but either way it showed a respect for the stranger now long forgotten in Europe. I felt sorry to go and, as they all disappeared around the bend in the platform, a phrase from Schopenhauer returned: 'in every parting comes an image of death.' Would these gainful, spirited childen of the twelfth and twentieth centuries survive the latest battle – for independence? As one Georgian friend had put it, 'While it is difficult for anyone to survive the twentieth century, here in Georgia we embrace it like we embrace everything we fear – too passionately.'

I wondered about their rocking emotions, their gallant quests for 'freedom' blotting out the sun of long-term planning and political strategy. I left feeling that they still skated across the thin ice of political inexperience, that this potential for mistakes held true right down to its most mundane actions, like driving across town. Here all life was precarious. Indeed, within a year of that scene of happy farewells on the platform, two of those faces were involved in serious road accidents and the mother of one was killed.

Finally the lights on top of Tbilisi's television tower slid away into the engulfing night. I acclimatized myself to that mournful grunting, creaking companionship of railways the world over, their moments of stretching time placing gaps between life's bigger moments. I always look forward to these strange in-betweens, the shuddering journeys along two metal shafts of no man's land, with all the extra time to catch up on one's crazily neglected life.

I felt Tbilisi receding behind me into the night like a gigantic, Gothic, toyland cathedral, shot with emotional lights streaming through its stained-glass windows. Out of its doors, citizens came and went in lustful worship of the past and its recurring tragedy. From inside, one heard those religious chords full of nationalism and fear for their future, a shout of alarm as the outside world threatened to engulf this grand old fortress with unsteady walls.

Now I headed towards West Georgia, the traditional outer limit of the country with its wide open border of sea. My spirits lifted. At the other end of the line lay Sukhumi, Georgia's first city on the Black Sea coast. I imagined subtropical heat, acres of light and relaxation. In the morning I would wake beside the sea from which Jason and his Argonauts had emerged in search of the golden fleece of Colchis, where today many of the former Soviet Union's privileged arrive in search of holidays and dachas (Gorbachev owned one at Musera).

But the Sukhumi I approached also contained a curfew and Soviet military patrolling its streets. Tomorrow morning I would also wake in the modern Autonomous Republic of Abkhazia, home of the newly reviled (by most Tbilisi Georgians) Abkhazians. Earlier, the Stalinist deep sleep had finally declared itself over with the first inter-ethnic flare-up within Georgia's own borders since the 1917 Revolution.

Some months had now passed since 9 April, and Georgian (and Abkhazian) blood had flowed again the following July as the two sides fought over the territory's sovereignty. But to say Georgian had fought Georgian would now be unacceptable for the Abkhazians. They regarded this violence as an indigenous population resisting a colonial power (Georgia), since Abkhazia had spent many centuries moving in and out of the Georgian federation. This was a humiliating and ironic

199

rebellion for the Georgians, whose own complaint against the Russians was thus mirrored within their own borders – this time with themselves as the brutalizing central power; (a conflict duplicating itself yet again in the more bloody Ossetian uprising of 1991).

In Sukhumi I wanted to try and understand why this emotion reared its head in another ancient nationality, which, like the Ossetians, could also live relatively peacefully within or beside Georgia – as it had for many years.

With me in the two-berth sleeper sat a powerfully built man in his late thirties. When one of my Georgian friends sat briefly on his bed at the station, he'd responded with an instant, 'Get off!' His eyes had glared back as if the territory of the bed was his alone and had been violated. Yet the moment the train left the station his mood changed. No longer aggressively dominating the small space between the beds, he behaved with absolute civility. Discovering I spoke only a few Georgian words, his face lit up with pleasure. I realized instantly that I shared my compartment with the enemy, an Abkhazian.

Via a mixture of Russian and several European languages, he told me he lived in the town of Novy Afon, just up the coast from Sukhumi, a former Greek community, and that he had come to dislike the Georgians, who, he felt, behaved like bullies.

'Georgians hate Abkhazians,' he said. 'They shout, "Abkhazia is ours", and treat us like property.'

I had been curious to hear the other side of the story ever since the day a liberal Georgian friend sneeringly described the Abkhazians as 'Russified Turks, with no culture of their own' (patently untrue).

'We're tired of being "ruled" by Georgia,' he said. 'We want to rule ourselves and maintain a friendship with Moscow. We're not crazy separatists like the Georgians.'

Yet statistics pointed to a serious problem here. The population of Abkhazia now stood at 44 per cent Georgian and only 17 per cent Abkhazian. At the same time the Autonomous Republic remained one of the most (if not 'the' most) rich, luxurious and profitably cultivated areas of the Soviet Union. The subtropical strip running along the western end of the Greater Caucasus caught plenty of sun and rain and the land was also favoured by a rich alluvial soil and long sandy beaches. On top of this, its coastline stood at the heart of 'the Russian Riviera', the 800-kilometre strip of coast from Batumi, in Georgia's south-west corner up to Novorossiysk in the Russian Federation.

In his angry expression I'd seen that same tirelessly rising sap of 'independence', the sublimated quest for individuality now saturating most of the Soviet bloc. To the outsider, watching it inflate the veins of a tiny autonomous republic within a republic, it seemed like madness. But then I'd not spent all my life penned down under Stalin's bludgeoning attempt to homogenize almost every aspect of private and public life.

After the lights went out, I lay back on my bunk wondering how on earth one solved this problem of self-definition. Here, surely, lay one of those terrible dilemmas of identity that could never be 'solved', only 'outgrown'. I racked my brain for anyone I'd ever met in the Soviet Union who had outgrown or stepped beyond this peculiar need for aggressive self-redefinition. As the train climbed towards the dark, invisible vales of the former West German kingdom of Imeretia, the mental screen remained quite blank. But, just as sleep threatened to slip in its place, suddenly a name flicked up: Sasha Bashlachov.

Yes, here stood a powerful alternative in the ideas of 'self' resurrecting itself in today's post-Soviet world, one that, during his tragically short life, he set out to announce as widely as possible. In the fashion of men like Maxim Gorky before him, Sasha Bashlachov had become a poetic vagabond, abandoning his work as a journalist on Cherepovets's newspaper the *Communist* to become a poet and singer.

I'll never forget our first meeting one wintry afternoon on St Petersburg's Nevsky Prospekt back in 1987. He'd stood there, a fierce, blue-eyed, gap-toothed poet wearing a Jim Morrison badge, speaking no English yet brimming with manic enthusiasm and passion. I asked, via a Russian friend, what he thought about the psychological "system" imposed by the Soviet government. He looked back half smiling and asked: 'Which system?'

I gestured to the buildings and streets all around.

'Oh, that . . . ,' he replied. 'I've got nothing to do with it. The word 'system' is a dead word for me. It's their word, not mine.'

Coming from anyone else, I might have suspected him of wishful thinking, but the peculiar zest of his speech, the intense burrowing look in his eye and the delight in the face of my friend as he translated somehow made it utterly believable.

I suddenly felt myself in the presence of the kind of imaginative freedom easily capable of withstanding any political system – except perhaps his own. He spoke intelligently with a wide-eyed fervour that sometimes placed his face centimetres away from mine, his fingers grasping the air to make his point. Eventually I'd asked about the struggles of self versus nationality in the USSR.

'We go to war, fight each other, kill,' he said, 'but it's like being with a woman. It's impossible to understand, so we fight in our frustration. For me the fight has turned to singing. To me this is like searching for a

201

woman's voice. You hear it when you're wrapped in the womb, then suddenly you're born into bright lights and noise. And you hear the screams, which were a part of you. You think they're delightful for her and you spend your life looking for that scream again: that is music. You come out of the womb with the question, how to find this voice again. But then you realize it's a mistaken question. Birth itself was your answer and you mistook it for a question.'

'And nationality?' I repeated.

'It's another cry, is the same!' he exclaimed.

He grabbed my notepad and wrote down two almost identical-looking Russian words. 'The first word, *strach*, means "fear",' he said with great purpose. 'The second word, *trach*, means "to make love". You see the connection?'

He stared back at me, full of a terrible, urgent, laughing need for me to understand.

'Death is in between both. To me it's also like a woman. Only a woman can really kill you, because only a woman can really love you. Death itself is just a brief physical event. It's easy. I try to die now, every day . . .'

If his songs hadn't been so marvellous, even in translation, if some of the USSR's greatest singers and writers hadn't praised him rapturously – Alla Pugacheva (the Soviet Barbra Streisand) had burst into tears when she first heard him sing, declaring him a genius – these may have sounded like the words of a madman. But everyone who came into contact with Sasha reported the same sense of genius, and bursting, impossible divination – in many ways too powerful for the world around it. This made it all the harder to accept his choice to indulge his curiosity towards life's biggest emotion of all with his suicide in February 1988.

I woke to the sight of fields of tea, sweetcorn and tobacco outside the window and the jagged white peaks above Lower Svaneti to the east. The temperature and the humidity had climbed dramatically during the 1,000-metre drop from Tbilisi and an entirely new climatic zone had been entered. The train now rattled through the terrible land of Abkhazia.

As the dense undergrowth, the flannel-like green leaves, the occasional bending palm, drifted peacefully by, I wondered about this nationality within a nationality now resisting the Georgians – a culture just as ancient, with a distinctive language linked not to Georgian but to the tribes of the northern Caucasus like the Circassians. The kingdom of Abkhazia had merged with West Germany many centuries ago for the sake of collective Georgian strength. Now, along with the rest of Georgia, identity seemed more important than strength. The train passed a cemetery with an extraordinary memorial – a garage-like shrine rising over a hideously crumpled car, a grim example of how the strength of modern technology can be ignored by Caucasians. I hoped these peoples didn't intend racing down the road to independence in the same way they drove to the shops.

Suddenly a huge space opened out in the left-hand window and with it came the smooth millpond of the Black Sea, sky and water melting peacefully together at the horizon. Before it, a long sandy beach followed the course of the railway, spreading unendingly north and south like a yellow bracelet wrapped around the sea. Yet, in spite of this balmy atmosphere, the September crowds had not arrived. I counted perhaps thirty holidaymakers along a 2-kilometre stretch of sand, only ten of whom were in the water. Sukhumi might be the Blackpool of the southern former USSR but it remained a far cry from the fearsome thrusts at entertainment and amusement so characteristic of the British seaside.

From the station I asked the cab to drive me straight to the seafront. Like a pilgrim to open space, I had first to soak in all the emptiness; and relax. I prayed for a secluded bench on a wide, carless esplanade, facing the water and Sukhumi, like all good seaside towns, provided exactly that. I sank down on to the seat close to the Hotel Abkhazia and, under some gently rustling palms, inhaled my first health-restoring gulps of Black Sea air.

Ahead spread the lazy landscape of gently rippling water stretching away to the place where the Soviet Union finally ended. The extraordinary calm of the sea's surface swept out before me like an enormous movie-screen, permanently running a feature of borderlessness, freedom, and the promise of uninhibited watery travel. I could feel its energizing message breathing over all the town and its ambling holidaymakers. Tideless, the Black Sea behaves more like a lake than a sea, its sinister depths (below 180 metres nothing lives) almost registering on the surface. Some say it takes its name from a lining of dark sediment and hydrogen sulphide occasionally stirred up by storms; others say it comes from the rusty black sand found on its southern beaches.

On either side of me, rows of chairs were filling with more blond heads than was usual, a sure sign of the heavy Russian presence in this far corner of the USSR. All eyes seemd to drift instinctively southward, following the Abkhazian coast towards the Muslim region of Adjaria, Batumi, the Turkish border and eventually, the West. The border was much trafficked by Georgians with relatives (imaginary or real) in northern Turkey and plenty of items to sell to the currency-bearing Turks.

I closed my eyes and tried to remember my background-reading on Sukhumi's history. According to archaeological evidence, the city had thrived as a population centre right back to the Stone Age. In the ancient kingdom of Colchis, it flourished as a focal point of local trade. When the Greeks arrived they changed its name to Dioscuria and the town became an international port which by the second century BC even minted its own coins. But the eroding advance of the Black Sea was to claim most of the original port and then, a few centuries later, the Romans saw to the rest. By the second century AD, it had evolved into their fortress-town of Sebastopolis, which subsequently fell to the Byzantines and then the Turks, and so on with the usual Caucasian ping-pong of conquest and reconquest, devastation and rebuilding, right up to the present century (in 1866 its population was reduced to 412 by the Turks during the Russo–Turkish War). During Soviet times, the city's capital status was restored and the population climbed back to a healthy 120,000.

Opening my eyes, I looked down the esplanade to see men and women wearing T-shirts emblazoned with slogans like 'Buggy' or 'Disco', now manufactured in the USSR, children eating ice-creams or clutching buckets and spades. A fully normalized image of modern seaside life. Yet I also knew that not far out under the water of Sukhumi bay lay an acropolis, a contemporary of the Parthenon apparently still standing.

Today the focal point of the seafront had to be its pier, with an entrance of elaborate neon-lit dolphins diving through a hoop. Beyond them stood the Amra Restaurant, striding out into the bay on stilts, with its breezy upstairs café and the word 'Restaurant' written in Abkhazian across the front. At first I mistook it for Russian, as the Abkhazian language uses an extended Russian alphabet, but I then noticed one of the peculiar nineteenth-century bulges on its newer letters.

On the avenue behind, the local car-culture flourished, roaming the streets in spite of the petrol shortage. I watched as a souped-up Lada with 'Duckham's' emblazoned across the bumper sang out its eight-note klaxon, then roared off angrily up Lenin Street, a roar suddenly hinting at the frustration bottled up along these city streets. I watched the dark eyes and eagle-like noses pass along the esplanade, asking myself which were Abkhazian, which Georgian?

A few minutes later a dark-haired Georgian came up to ask me the time in an aggressive, rough Russian. I smelt alcohol on his breath.

When I held up my wrist for him to look, he spat on the ground and walked away. He wished to make the point that we Russians (the wine made him mistake my blond hair as Slavic), waving our cameras as if nothing were going on, should not feel welcome in *his* seaside resort. Georgians resented the Russians in Sukhumi for what they saw as their support for the Abkhazian cause, believing the Russians put the Abkhazians up to their rebellion to deliberately sabotage the Georgian call for independence. During the taxi ride from the station I'd passed several Soviet Army armoured cars manning roadblocks, searching vehicles for weapons. Here were yet more targets for Georgian resentment.

Sitting amid this blend of the murderous and the happy, I noticed a boy of about eight years old on the beach, playing a new game with an enormous grandmother. She threw stones and he dodged them. I watched fascinated as the sport grew steadily more determined. He shouted at her to throw the stones harder. She laughed but did as she was told until, after a few minutes, I could tell she genuinely tried to hit him and he genuinely had to leap hard and wide to dodge these phoney bullets.

I wondered if this might be the game now played throughout the city – provocation and counter-provocation as the two populations threatened to pull the city apart and create a Belfast by the Black Sea.

My home in Sukhumi turned out to be a room in the Fifteenth Congress Holiday Home on the Tbilisi road. I'd arranged to join another tourist group accommodated at this miniature Soviet Butlin's, comprised of two tower blocks, a large communal eating-hall, outdoor dance area and public address system, all surrounded by a high metal fence and gates. On the other side of the gates, just across the Tbilisi road, the Black Sea slopped amiably against the sand.

The real difference between this institution and Butlin's came in bookings. Most holidays here came as an integral part of employment. Years of service automatically assured workers a spell at a state camp in the sun like this. Today, however, they locked the gates at 11 p.m., due solely to the curfew, so they told us.

That evening, fearing the lock-out, I had no alternative but to lean against the alcohol-free bar and watch the organized entertainment. It began with a dance. A smartly dressed band playing ballads and polite rock and roll as a group of very reserved couples swayed on the floor. This apparent unemotional mixing of men and women took place in a camp dotted with noticeboards exhorting inmates not to drink, to follow camp rules and the Congress ideology – like a prepschool for

205

grown-ups. Watching the dance, I remembered George Orwell's term for love-making in *1984* – 'our duty to the party' – knowing here was one area in which he sorely misjudged: Soviet Russia had evolved as a hugely promiscuous society and these apparently passionless public spectacles belied a corresponding abandon in private.

This camp, virtually unchanged since Brezhnev's day, conveyed with impeccable authenticity the good clean atmosphere of obedience of the last seventy years, right down to the distance between the dresses and brown nylon trousers on the dance-floor. But now, just outside the perimeter fence, I sensed the awakening winds of change, the complaint of the Caucasian tribes threatening to break in, like natives dancing round the stockade.

For someone (like myself) accustomed to the raggedly extroverted night-life of London, this subdued dance atmosphere appeared quite unreal. Absent were the cans of lager, the lingering air of aggression, of coked-up over-confident faces or sweeping narcissistic displays of style, as if here the idea of 'fun' had turned deliberately away from our Dionysian ideal, back to one in which human emotion remained restrained and considered.

Clutching my paper cup filled with cherry juice, I engaged in conversation with a schoolteacher from Moscow who spoke quite passable English. I noticed his cup full of wine. I asked him where on earth he bought it.

'Here.'

He smiled and lifted the bottle from beside his feet, then, taking hold of another cup, filled it for me.

'They don't care,' he said throwing a glance to the staff behind the bar, 'because they didn't serve it. They won't get in trouble.'

'But you will,' I suggested.

He smiled sweetly. 'What are they going to do? Throw me out? There's a curfew! Besides everybody here is drunk.'

At first I didn't believe him, having watched those stiff, restrained dancers. But he proved to be absolutely right. The alcohol, rather than liberating people, had simply sunk them deeper into their introspection. Confirmation then arrived with the night's organized entertainment, 'The Love Competition'. The band stopped playing and a camp attendant clutching a microphone stepped forward to explain the rules. 'First of all we need an attractive young woman,' she said and walked straight over to a blonde girl in the audience, took her by the arm and positioned her at the front of the dance floor. She asked the girl her name.

'This is Tanya. She's from Minsk,' she said into the microphone.

'Now, which men would like to have a date with her?'

There followed a moment of terrible silence, as the sodden introversion deepened. But finally a couple of isolated hands rose sheepishly out of the crowd. Seeing this, a few other men who would not have dared to admit such desires in public gingerly lifted theirs.

'OK, you, you, you and you,' said the compere, pointing to various hands in the audience and beckoning them to step forward. She then positioned these male suitors at the opposite end of the floor from the girl.

'Now you must take a step forward and tell the girl just how much you like her.'

She told the girl at first to encourage the men, listen to each entreaty, then to cut it off when she felt she had heard enough and pass on to the next. For every ten seconds of speaking the suitors could take a step forward. Thus she produced a staggered line of suitors, frozen in their headlong rush towards their feminine goal.

The compere handed the microphone to the first man, who introduced himself as Serge from Kiev in very slurred speech. He took his step forward, then dried up completely. The compere tried to help.

'Tell her how beautiful she is, how much you would like to meet her, what you have to offer her.'

Serge held the microphone to his lips, opened his mouth but no sound came out. He just stood there open-mouthed, either too drunk or too shy to say more than his name. The microphone was quickly passed to the next.

A tall, tanked-up Czech took several huge strides forward amid a torrent of soulful promises, claims and gross flattery until he too was stopped, a good 2 metres ahead of the Ukrainian. After this, the microphone was handed to a casual, smooth-talking Georgian from Tbilisi who, focusing his attention on the girl, walked forward, speaking in the most charming and persuasive tones, as if not playing a game at all. He was allowed two good strides beyond the Czech.

My companion from the bar made a wry observation: 'Russian women always seem to like Georgian men – why, I don't know!'

'Perhaps they're more charming?' I suggested.

'I don't call their love of Stalin very charming,' he replied gruffly.

But his words turned out to be prophetic because, on the third round, the Georgian went on to win convincingly. I asked my companion what he thought about the Georgian charm in relation to the Abkhazians, and the problem now closing in on the camp gates.

'The Georgians are crazy,' he said with some distaste. 'They're trying to force the Abkhazians to speak Georgian. They put forward a new programme at the university only in Georgian, so the Abkhazians would have to learn. This led to the fighting. Because, you see, the conflict is really only because the Abkhazians won't join them in their plans to separate from the Soviet Union. Their refusal made the Georgians furious, and they started shouting, "Abkhazia is ours" and that the Abkhazians are devils, collaborators with the evil Russians.'

He smiled briefly, then shrugged his shoulders. 'They're crazy,' he repeated. 'They're like little Stalins. They have, what do you say ... inferiority complex. Give them power and overnight they become capable of great cruelty, like their Stalin.'

I thought it strange that Stalin had suddenly become nothing to do with Russia, a purely Georgian phenomena.

I heard a metallic sound behind us, and turning round, saw two Ministry of Interior soldiers not a couple of metres away, clutching Kalashnikovs, as if just sprouted from the public-address speakers. They stood in full uniform watching the entertainment. A few minutes later I found out why. The band suddenly stopped playing and the public-address system came to life.

'It is now 11.00 p.m.,' announced a stiff school-marmy voice. 'Due to the extraordinary situation will you all now please return to your rooms.' From her tone I almost expected to hear her add, 'And then wash behind your ears.'

With that announcement, all life in the camp suddenly evaporated. My companion at the bar shrugged again, picked up his bottle and said grimly, 'See you at breakfast!' He walked off.

I waited a few minutes while people dispersed. From down beside the main gate came the sound of jeeps driving up and down the seafront, with megaphoned voices announcing the curfew. From the main gate came the sounds of angry shouts as a small group of Georgians were hustled out of the camp. Their body language indicated that they were looking for trouble. I saw one slam his fist into the palm of his hand, then look around wildly for a target until a friend grabbed his shoulder, calming him down. The young soldiers holding their weapons glanced about nervously.

The next morning brought with it the realization that my journey through Georgia was reaching its end. The following afternoon I would sit on an Aeroflot flight bound for Moscow and that evening I would be on my way to London. I walked out on to my balcony and looked down at the camp's wispy pines and palms, the speakers tied to the trees, the glimpses of Black Sea beyond. I inhaled the heavenly sweet fragrance of osmanthus now floating across the city. All signs of any curfew or trouble in the nation of Georgia had completely disappeared. The sea breathed in and out with the same voluminous tranquility as it had for millions of years. Would the ethnic problems of these mountains just fade away as easily as the arrival of this soothing dawn after last night's curfew? Instinct still told me 'no'.

I walked into the town and, searching for a short cut to the beach, accidentally wandered into a large private holiday camp for Party officials and Army officers. On the beach at the end of an elegant palm-lined walkway a couple of junior officers stood stretching on the sand; another dried himself with a large red towel. I imagined these younger men in the lower military (possibly KGB) echelons eventually returning to their modest flats in Moscow, with walls and kitchens decorated with the hardware of our 1960s in the West. I, on the other hand, would be returning to their future and the land of black-market goods. In so many ways, this experience in the Soviet deep south had been like entering a time capsule.

I watched an old military man jogging along the seafront at walking pace, his bleach-white belly wobbling in the morning light. Still the old body tried to keep itself alive, as its political life-support system now disintegrated. It occurred to me that Abkhazia had been the right holiday choice for these men. The nation is famous for its centenarians and its history of longevity – people live longer here than almost anywhere in the world. These old generals and KGB colonels now breathing in this balmy air might well out-live the system which they had nourished and then inadvertently killed.

Later that day, at the Abkhazian State Museum, I saw a photograph of a man looking remarkably like that old jogger, with a caption beneath it reading '150 years old'. Next to it came another picture of two-dozen centenarians dressed in Caucasian Mountain dress, with Phaphahi wool hats, Masra cartridge-belts, moustaches and daggers lying across their knees. It may have been appropriate that the museum also filled itself with numerous fossils, Palaeolithic finds, and collections of stuffed local animals. In one display, as I confronted a Caucasian auroch, an imperial eagle, an ibex and a bear, I remembered the words of a Georgian friend: 'I look forward to the day when museums will display nature's strangest creation of all, *Homo sovieticus.*'

Outside the Museum's entrance stood a large dolmen to remind visitors just how imponderable Sukhumi's history was. It dated back to Palaeolithic times. Many of these antiquated tombs could be found scattered among the nearby hills, as well as (so we were told) some remarkable 2-metre-tall stone penises – not on display in the museum –

although I once bumped into one hidden away from embarrassed Intourist guides at the bottom of Tbilisi's Architectural Park.

Later, visiting the State Institute for Gerontology with the tourist group, I asked the resident professor for a more specific indication of these claims of longevity in Abkhazia. As an amiable, remarkably relaxed academic he replied casually: 'We've found that Abkhazia averages thirty-eight centenarians per 100,000 of the population, while the rest of the world averages about fifteen per 100,000.'

And how did he arrive at these figures?

'In this institute we've studied about 1,500 cases in depth since 1974,' he said. 'We've learned to be very careful because our research shows that 56 per cent of old people give a wrong date of birth and, generally, once over eighty, feel they've earned the right to add on a few more years to their total.'

Still not entirely convinced, we asked how they verified age.

'The most accurate method of dating them is by their teeth,' he said, and then he smiled. 'But most have already lost them.'

'What about the photographic evidence?' someone interjected, 'like the two-dozen centenarian men and the two 150-year-olds in the museum?'

'A good example of exaggeration,' he said calmly. 'It's interesting to remember there are twice as many women as men, and how many photographs of women did you see in the museum?'

I didn't remember seeing any, and suddenly I found myself inclined to believe this Soviet scientist.

'The oldest properly documented person we have living in Abkhazia at the moment is 107. But if you ask him his age he'll tell you he's 140. I personally don't believe it's possible to live beyond 120.'

From here the conversation grew steadily more fascinating and I found my notebook filling up rapidly, as did many others in the room. Under the 'advice' section my remarks ran as follows: 'Centenarians rarely smoke. They eat a wide variety of vegetables, prefer maize bread to wheat, like yoghurts, cheeses, beans and natural wines – they drink two or three full glasses a day(!) Honey seems to play a part in their diet. Never been a fat centenarian. All are slim, active and have usually lived a full married life. Not many bachelor centenarians. They hunt or pick the fruit. They drink coffee only for medicinal purposes. The world's oldest man liked to drink half a pint of hard liquor before going to bed every night...'

Then came the bad news. 'They all lived in villages most of their lives where the air is clean.'

He then gestured to an old woman sitting quietly in the corner who for some reason I'd assumed to be the cleaner. 'This woman is ninety,' he said, 'and she's still very active and in good health. Ask her your questions if you like.'

At this moment her face suddenly came alive and I instantly recognized those signs of depth and beauty so unique to the old. Her eyes sparkled with as much vitality and sensitivity as a teenager. The muscles tugged and relaxed around them like delicate bell-ropes as she listened, more to the tone of our questions than the words.

How long do you sleep? Do you read the newspapers? Do you drive a car?

Here the professor interrupted. 'Not one of our centenarians has ever driven a motor-car.'

In Georgia, this didn't surprise me in the least.

'Do you have any tips for a long life?' someone finally asked.

She replied in a matter-of-fact way through the translation of our Abkhazian guide. 'I think you should eat a good diet, and be well respected by your family,' she said simply. Then, raising her voice just a trace, she added: 'And most important of all, you must do only good to people, you must live with a moral purity.'

There followed a moment of animated discussion between our Abkhazian guide (a fierce supporter of the Soviet regime) and the professor. He seemed to have spotted a mistranslation – even though I thought he couldn't speak English. The professor then asked the group's St Petersburg guide – a far better representative of *glasnost* – to retranslate the last line.

'She says you must live with a *clear conscience*,' she corrected, and the professor agreed.

At last, I thought, the habitual old lies and mistranslations of the seventy years were being spotted.

I noticed the old woman showing a glimmer of a smile as if she'd noticed too. I looked at her wrinkled features, trying to guess at the stock of natural philosophy lying behind those last two words. These eyes had grown up surrounded by Tsarist Georgia; had watched the revolution slowly ferment, arrive, then with its apparent *glasnost* and *perestroika*, be followed by Georgia's Menshevik government. Her fingers would briefly have used the new coinage of independent Georgia, before the Bolsheviks snatched it away and switched to the currency of Soviet Russia. She, like everyone, would then have felt the grip of Stalin steadily tighten around daily life, culminating in the terrible purges of 1937. Now, once again, she saw the nation close in on a new *fin-de-siècle* phase, amid more revolution, *perestroika* and the arrival of another independent Georgia. No wonder this old woman had asked, with a certain degree of determination, for a clear conscience. The political behaviour of humankind she'd witnessed so far had shown little evidence of it.

On my final afternoon in Georgia, the Intourist bus took us up the coast in the direction of the luxurious resorts of Pitsunda and Gagra. Following the winding Black Sea Highway for half-an-hour we arrived at another balmy, palm-studded resort, the former Greek colony of Novy Afon (which translates as New Athens). Here swans decorated the roadside 'water gardens' and an enormous 'tourist attraction' cavern lurked deep inside its holy Mount Iveri, awaiting coaches like ours. My official Intourist introduction to Georgia had described these caves tantalizingly as 'an Aladdin's kingdom with fairy palaces'.

As the bus wheeled round the coastal hairpin bends, past the numerous citrus and persimmon orchards, olive and cherry groves, so we began to see the red flags of Communism hanging from house windows, instead of the magenta, black and white of independent Georgia – a sure sign of leaving the area of the Georgian majority.

Black Sea coast.

'This is the road that Maxim Gorky helped construct,' our guide interrupted my thoughts.

I remembered how the young Gorky returned to the Caucasus several times as the 1917 Revolution was brewing among these very same houses. He'd spent his time living as a virtual tramp, paying his way from job to job, priming his imagination with its deeply romantic supercharge. I imagined the young writer digging out these very embankments along the Sukhumi Military Highway, now permitting us our air-cushioned race between tourist resorts, labour that also permitted the Bolshevik Red Army (that he supported, like many young writers – only to abandon it quickly after the Revolution) to attack Georgia in its three-pronged assault, bringing down the liberal Menshavik government in ten short days.

I remembered his over-the-top descriptions from *The Birth of Man*, written while sitting near here, recovering from bee-stings, triumphantly dipping bread into a pot of honey. When he looked up, he saw Georgia as a kingdom full of 'jewels, silk and happy children', 'sowing it with kaleidoscope treasures', and the Caucasus mountains as a magnificent church built by sinners 'to conceal their past from their own conscience'. Chekhov also had passed through Abkhazia, declaring 'the scenery is maddeningly beautiful . . . every little bush, every shadow in the mountains, all the delicate shades of the sea and sky offering me a thousand plots'.

I hoped my last tourist moments in Georgia, at the Novy Afon caves, might offer more opportunities for rapture. Unfortunately, it seemed that the local conscience had still to clear. At their entrance we pulled up into an enormous and completely deserted car-park.

'There must be a strike,' said our Abkhazian guide flatly. 'Part of the troubles.'

We descended from the bus and milled around the locked reception-centre, with that so-near-and-yet-so-far feeling. Then I happened to glance across the valley and saw to my astonishment a huge 'fairy palace', not once mentioned by our guide: a delirious fantasy of a building with silver domes bubbling up out of the mountainside, its walls painted in rich yellows and red, crowned by spires. What, we all asked her excitedly, was *this*?

'It's the old Novo Afonsky Monastery,' she said, adding casually, 'It's not interesting.'

She seemed greatly surprised by our desire to visit it.

'It's just been repainted,' she said. 'It only looks good on the outside but there's nothing there.'

But she convinced no one. The bus was turned round and driven to

213

the bottom of the hill.

'Well, if you really want to visit it, you'll have to walk up the hill,' she said unhelpfully. But to her surprise, everybody did just that.

And not in vain, for at the top came my last memorable experience of the nation of Georgia, now poised on the edge of transformation. For this majestic monastery, built in 1886, its multidomed courtyard surrounding an enormous, cathedral-sized church, had been converted into a Soviet holiday camp. But this was not the high-class, executive Communist Party palace one might expect; instead a down-market two-star workers' accommodation. Walking around the converted, decaying dormitories, trying to peer in through the windows of the locked church (now a 'museum'), one tasted again how functionalism had triumphed over imagination – to everyone's detriment.

I thought to myself, Gorky's 'mighty church' of the Caucasus been built here, only to have its conscience publicly stripped naked by the Communists a few years later. In the place of a wasted human belief in God, they had imposed even less convincing belief in man – dressed up as the dictatorship of the proletariat. The monastery was now converted into the atheists' heavenly reward (no longer hidden away in the afterlife, the heaven of the evil capitalists) but back on tangible earth, and right on the site of the church.

Yet the untidiness of that inner courtyard, the caravans standing in a haphazard row, the obvious lack of organization, told that the point was still being made. This fine old building still needed to be shamed.

I walked up to two enormous 6-metre-high doors and, pushing gingerly, found to my surprise that they swung open. I stepped into what used to be the refectory and now had become the camp canteen. This once magnificent room, with tall stained glass windows, paintings of the saints and apostles and a huge fresco of The Feeding of the Five Thousand had been converted into a self-service café. The frescoes of the apostles surrounding the eaters had been partially painted over and defaced by the new regime, just as the frescoes at Vardzia had been attacked by the Muslims. Electrical conduits ran straight through the Patriarch's faces, a plug had been positioned on an apostle's stomach and, connected to it, just below where the serene face had once looked back from under its halo, an old plastic speaker had been tacked to the wall. Walking by, I heard a faint music trying desperately to crackle out of its dirty grille. Stopping to listen, to my surprise I just recognized Vivaldi's 'Dixit Dominus'. Suddenly that eerie sense of unconscious theatricality so saturating the Soviet world was back, the drama so deliberately blind to its own ironies. Could it be the just-surviving voice of the religion, held captive inside the walls for seventy years, now struggled to re-emerge?

In my state of suspended disbelief, I noticed one of the senior kitchen staff staring at me. I gestured casually at the speaker, trying to point out this extraordinary paradox. But I received only a quizzical look.

Do you want the station changed?' he asked, trying to be helpful. 'Would you like it turned off?' suggested his friend.

Before I had a chance to stop them, they'd switched over to another station playing Western rock music. Suddenly I heard Madonna's voice belting out 'I'm a Material Girl' from the space formerly filled by the saint's halo.

'That's better,' they all agreed.

POSTSCRIPT

I made one more trip to Tbilisi shortly before handing in this manuscript, to catch up on the manic history of Georgia. So much had changed – even the name. Now the Soviet Socialist Republic of Georgia had become the Republic of Georgia. The Communist Party had lost power in the 1990 democratic election, and a new government formed by Zviadi Gamsakhurdia, had declared its independence from the USSR and was now locked into a battle with Moscow. Georgia was trying desperately to shake itself free from the remaining Communist structures that still solidly underpinned it.

Yet the changes were more than just political. The first sign of a shift in everyday life hit me at Moscow's Vnukovo Airport. There, at the Aeroflot desk, I met a Georgian woman in the middle of the usual furious battle with Aeroflot officials, trying to ensure her place on a flight to Tbilisi. Due to our similar plight – my plane had been delayed eight hours, until 4.00 a.m. – that instant friendship, possible with any Georgian, immediately established itself. After several, highly frank discussions on the 'war' in Ossetia, the unstable political situation in the crumbling USSR, the various personalities in the government, I finally asked the profession of her father.

'He's with the Ministry of the Interior,' she said cheerfully (Ministry of Interior was then almost tantamount to saying KGB).

'Oh no,' I said, unable to prevent myself.

She just smiled. 'You don't have to worry. Now it's the *free* democratic Republic of Georgia!'

'You mean even the KGB is for independent Georgia?' I joked.

'Yes, it is,' she said. 'It's officially separated itself from Moscow. Now it's the Georgian KGB.'

Not quite certain how to take this, I decided to keep my ear close to the ground on arrival. As I boarded the jet, I wondered why that old edifice of fear had changed its name – and if other such organizations would also simply redesign their frontispiece?

At the other end of the two-and-a-quarter-hour flight, I found a capital city now offering up a good deal more than a simple facelift. First came a sight most Georgians never expected to see in their lifetimes – the magenta, black and white flag of independent Georgia flying on the Stalinist Government Building on Rustaveli Avenue (Georgia was the first republic to elect a non-Communist state government – in November 1990). Then came a sight I never expected to see – Lenin Square without Lenin. In his place was a small, cheerful patch of grass; Lenin Square had been renamed Freedom Square to honour the event. Progress too had graced the shops: goods once black-market (Western cigarettes, video-tapes, cassettes) were now on sale for roubles – if a good many of them.

Yet I was to quickly realize that the 'democratic forces' that replaced the rapid decline of Communist power had not arrived without exacting a price. On the first evening, trying to catch a taxi on Rustaveli Avenue I experienced a dilemma never encountered before in Georgia. The taxis no longer stopped. Dozens of people lined the roadside, leaning out ever more eagerly towards the hurtling Ladas, but in vain. The cars drove on by empty, or occasionally stopped to pick up women. But single men standing alone – almost never. Why? At the house of a Georgian friend I received the answer.

'The streets aren't safe like they used to be,' he said. 'Taxis are being held up, people are being robbed, many have guns now. Our situation is not good.'

In spite of the tendency for Georgians to over-dramatize, I realized the psychological climate had already changed radically. The new individuality had started to bring with it sense of self-gain and steeply-rising crime statistics.

My friend told me the number of weapons in the country had risen substantially, due in part to the 'war' in Ossetia and the arming of the new Georgian National Guard, and in part to the entry of many disaffected Red Army conscripts into a proliferating black-market.

'For you, a Kalashnikov will cost $250 if you want,' he said.

To my expression of surprise at the low figure, he just laughed.

'The other day I heard of a Russian officer trying to sell his armoured car!' Then he went on to explain. 'The situation in Ossetia, in Tskhinvali, was pretty bad. Many houses had been burnt and people killed. Moscow was supplying the Ossetians with weapons and the Georgian National Guard had been fighting against them. Now the Red Army are there in force protecting the Ossetians.'

(When Georgian South Ossetia had declared its intention to unify with its northern part in the Russian Federation, the new government of Gamsakhurdia declared Georgia would no longer recognize South Ossetia as distinct from Georgia and blockaded the region.)

To me it seemed like another Abkhazia, a situation which, after its initial flare-up, had now quietened to an uneasy stalemate. But discussions among new and old Georgian friends revealed that several radicals, previously calling for uncompromising collective action against the Soviet regime had started to back-pedal. Now anti-Sovietism had become government policy. It threatened to spill over the top into a pointless fanaticism and bloody confrontation.

My friend (who preferred to remain anonymous) said: 'It was one thing for our leaders to pump up emotions in cries for "independence". It's quite another to convert them into serious strategies for reform. Our new government hasn't learned the second stage yet. They're still stuck in the habit of confrontation.'

Gamsakhurdia had already unleashed some crazily nationalistic ideas on his parliament; like suggesting that Georgian citizenship should only be granted to those with family roots in the country before the Russian arrival in 1801. His former liberal support had ebbed away, some even suspecting him of encouraging the Ossetian 'war', which he portrayed as a Russian plot using the Ossetians to capture more Georgian territory. (When in August 1991 he appeared to support the authoritarian Moscow coup, his former allies in the Georgian National Guard switched allegiance to the opposition National Democratic Party, splitting the population down the middle.)

Later that night, I found myself again stranded on the edge of a Tbilisi street trying to stop a car, this time after visiting friends about a kilometre from the hotel. My concerned hostess had insisted the Tbilisi streets were no longer safe to walk at night (although subsequently I had no trouble at all). She accompanied me outside at 2.00 a.m., to wave furiously at the traffic. Delighted when a car finally stopped for her, she bundled me into the back and, hardly looking at the occupants, shouted the name of my hotel. Stepping back, she then slammed the door and waved a cheery goodbye from the kerb.

As the car lurched off, I glanced forward to see two members of Tbilisi's swarthy, wild-eyed youth in the front seats. The one in the passanger seat then turned and said in an alcohol-tinged, mafioso voice,

'Hotel Tbilisi, *da?*'

The words were spoken aggressively out of the corner of his mouth, with as much distaste for the Russian language as the Russian government. Did he know I wasn't one? The driver then swerved round the corner and, reaching down to steady myself, I placed my hand straight on to the snub barrel of an Uzi machine-gun, lying on the back seat.

As we accelerated down the road, I began to sense those flashes of anarchy that sometimes ignite across nations, after resounding victories. These two night-cruising heroes had won back Georgia; now they patrolled it with their Israeli-made toys of death. I guessed from the earnest glint in his eye that this kid (nineteen at most) had seen some kind of combat action (Vietnam veterans called it the '1000-yard look'). I asked if they'd been to Tskhinvali.

'*Da*,' came back the stark reply.

I began to realize that these wild boys, who initially expected to pick up a woman, had been confused by this alternative – me. What should they do?

They were the law, and here were a law completely unto themselves. But before they could find an excuse not to drop me off, the hotel loomed in the windscreen with alarming speed.

'Cigarette!' the driver demanded in another gruff voice.

For the privilege of releasing me unscathed he at least wanted Western payment. But I'd absolutely no cigarettes left – having given them all to my evening's hosts. I also had no dollars, having left them behind in my room. Digging deep into my bag, I found a lone pack of chewing-gum and handed it up front. They took this pathetic gesture without a word. When we drew up level with the hotel, instead of slowing down the car accelerated. Had they found their excuse?

Reaching forward I tried another tactic, offering my hand in the gesture of friendship and, with my sincerest smile, I thanked them for the ride, although my hotel was now several hundred metres behind us.

It had an unexpected effect. Rather than shunning the gesture as I had expected, both faces instantly lit up with huge smiles. The breaks were applied, an illegal U-turn effected, and the car screeched to a halt right outside the hotel front door. They both then shook my hand vigorously, wished me well and squealed the tyres off into the night.

The following evening I walked up Rustaveli Avenue again, this time towards the yellow-and-red walled Paliashvili Opera House. Outside it, I encountered a large gathering of Georgian faces clutching banners that read 'Free our Political Prisoners!', slogans now directed not against the Communists, but against the new non-Communist government of Gamsakhurdia and the Round Table Coalition. It turned out that the leaders of two opposition parties had been arrested, apparently for advocating armed resistance.

Although no more than the primitive signals of democracy, I realized that this was a sure sign that the hard rock of united hostility against the

Soviets had begun to crack, crumbling into numerous competing factions. At the same time, I couldn't quite believe that a new form of political dictatorship would simply replace the old. Talking to members of that upset gathering, I met several Georgians strongly criticizing Gamsakhurdia. One described the victory of the Round Table Coalition as the victory of 'the shouting party'; another expressed a real fear that his brand of nationalism came closer to fulfilling the Georgian bitterness against the Russians than constructing a positive alternative. Then he added: 'Real democrats don't imprison their rivals, no matter what they say.'

I replied that at least they didn't imprison him for saying so. Then I asked about the alternative parties. He said they were temporarily losing their way. And what about the Communist Party, I asked.

'They came up with a new title,' he said, half smiling. 'Trying to make themselves sound better. "The National Socialist Party!" Then someone told them about Hitler's party!'

I felt the recreating Georgian nation all around me. It had begun just as Western observers had predicted: in a blaze of confusion, mistakes, good intentions, bad intentions and impulsive zeal. Already the long established scapegoat, of blaming 'the Kremlin' as the source of all Georgia's problems, had begun to fail, as the country lurched in its first difficult step towards political pluralism. The deep split within the population, that would lead to crude government censorship and running street battles by the end of 1991, had already opened. In January 1992, Georgia's re-armed population would explode across the world's TV screens as a mini-civil war raging along Rustaveli Avenue. Having fulfilled his role as a blazing nationalistic figurehead leading Georgia to feedom from the Communists, Gamsakhurdia's political inexperience caused him to end up stuck underground in a Government Building bunker. With his calls for help increasingly unheeded he eventually had to flee Tbilisi, only eight months after his election with an 87 per cent majority. This same soil of Georgia, having nurtured the seed of nationalism, had now dropped its first shining, inflated fruit to the ground and discarded it. The new culture had yet to stumble into its own blueprint of subliminal checks and balances.

Stepping away, I noticed the interior of the opera ablaze with light. Had these feelings in any way transferred themselves into the arts? I stepped up to the front door and encountered a *babushka* demanding my ticket.

'What, no ticket!' she exclaimed, then suddenly smiled and waved me through, as if tickets, like Communism, were now an old joke.

For the next fifteen minutes I wandered around inside the reconstruction of a Moorish palace. Founded in 1851, burnt down mysteriously and then rebuilt in the 1970s, its walls were stuffed with beautiful arabesque mirrors, turquoise mosaics, gold reliefs and fabulous chandeliers. Eventually my curiosity about the auditorium itself overcame my guilt at having no ticket.

Expecting it to be empty, I pushed open one of the balcony doors. I stepped into the plush 1,100-seat auditorium, where to my enormous surprise, a large cast and orchestra sang out in mid-scene to an almost completely empty theatre. I counted seventy performers on the stage, all in full costume, outnumbering the audience by about five to one. I watched in amazement as a soprano reached the climax of an aria, then sank down on her knees in a passionate plea to the empty rows of seats. Was this a plea for an audience? What had happened to everyone?

At that second, I heard the crash of a bucket in the hall outside. I turned to see a Russian cleaning lady push open the door and step in, mop still in her hand, and walk up to the edge of the balcony. She stood silently for a few minutes watching, then clopped out again, resuming her work.

Was this it? The other Georgian audience, the drama-lovers, had at last found a performance more vivid than anything the theatre could now offer. Outside on the streets, the real Georgian opera continued unabated.

I decided to return to the hotel to try to catch up on the news of my former Tbilisi friends via the telephone. Getting through first to Manana, she told me her marriage had passed off as planned.

'Now I'm eight months' pregnant,' she said. 'I'm taking a break from my career.'

Next Ilya told me he now planned to educate his children in the West – although how I had no idea. Marika, who in between times had visited London, remained the same as ever, absorbed in her love of Georgian art. Tamoona's phone didn't respond any more.

There could be no doubt, the kingdom of Georgia had taken another large step towards our own. How much longer, I found myself wondering, before their greatest son, Stalin, would turn into the subject for just another opera worthy of such an audience? Now, with a zeal the old Bolsheviks would have envied, the new government set about taking over, transforming or abolishing nearly every institution, organization and structure of the Communist era. I wondered if they realized how deeply this ideology had left its footprint in the Caucasian soil.

Some time later, back in England I heard an ex-patriate Georgian even give utterance to a burst of nostalgia for those 'lazy days' of

Communism; the period when everything fun was illegal and caviar was cheap, when nobody had to work hard, earn money for rent, the phone bill. The years when rebellion was pure, noble and simple against the wicked Russians. She told me she felt a duty to inform her still starry-eyed cousins back home of the reality of life in the West. Our streets were not lined with gold. And nor would theirs be.

The final statement must lie with another Georgian friend who described to me with great emotion the moment when Lenin was finally removed from Tbilisi's Lenin Square. An enormous crowd had gathered to witness this momentous event. She told me about the great cheer that rose up across Tbilisi as the monstrous statue was finally uprooted from its position in the centre of their city. Then suddenly she paused, looking wistful, a little uncertain: 'But you know, there was a funny moment in the ceremony. When the crane tried to lift Lenin away, his feet stuck themselves inside the base, they wouldn't free from Georgian soil.'